# HEAVEN'S DESIGN TEAM

## VOL.02

BY ► HEBI-ZOU & TSUTA SUZUKI

ART BY ► TARAKO

HEAVEN'S DESIGN TEAM

# CHARACTER PROFILES

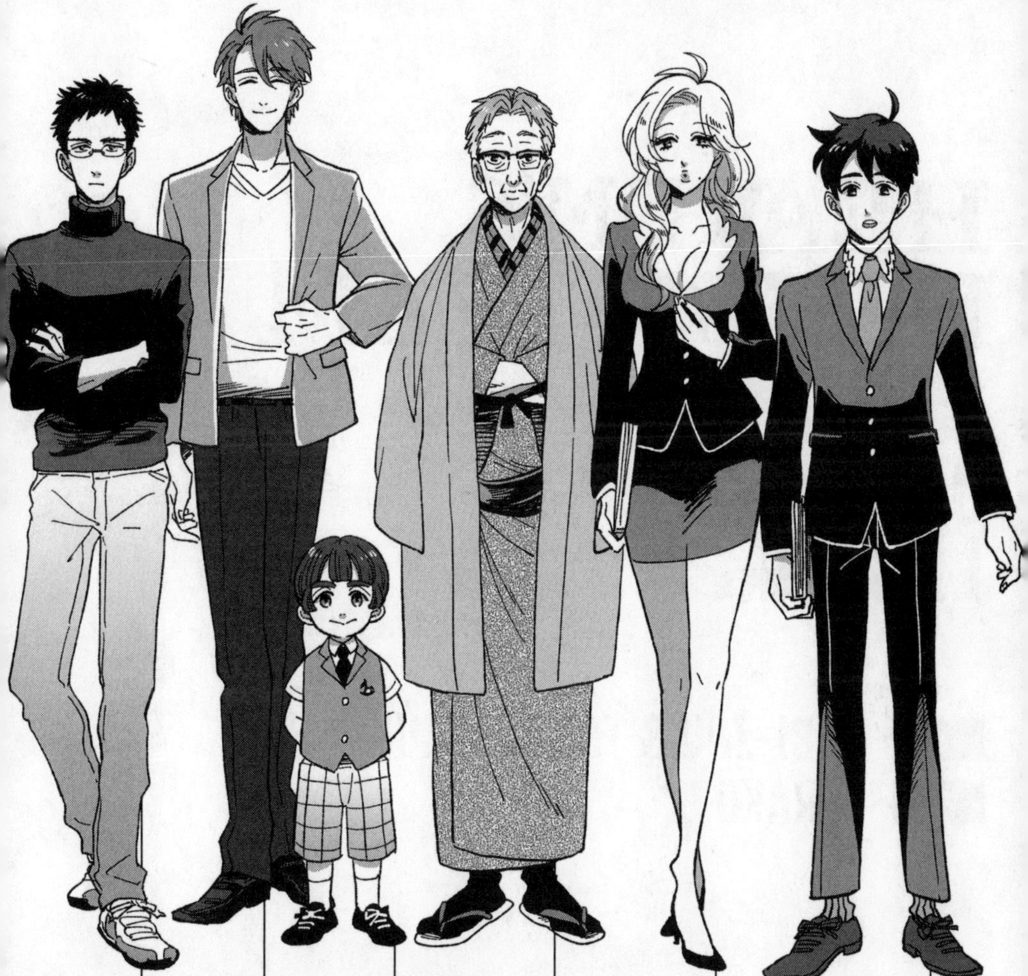

**MERCURY**

A designer. His masterpiece: the snake.

**JUPITER**

A designer. His masterpiece: the cow.

**MR. SATURN'S GRANDSON**

Mr. Saturn's grandson, Kenta. A horse fan, just like his grandpa.

**MR. SATURN**

A designer and the head of the Design Department. His masterpiece: the horse.

**UEDA**

Shimoda's supervisor. An angel who acts as a liaison between God and the Design Department.

**SHIMODA**

The new angel. Serves as a liaison between God (the client) and the Design Department.

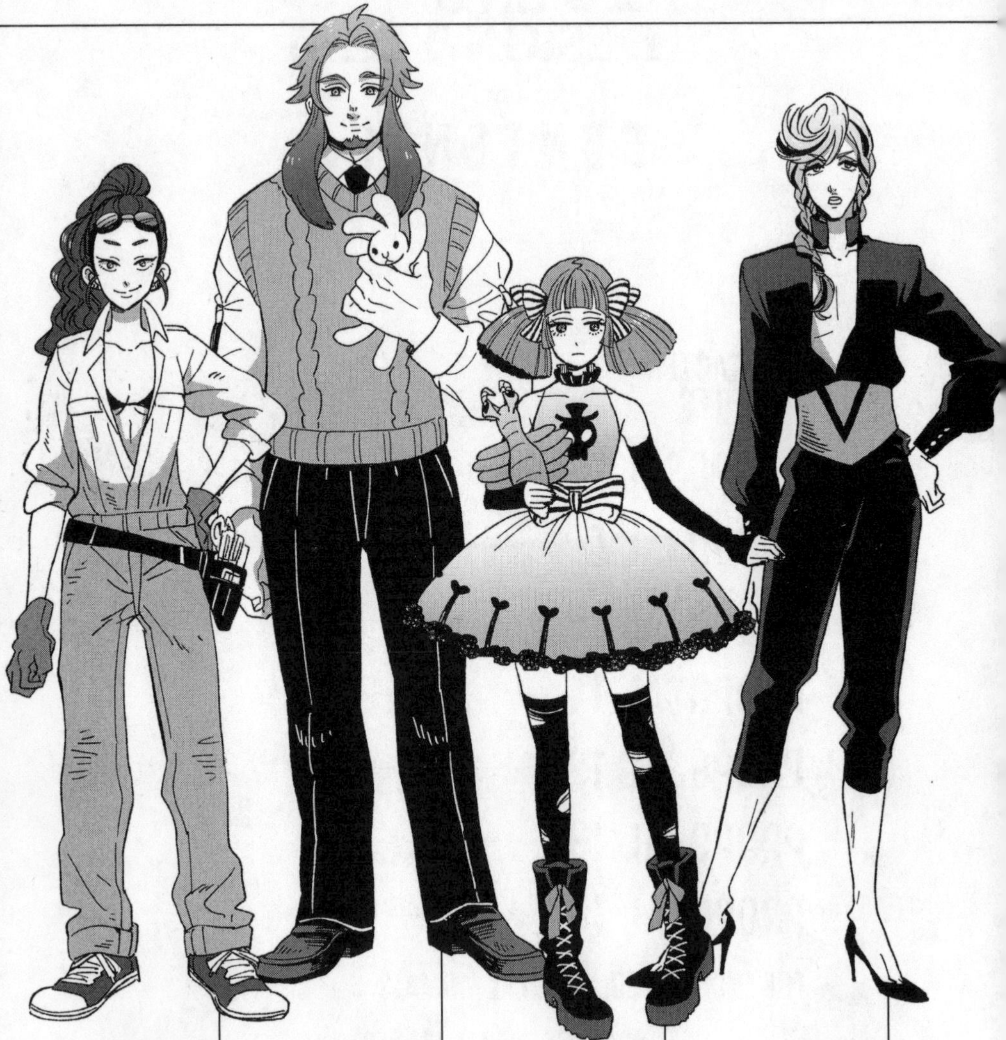

**MARS**

An engineer. Tests whether the animal designs will actually function in the physical world. The hardest worker in the office.

**NEPTUNE**

A designer. His masterpiece: the kangaroo.

**PLUTO**

A designer. Her masterpiece: the poisonous frog.

**VENUS**

A designer. Nicknamed "Ven." Their masterpiece: the bird.

# HEAVEN'S DESIGN TEAM

✦

# CONTENTS

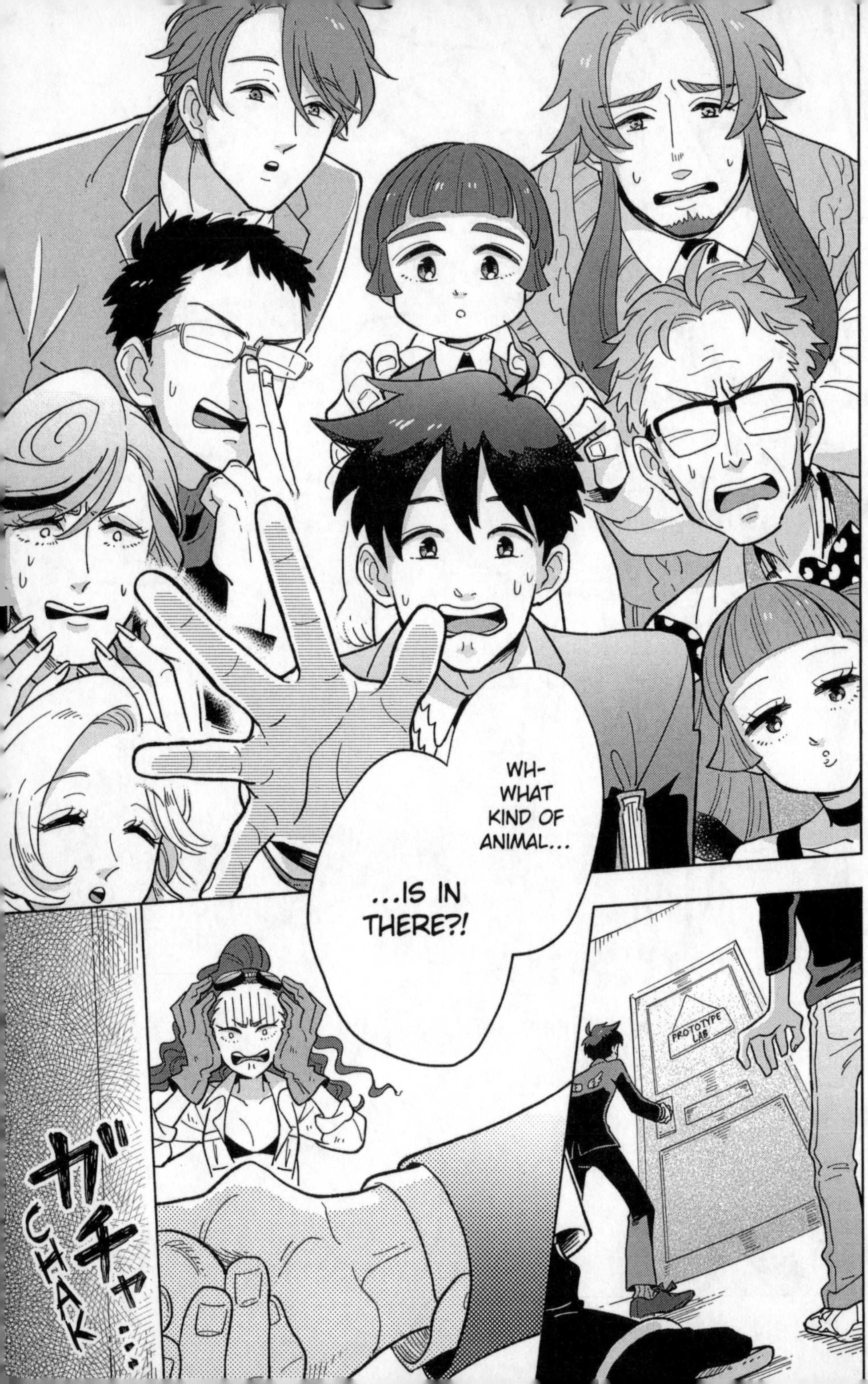
WH- WHAT KIND OF ANIMAL...
...IS IN THERE?!
PROTOTYPE LAB
ガチャ...
CHAK

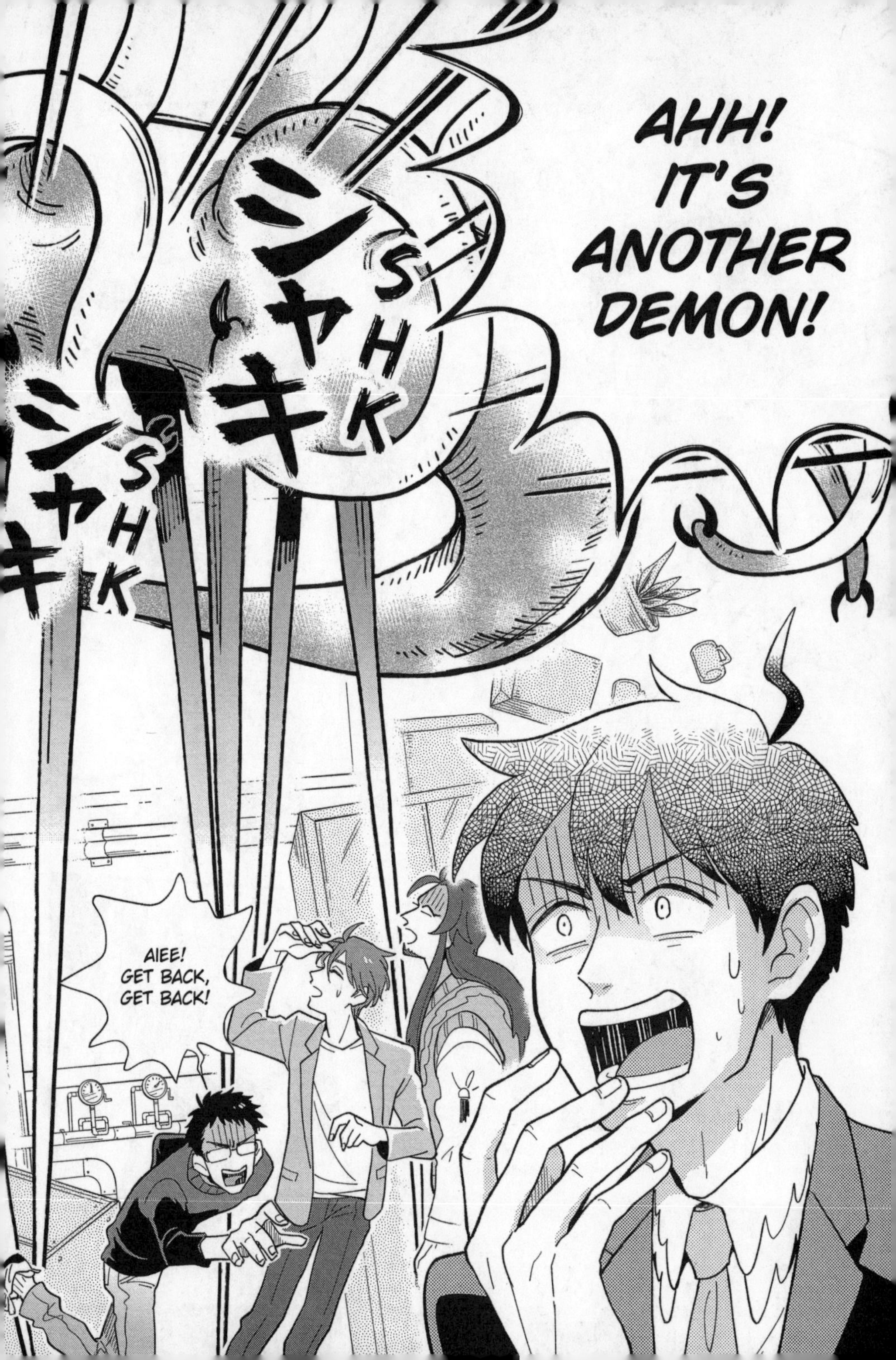
AHH! IT'S ANOTHER DEMON!
シャキ SHK
シャキ SHK
AIEE! GET BACK, GET BACK!

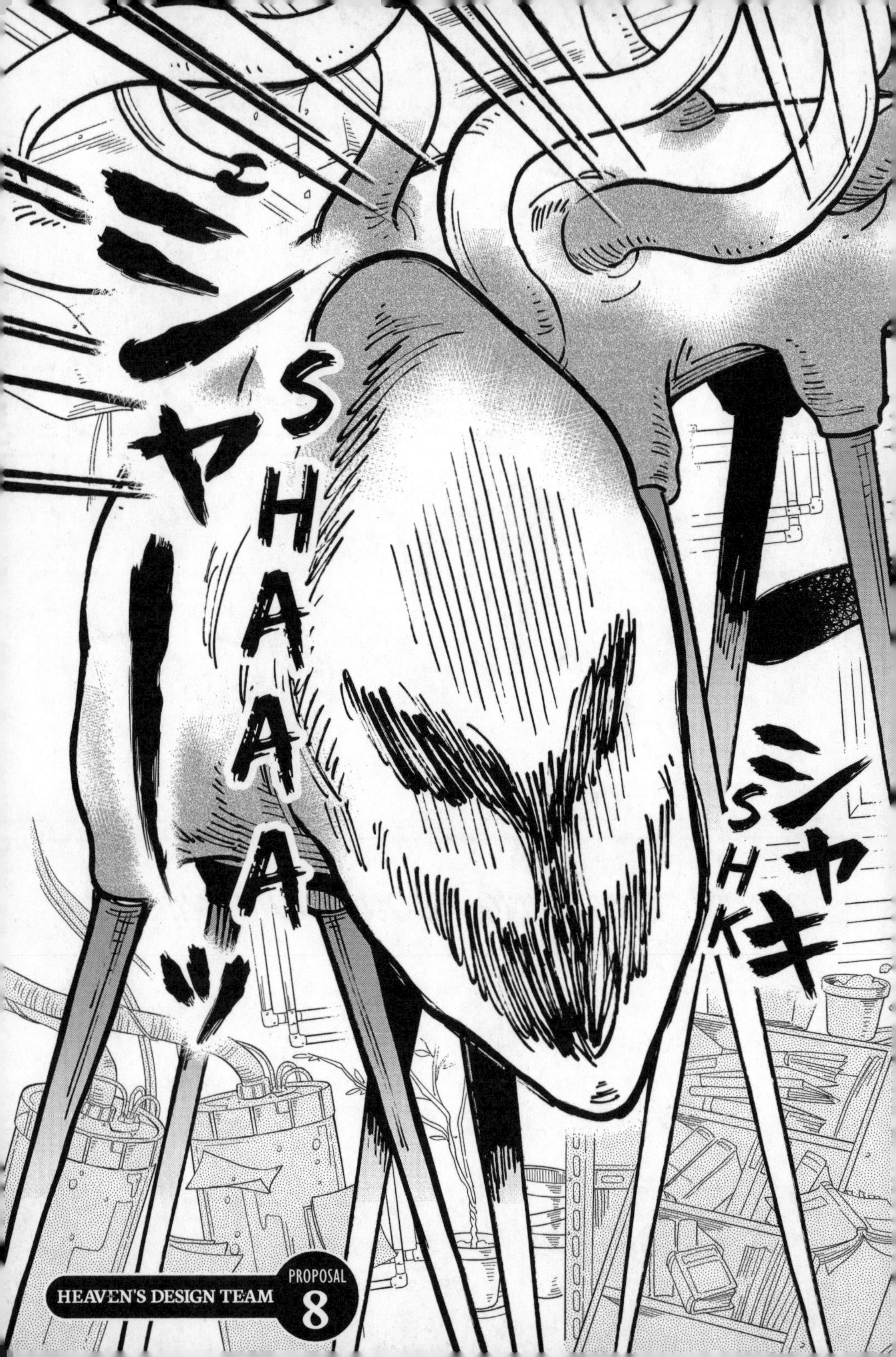
シャーッ
SHAAAA
シャキ
SHK
HEAVEN'S DESIGN TEAM
PROPOSAL 8

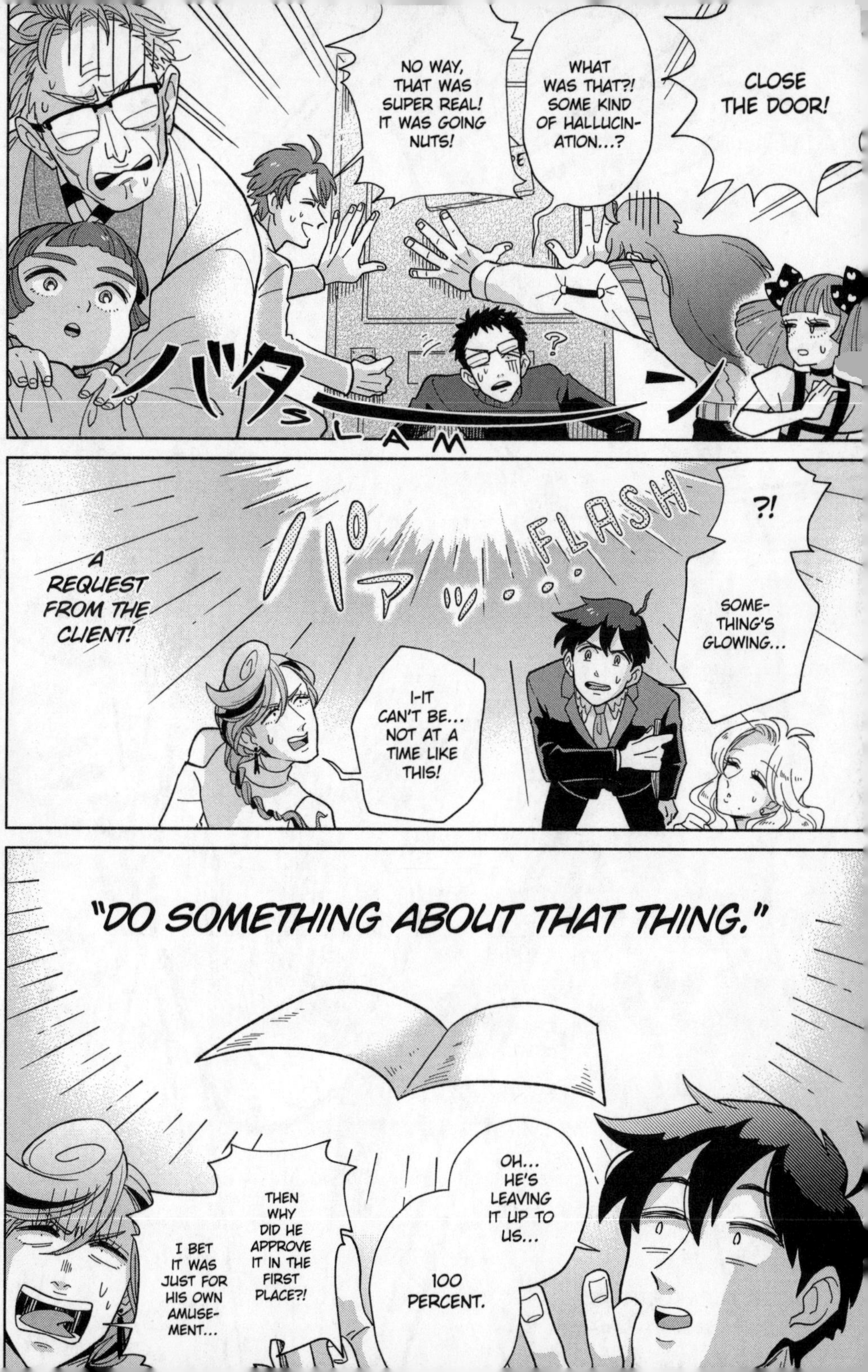
CLOSE THE DOOR!
WHAT WAS THAT?! SOME KIND OF HALLUCINATION...?
NO WAY, THAT WAS SUPER REAL! IT WAS GOING NUTS!
バタン
SLAM
?!
SOMETHING'S GLOWING...
パァッ...
FLASH
I-IT CAN'T BE... NOT AT A TIME LIKE THIS!
A REQUEST FROM THE CLIENT!
"DO SOMETHING ABOUT THAT THING."
OH... HE'S LEAVING IT UP TO US...
THEN WHY DID HE APPROVE IT IN THE FIRST PLACE?!
I BET IT WAS JUST FOR HIS OWN AMUSEMENT...
100 PERCENT.

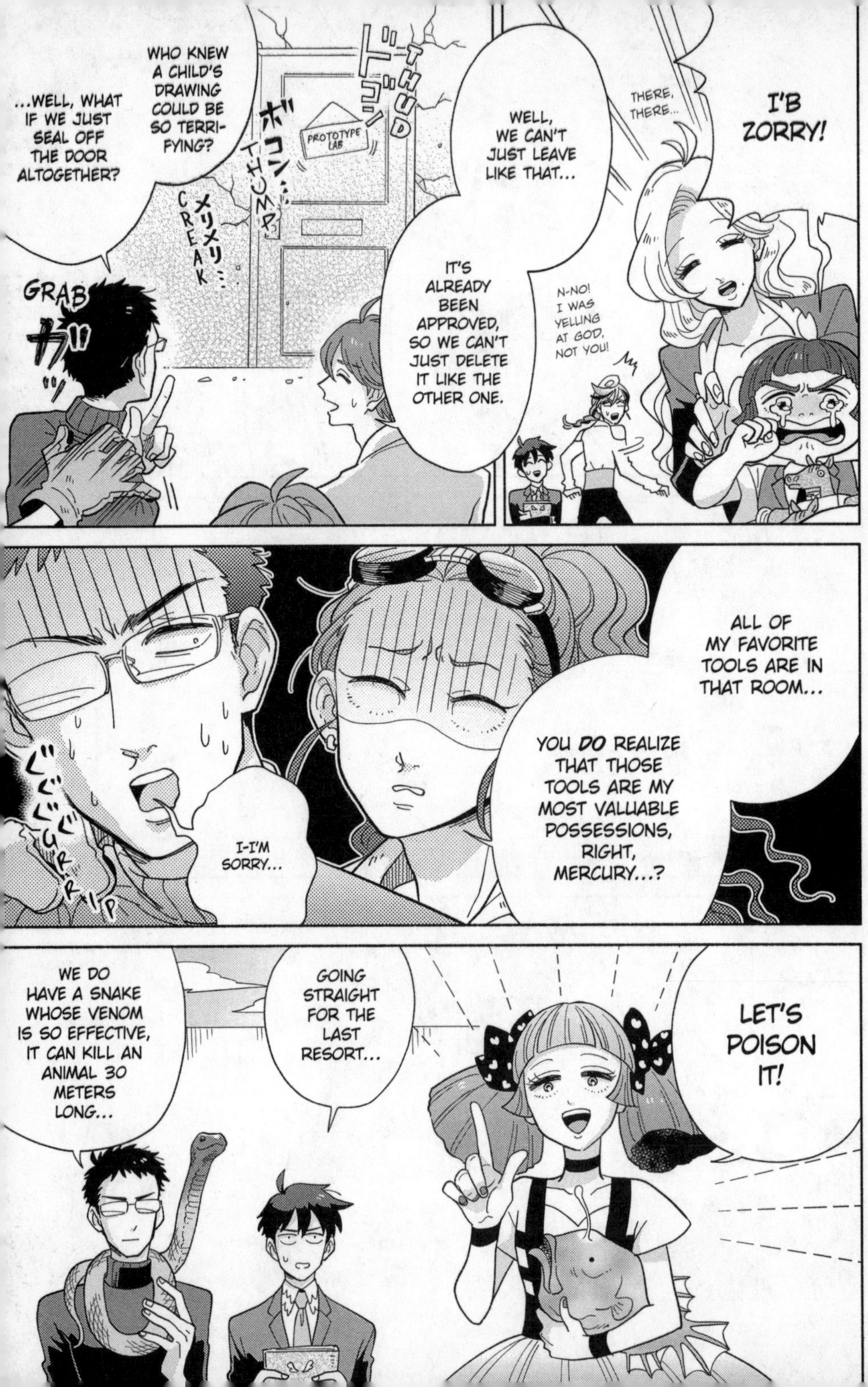

I'B ZORRY!
THERE, THERE...
N-NO! I WAS YELLING AT GOD, NOT YOU!
WELL, WE CAN'T JUST LEAVE LIKE THAT...
IT'S ALREADY BEEN APPROVED, SO WE CAN'T JUST DELETE IT LIKE THE OTHER ONE.
PROTOTYPE LAB
ドゴン THUD
ボコン THUMP
メリメリ CREAK
WHO KNEW A CHILD'S DRAWING COULD BE SO TERRIFYING?
...WELL, WHAT IF WE JUST SEAL OFF THE DOOR ALTOGETHER?
GRAB ガッ
ALL OF MY FAVORITE TOOLS ARE IN THAT ROOM...
YOU ***DO*** REALIZE THAT THOSE TOOLS ARE MY MOST VALUABLE POSSESSIONS, RIGHT, MERCURY...?
I-I'M SORRY...
ぐぐぐぐ GRRRIP
LET'S POISON IT!
GOING STRAIGHT FOR THE LAST RESORT...
WE DO HAVE A SNAKE WHOSE VENOM IS SO EFFECTIVE, IT CAN KILL AN ANIMAL 30 METERS LONG...

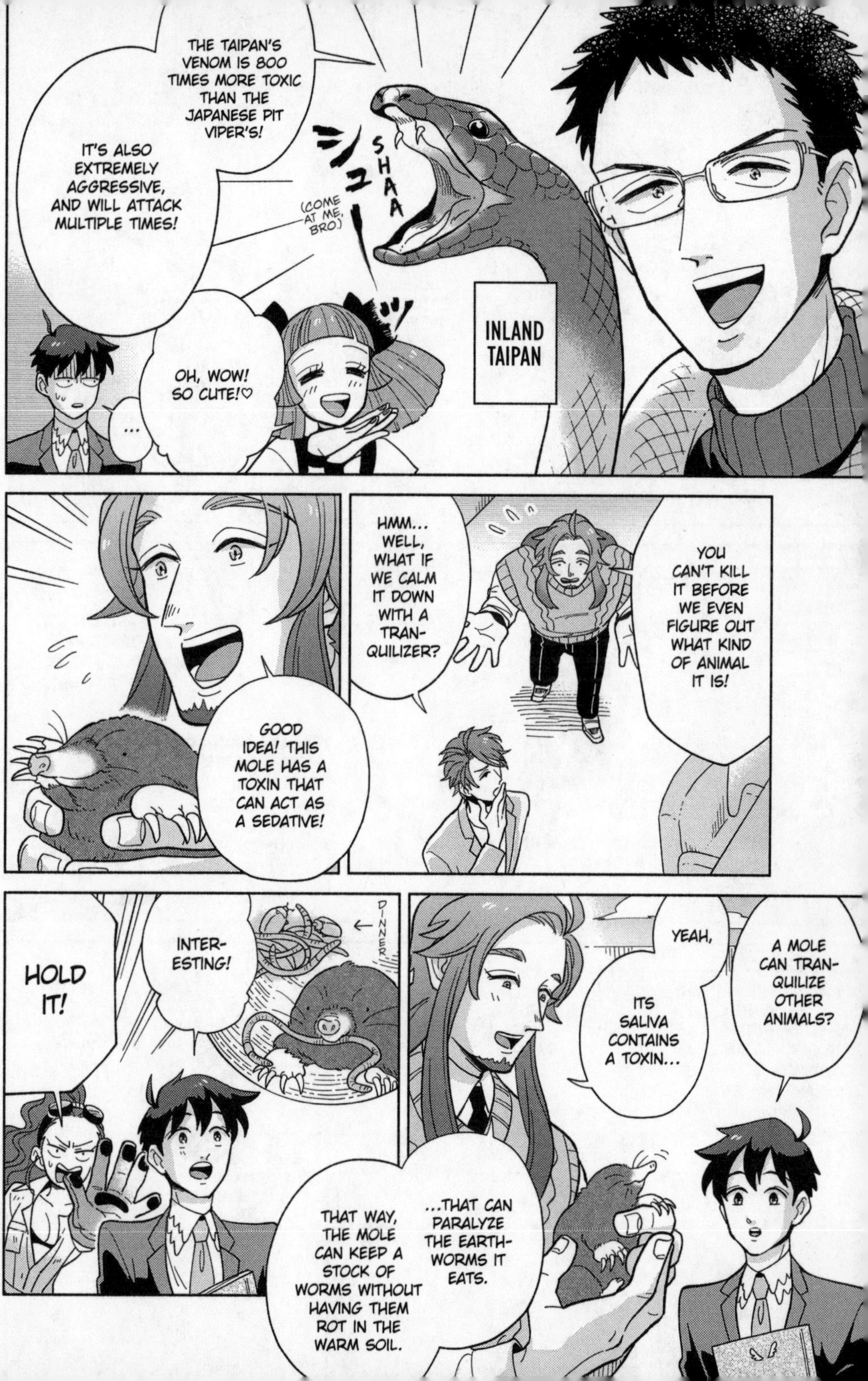
THE TAIPAN'S VENOM IS 800 TIMES MORE TOXIC THAN THE JAPANESE PIT VIPER'S!
IT'S ALSO EXTREMELY AGGRESSIVE, AND WILL ATTACK MULTIPLE TIMES!
SHAA
(COME AT ME, BRO.)
INLAND TAIPAN
OH, WOW! SO CUTE!♡
...
YOU CAN'T KILL IT BEFORE WE EVEN FIGURE OUT WHAT KIND OF ANIMAL IT IS!
HMM... WELL, WHAT IF WE CALM IT DOWN WITH A TRAN-QUILIZER?
GOOD IDEA! THIS MOLE HAS A TOXIN THAT CAN ACT AS A SEDATIVE!
A MOLE CAN TRAN-QUILIZE OTHER ANIMALS?
YEAH,
ITS SALIVA CONTAINS A TOXIN...
...THAT CAN PARALYZE THE EARTH-WORMS IT EATS.
THAT WAY, THE MOLE CAN KEEP A STOCK OF WORMS WITHOUT HAVING THEM ROT IN THE WARM SOIL.
DINNER
INTER-ESTING!
HOLD IT!

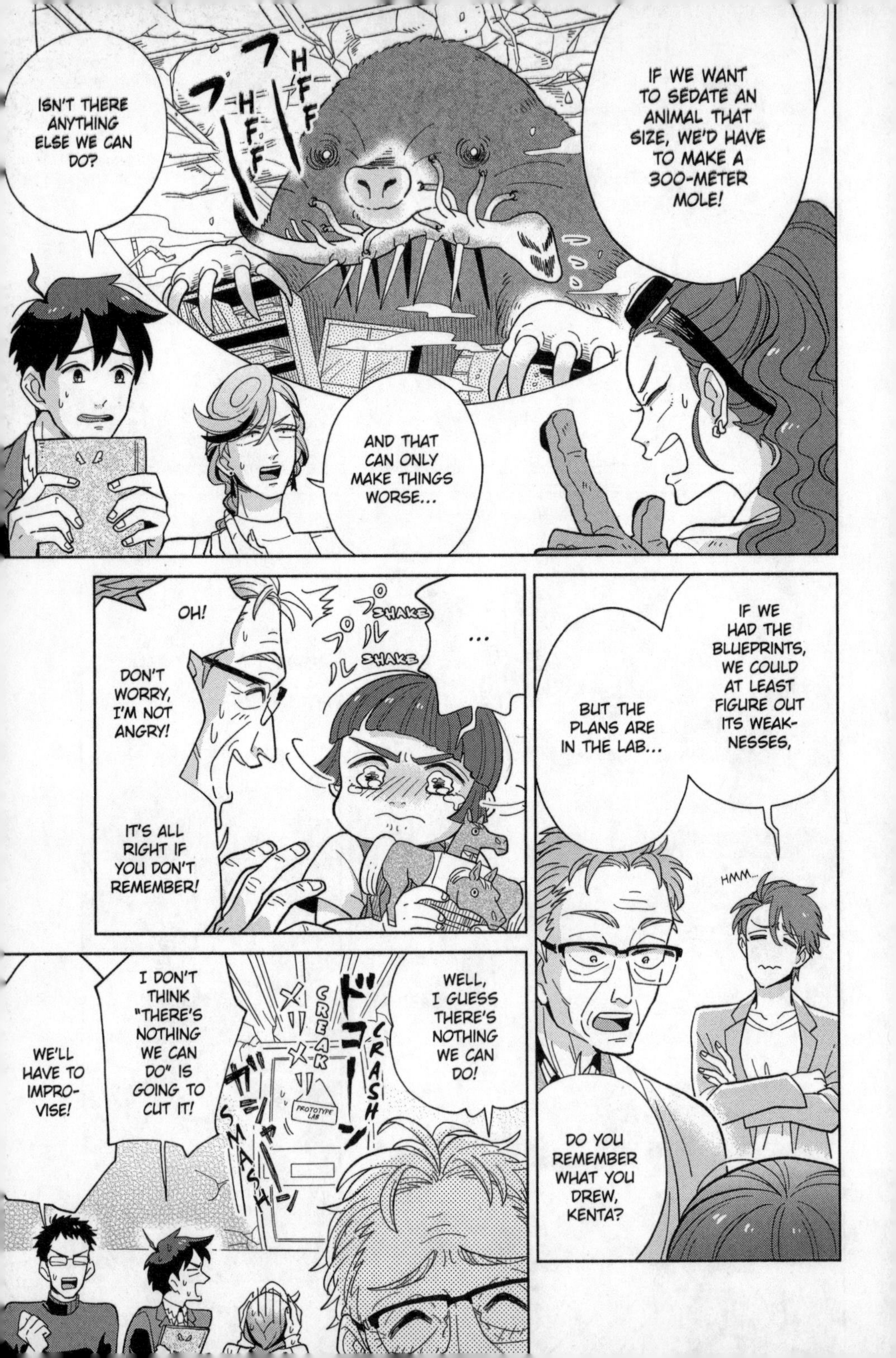

IF WE WANT TO SEDATE AN ANIMAL THAT SIZE, WE'D HAVE TO MAKE A 300-METER MOLE!
HFF HFF
AND THAT CAN ONLY MAKE THINGS WORSE...
ISN'T THERE ANYTHING ELSE WE CAN DO?
IF WE HAD THE BLUEPRINTS, WE COULD AT LEAST FIGURE OUT ITS WEAK-NESSES,
BUT THE PLANS ARE IN THE LAB...
HMM...
DO YOU REMEMBER WHAT YOU DREW, KENTA?
...
SHAKE SHAKE
OH!
DON'T WORRY, I'M NOT ANGRY!
IT'S ALL RIGHT IF YOU DON'T REMEMBER!
WELL, I GUESS THERE'S NOTHING WE CAN DO!
CRASH
CREAK
SMASH
PROTOTYPE LAB
I DON'T THINK "THERE'S NOTHING WE CAN DO" IS GOING TO CUT IT!
WE'LL HAVE TO IMPRO-VISE!

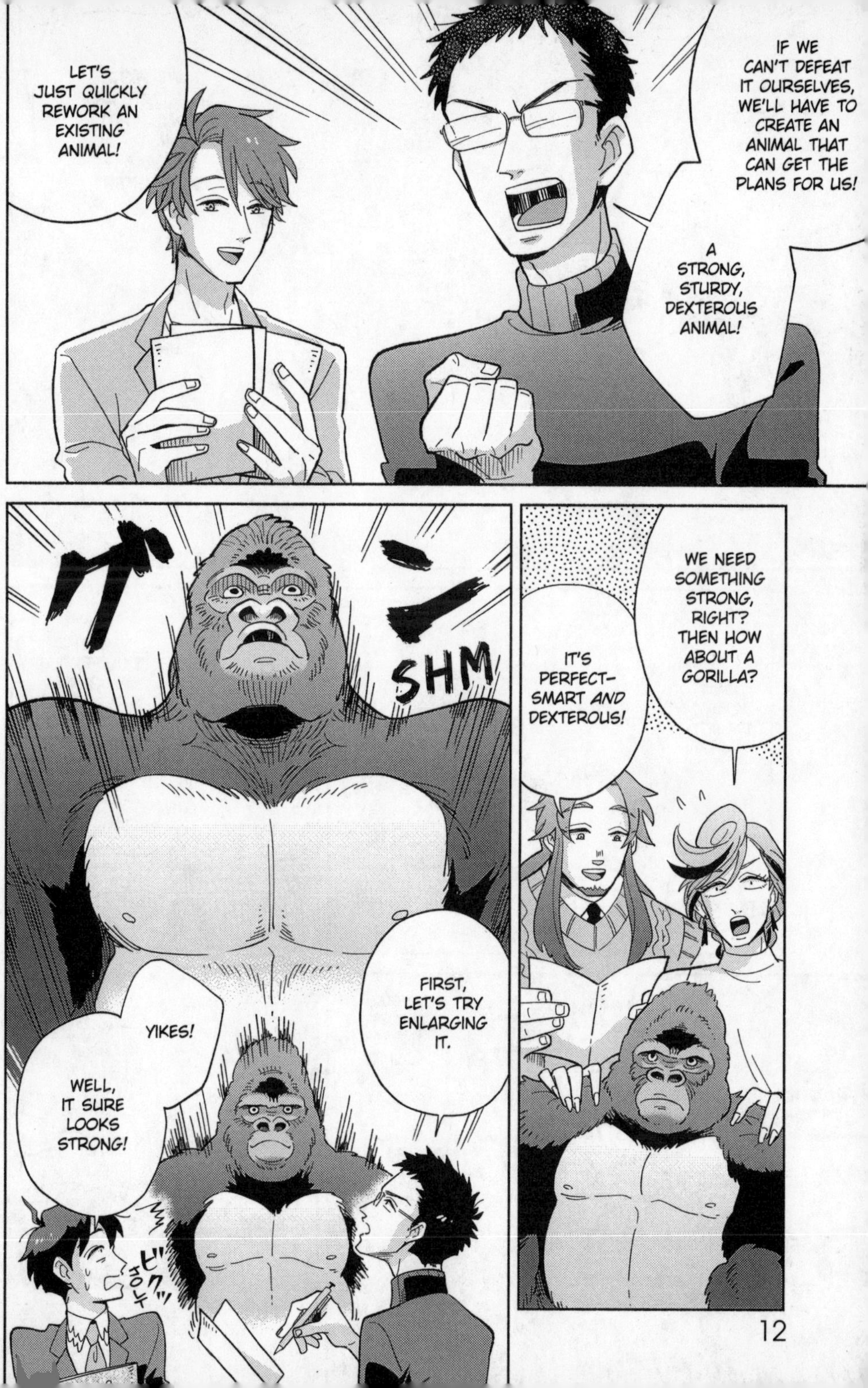
IF WE CAN'T DEFEAT IT OURSELVES, WE'LL HAVE TO CREATE AN ANIMAL THAT CAN GET THE PLANS FOR US!
A STRONG, STURDY, DEXTEROUS ANIMAL!
LET'S JUST QUICKLY REWORK AN EXISTING ANIMAL!
WE NEED SOMETHING STRONG, RIGHT? THEN HOW ABOUT A GORILLA?
IT'S PERFECT- SMART AND DEXTEROUS!
SHM
FIRST, LET'S TRY ENLARGING IT.
YIKES!
WELL, IT SURE LOOKS STRONG!

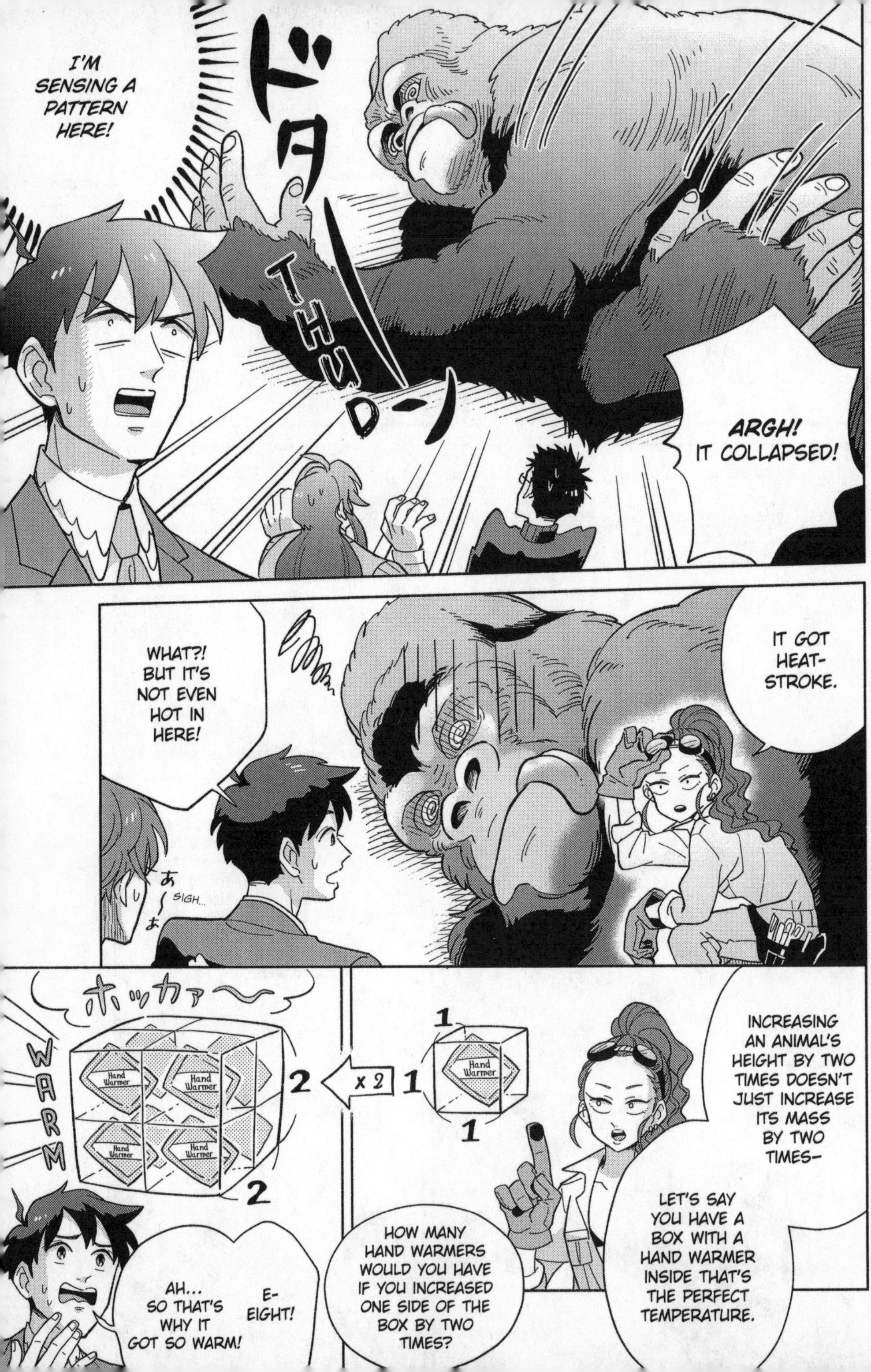
ドタ
THUD
ARGH! IT COLLAPSED!
I'M SENSING A PATTERN HERE!
IT GOT HEAT-STROKE.
WHAT?! BUT IT'S NOT EVEN HOT IN HERE!
あ〜あ
SIGH...
INCREASING AN ANIMAL'S HEIGHT BY TWO TIMES DOESN'T JUST INCREASE ITS MASS BY TWO TIMES—
LET'S SAY YOU HAVE A BOX WITH A HAND WARMER INSIDE THAT'S THE PERFECT TEMPERATURE.
1
Hand Warmer
1
1
x 2
HOW MANY HAND WARMERS WOULD YOU HAVE IF YOU INCREASED ONE SIDE OF THE BOX BY TWO TIMES?
ホッカァ〜
WARM
Hand Warmer
Hand Warmer
Hand Warmer
Hand Warmer
2
2
E-EIGHT!
AH... SO THAT'S WHY IT GOT SO WARM!

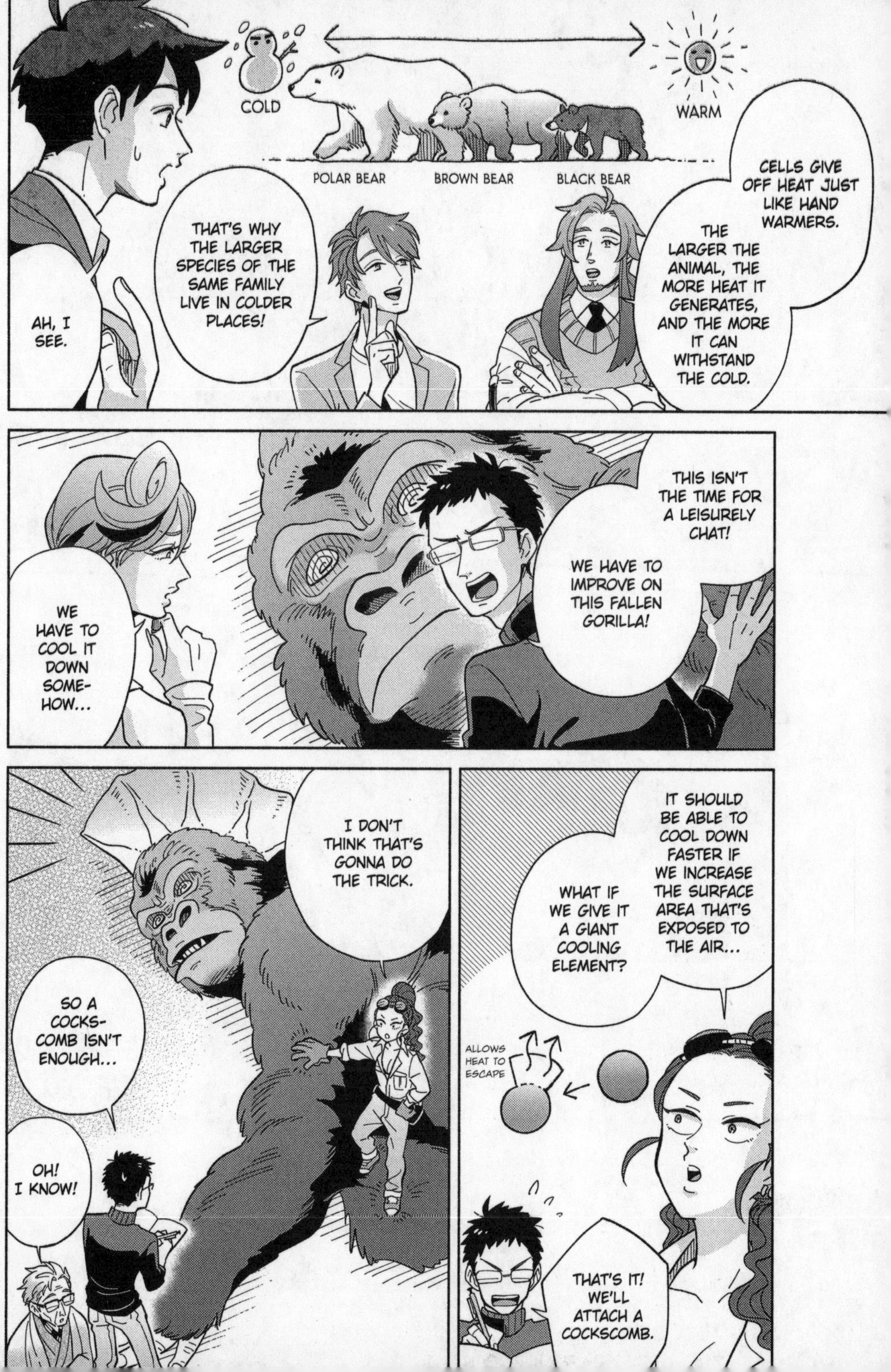
COLD
WARM
POLAR BEAR
BROWN BEAR
BLACK BEAR
CELLS GIVE OFF HEAT JUST LIKE HAND WARMERS.
THE LARGER THE ANIMAL, THE MORE HEAT IT GENERATES, AND THE MORE IT CAN WITHSTAND THE COLD.
THAT'S WHY THE LARGER SPECIES OF THE SAME FAMILY LIVE IN COLDER PLACES!
AH, I SEE.
THIS ISN'T THE TIME FOR A LEISURELY CHAT!
WE HAVE TO IMPROVE ON THIS FALLEN GORILLA!
WE HAVE TO COOL IT DOWN SOMEHOW...
IT SHOULD BE ABLE TO COOL DOWN FASTER IF WE INCREASE THE SURFACE AREA THAT'S EXPOSED TO THE AIR...
WHAT IF WE GIVE IT A GIANT COOLING ELEMENT?
ALLOWS HEAT TO ESCAPE
THAT'S IT! WE'LL ATTACH A COCKSCOMB.
I DON'T THINK THAT'S GONNA DO THE TRICK.
SO A COCKSCOMB ISN'T ENOUGH...
OH! I KNOW!

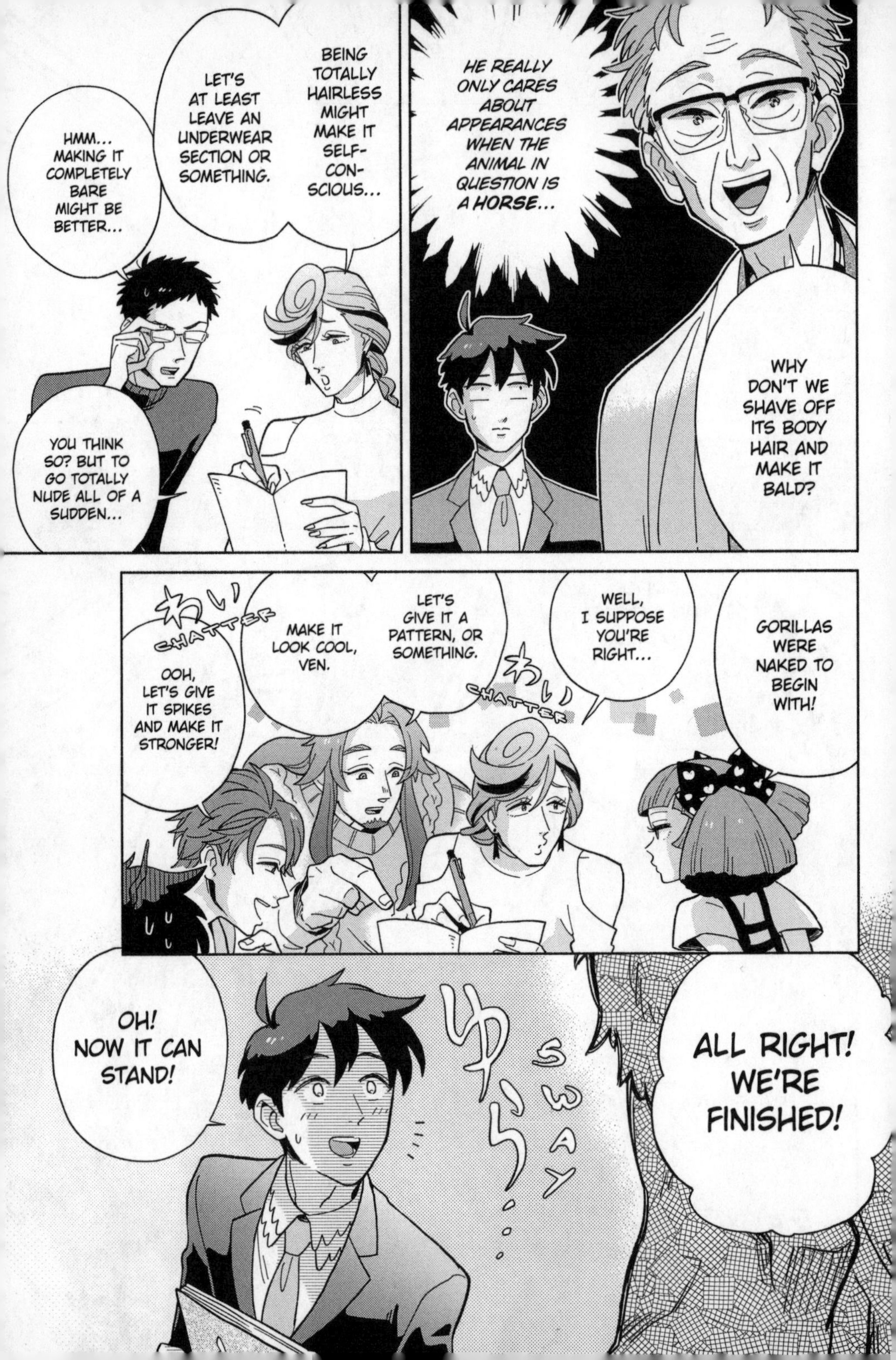
WHY DON'T WE SHAVE OFF ITS BODY HAIR AND MAKE IT BALD?
HE REALLY ONLY CARES ABOUT APPEARANCES WHEN THE ANIMAL IN QUESTION IS A HORSE...
BEING TOTALLY HAIRLESS MIGHT MAKE IT SELF-CONSCIOUS...
LET'S AT LEAST LEAVE AN UNDERWEAR SECTION OR SOMETHING.
HMM... MAKING IT COMPLETELY BARE MIGHT BE BETTER...
YOU THINK SO? BUT TO GO TOTALLY NUDE ALL OF A SUDDEN...
GORILLAS WERE NAKED TO BEGIN WITH!
WELL, I SUPPOSE YOU'RE RIGHT...
CHATTER
LET'S GIVE IT A PATTERN, OR SOMETHING.
MAKE IT LOOK COOL, VEN.
CHATTER
OOH, LET'S GIVE IT SPIKES AND MAKE IT STRONGER!
ALL RIGHT! WE'RE FINISHED!
SWAY
OH! NOW IT CAN STAND!

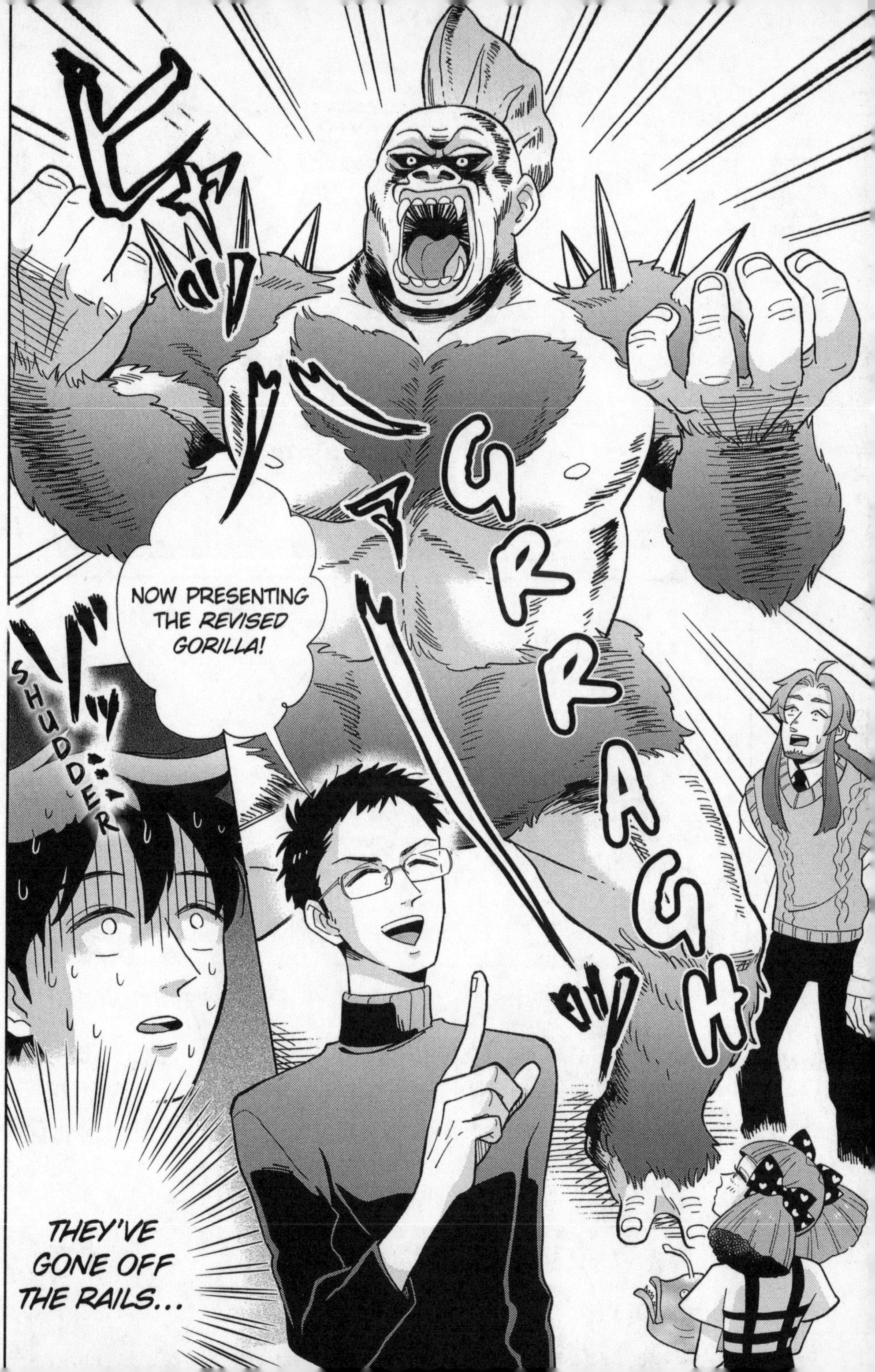
GRRRAAAGH
NOW PRESENTING THE REVISED GORILLA!
SHUDDER
THEY'VE GONE OFF THE RAILS...

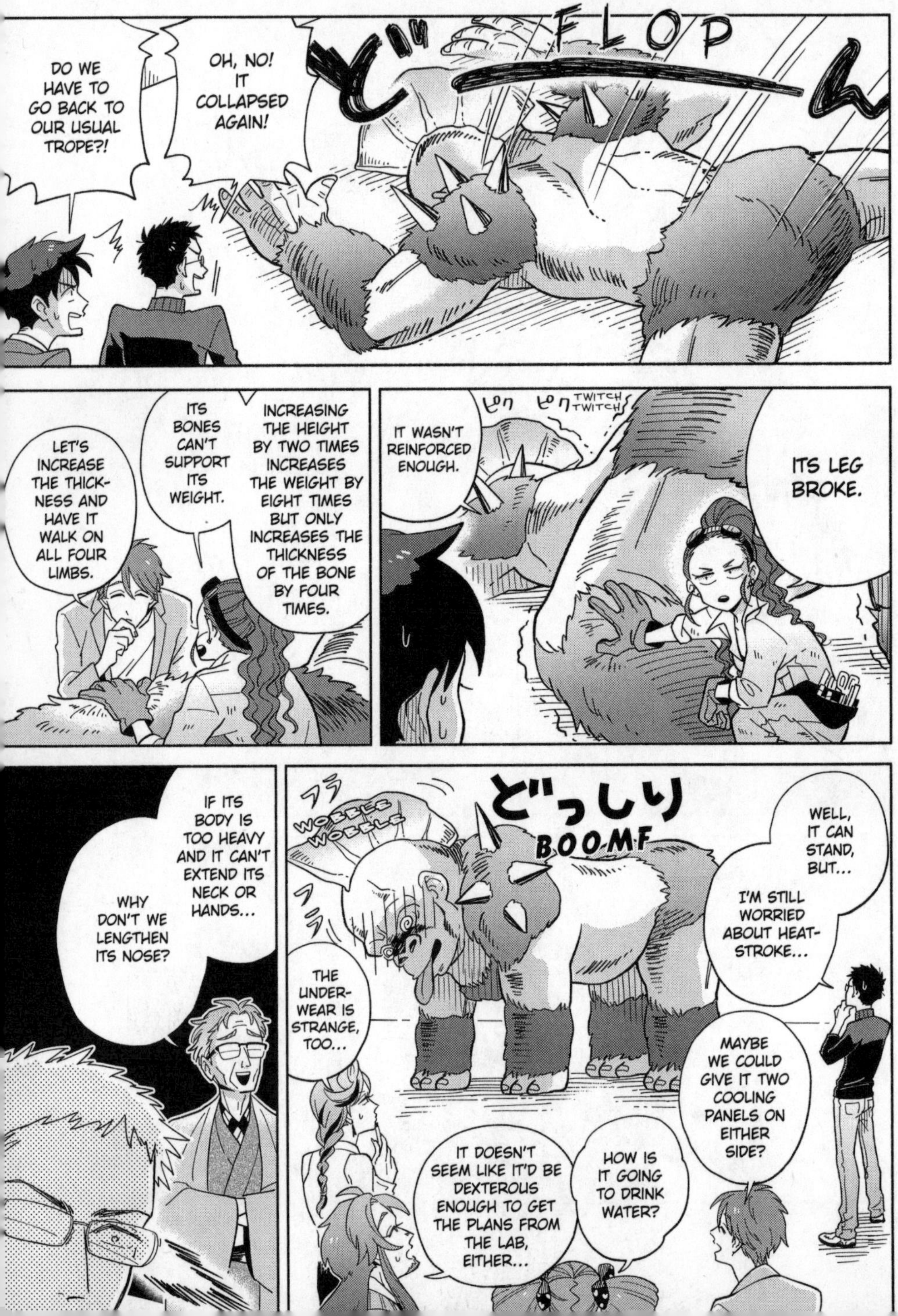
FLOP
OH, NO! IT COLLAPSED AGAIN!
DO WE HAVE TO GO BACK TO OUR USUAL TROPE?!
ITS LEG BROKE.
ピク ピク
TWITCH TWITCH
IT WASN'T REINFORCED ENOUGH.
INCREASING THE HEIGHT BY TWO TIMES INCREASES THE WEIGHT BY EIGHT TIMES BUT ONLY INCREASES THE THICKNESS OF THE BONE BY FOUR TIMES.
ITS BONES CAN'T SUPPORT ITS WEIGHT.
LET'S INCREASE THE THICK-NESS AND HAVE IT WALK ON ALL FOUR LIMBS.
WELL, IT CAN STAND, BUT...
I'M STILL WORRIED ABOUT HEAT-STROKE...
どっしり
BOOMF
フラ フラ
WOBBLE WOBBLE
MAYBE WE COULD GIVE IT TWO COOLING PANELS ON EITHER SIDE?
THE UNDER-WEAR IS STRANGE, TOO...
HOW IS IT GOING TO DRINK WATER?
IT DOESN'T SEEM LIKE IT'D BE DEXTEROUS ENOUGH TO GET THE PLANS FROM THE LAB, EITHER...
IF ITS BODY IS TOO HEAVY AND IT CAN'T EXTEND ITS NECK OR HANDS...
WHY DON'T WE LENGTHEN ITS NOSE?

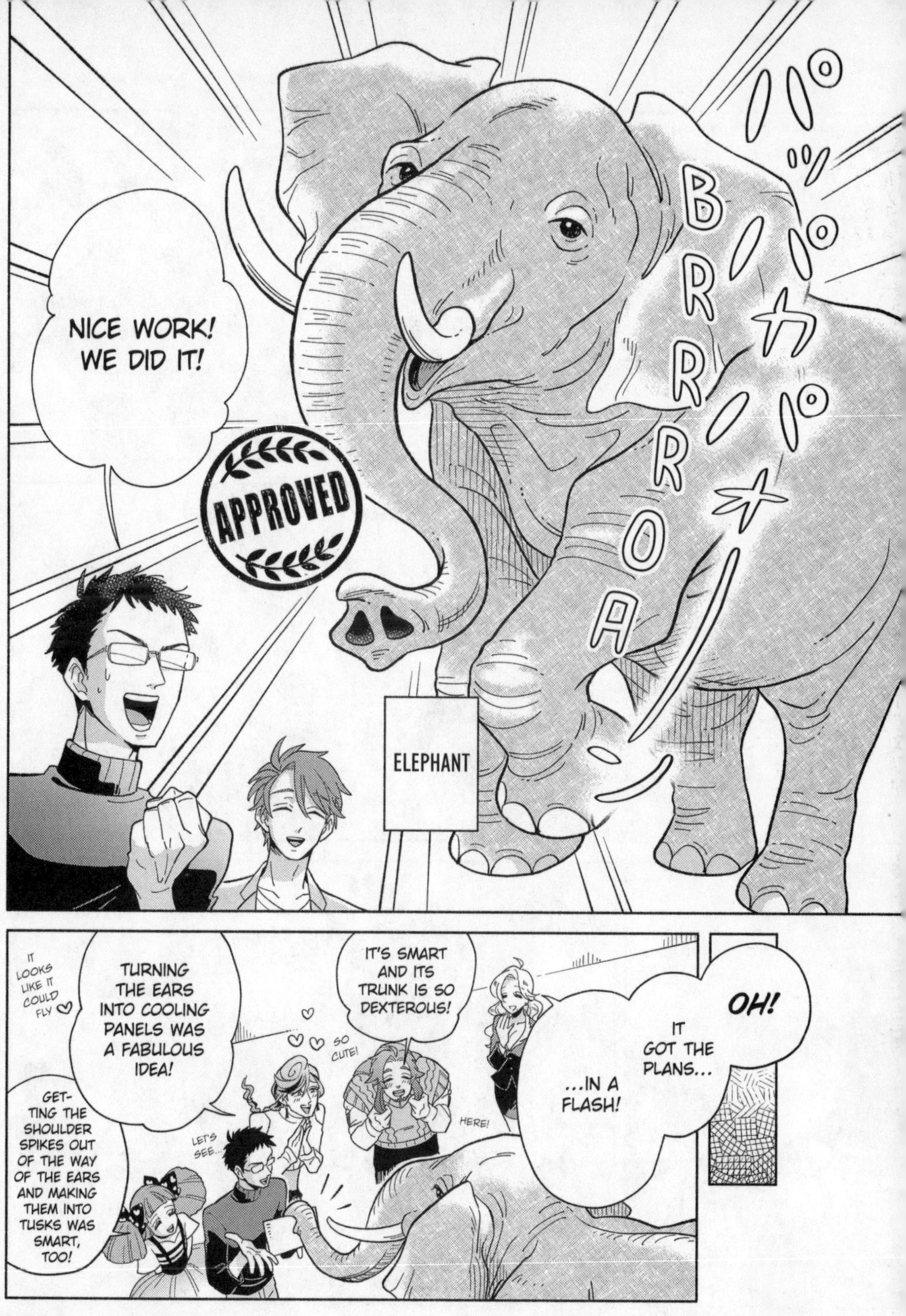
BRRROA
NICE WORK! WE DID IT!
APPROVED
ELEPHANT
OH! IT GOT THE PLANS... ...IN A FLASH!
HERE!
IT'S SMART AND ITS TRUNK IS SO DEXTEROUS!
SO CUTE!
TURNING THE EARS INTO COOLING PANELS WAS A FABULOUS IDEA!
IT LOOKS LIKE IT COULD FLY ♡
LET'S SEE...
GET-TING THE SHOULDER SPIKES OUT OF THE WAY OF THE EARS AND MAKING THEM INTO TUSKS WAS SMART, TOO!

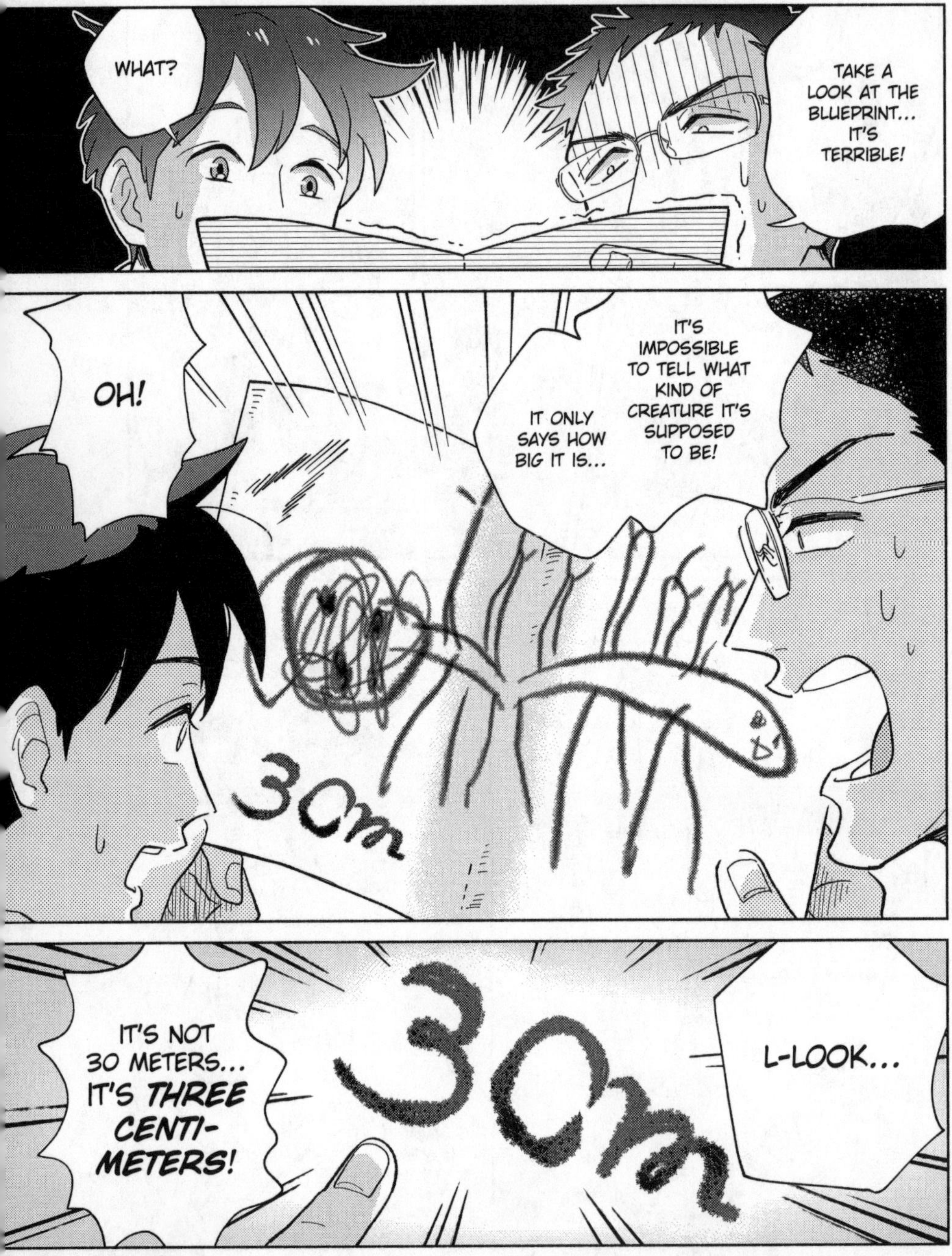
TAKE A LOOK AT THE BLUEPRINT... IT'S TERRIBLE!
WHAT?
IT'S IMPOSSIBLE TO TELL WHAT KIND OF CREATURE IT'S SUPPOSED TO BE!
IT ONLY SAYS HOW BIG IT IS...
OH!
L-LOOK...
IT'S NOT 30 METERS... IT'S *THREE CENTI-METERS!*

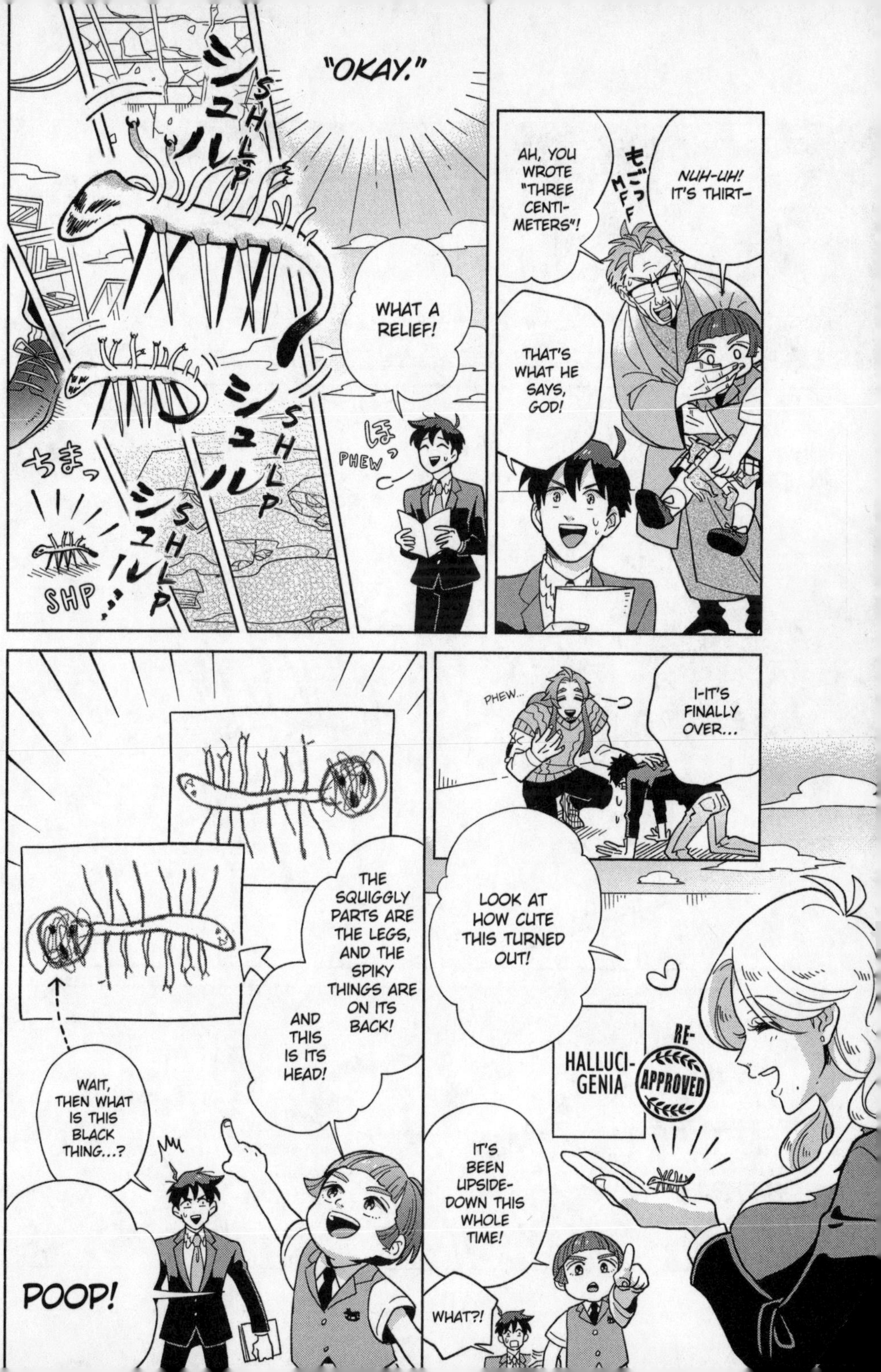

NUH-UH! IT'S THIRT-
もごっ MFF
AH, YOU WROTE "THREE CENTI-METERS"!
THAT'S WHAT HE SAYS, GOD!
"OKAY."
WHAT A RELIEF!
ほっ PHEW
シュル SHLP
シュル SHLP
シュル SHLP
ちまっ SHP
I-IT'S FINALLY OVER...
PHEW...
LOOK AT HOW CUTE THIS TURNED OUT!
HALLUCI-GENIA
RE-APPROVED
IT'S BEEN UPSIDE-DOWN THIS WHOLE TIME!
WHAT?!
THE SQUIGGLY PARTS ARE THE LEGS, AND THE SPIKY THINGS ARE ON ITS BACK!
AND THIS IS ITS HEAD!
WAIT, THEN WHAT IS THIS BLACK THING...?
POOP!

# THE ENCYCLOPEDIA OF REAL ANIMALS 08

## ANIMAL 22 | ELEPHANT

An African elephant (top) and an Asian elephant. The African elephant has larger ears.

Photo: John Warburton-Lee/Aflo

THE REAL THING

Photo: Minden Pictures/Aflo

NICE WORK! WE DID IT!
APPROVED
ELEPHANT
BRRROA

There are three species of elephant, including the Asian elephant, the African bush elephant, and the African forest elephant (the Indian elephant belongs to the Asian elephant species). Their large ears help cool their body temperature, and African elephants, which inhabit a comparatively warmer climate, have larger ears than their Asian counterparts. With their extremely large bodies, their heads alone can weigh up to one ton and their necks are very thick and short, making it difficult to reach the ground. It's believed that this is why their trunks became so long.

| | |
|---|---|
| **[Name]** | Elephant |
| **[Classification]** | Class: Mammalia<br>Order: Proboscidea<br>Family: Elephantidae |
| **[Habitat]** | Sub-Saharan Africa, India, South East Asia |
| **[Height]** | 5-7 m (16.4-23 ft) |

## ANIMAL 23 | HALLUCIGENIA

The picture below shows the hallucigenia both upside-down and backwards.

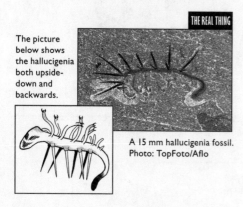

THE REAL THING

A 15 mm hallucigenia fossil.
Photo: TopFoto/Aflo

The first hallucigenia fossil was discovered in Canada in 1911. It lived around 500 million years ago, and its name derives from the Latin word "hallucinatio." Just like in this chapter, it was originally thought that the spines on the hallucigenia's back were its legs. It was later reinterpreted the right way up. In 2015, it was also determined that the area once thought to be the head was actually a stain (decay fluids squeezed out of the organism).

**[Name]**      Hallucigenia
**[Temporal range]**      500 million years ago
**[Length]**      1-5cm (0.4-2 in)

---

## ANIMAL 24 | MOLE

Though moles are nearly blind, they have an excellent direction-al sense of smell. Their front legs extend outwards and are ideal for digging and shoveling dirt away to either side. Some species are also skilled swimmers. Members of the Talpidae family use their toxic saliva to paralyze earthworms, which allows them to store their prey alive in special larders in their burrows.

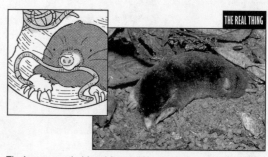

THE REAL THING

The Japanese mole (above) lives in Western Japan, while the small Japanese mole inhabits Eastern Japan.

Photo: Gakken/Aflo

**[Name]**      Mole
**[Classification]**      Class: Mammalia
     Order: Eulipotyphla
     Family: Talpidae
**[Habitat]**      Northern Hemisphere
**[Length]**      7-16 cm (3-6.3 in)

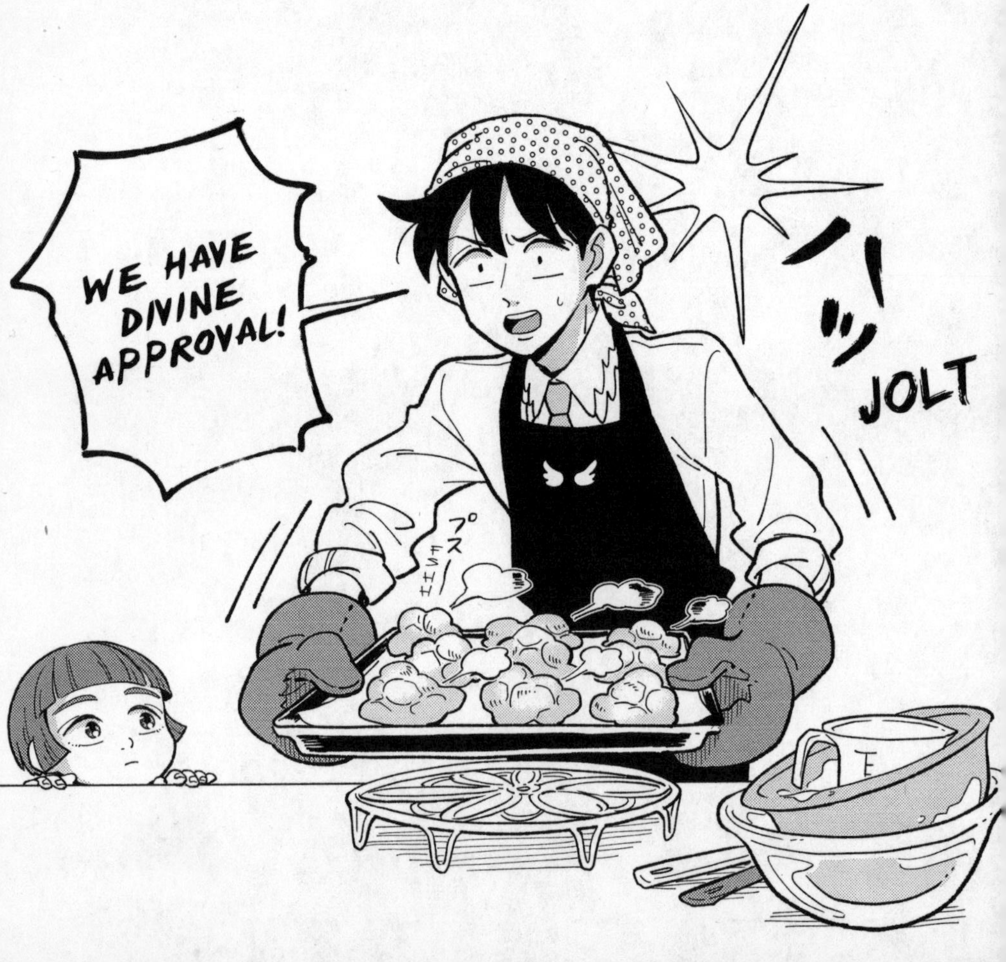

ハッ
JOLT
WE HAVE DIVINE APPROVAL!
プス

# HEAVEN'S DESIGN TEAM

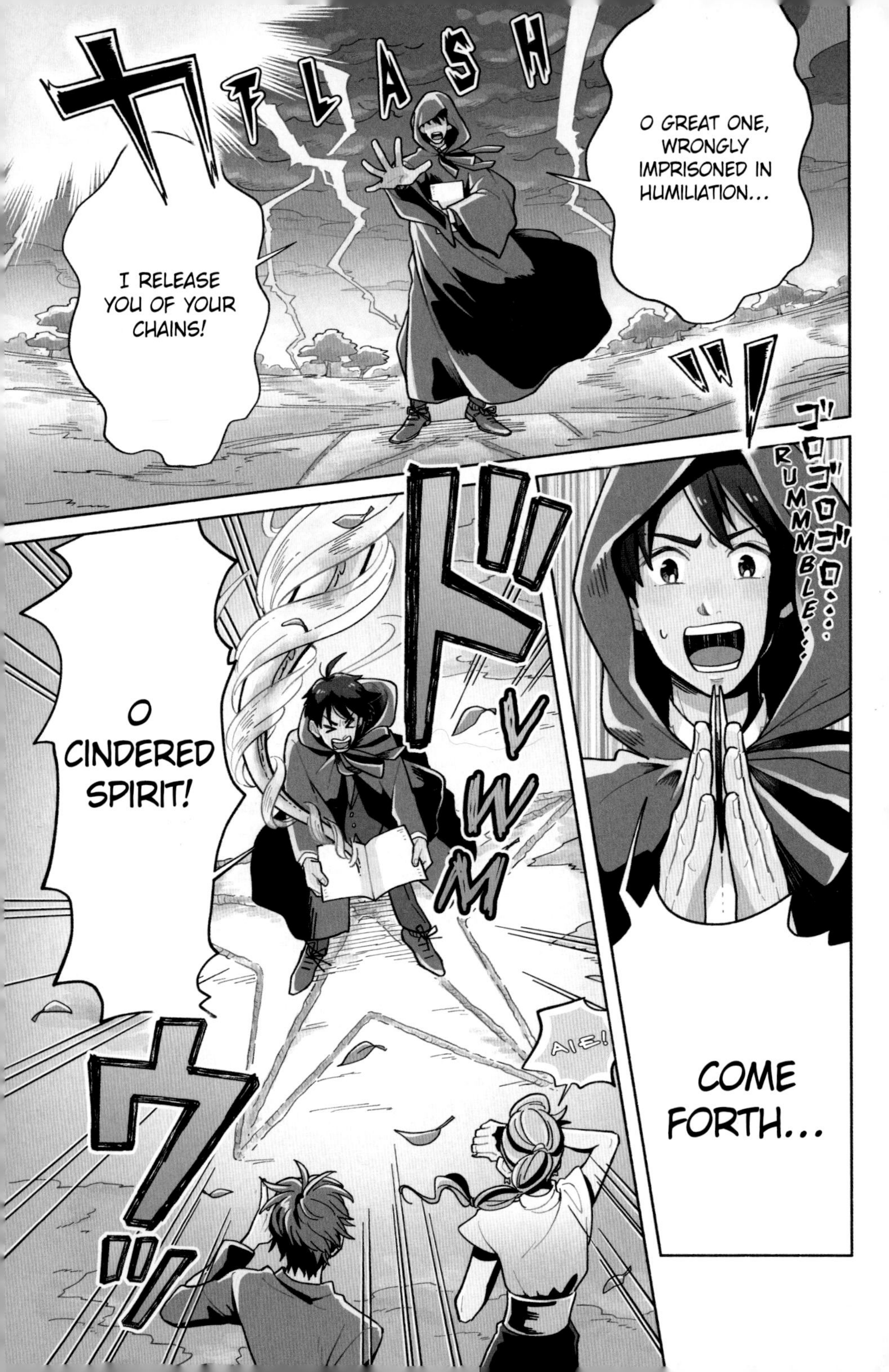
O GREAT ONE, WRONGLY IMPRISONED IN HUMILIATION...
カッ
FLASH
I RELEASE YOU OF YOUR CHAINS!
ゴロゴロゴロ…
RUMMMBLE...
COME FORTH...
ドウッ
VWM
O CINDERED SPIRIT!
AIE!

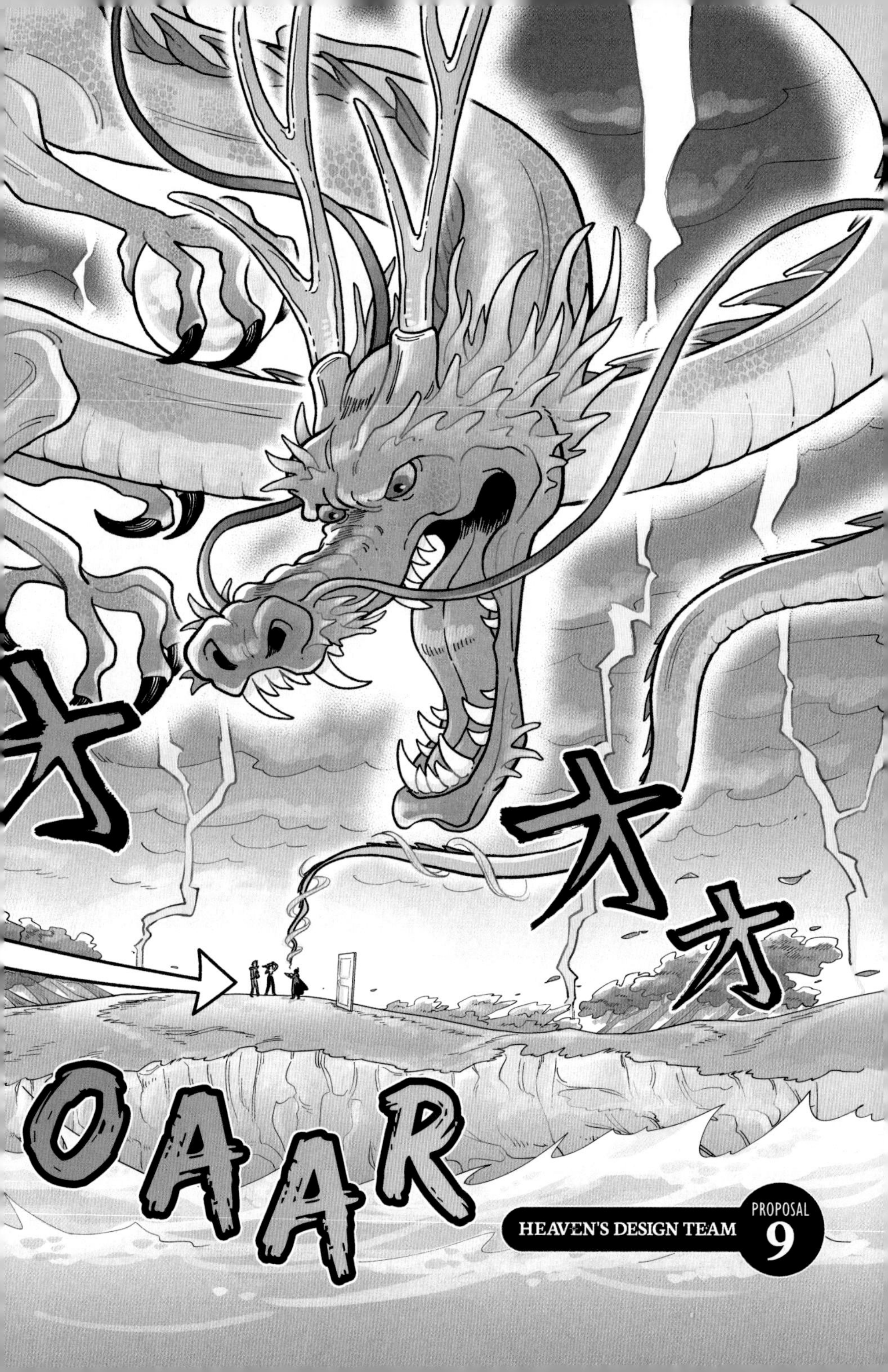

オォォ
OAAR
HEAVEN'S DESIGN TEAM
PROPOSAL
9

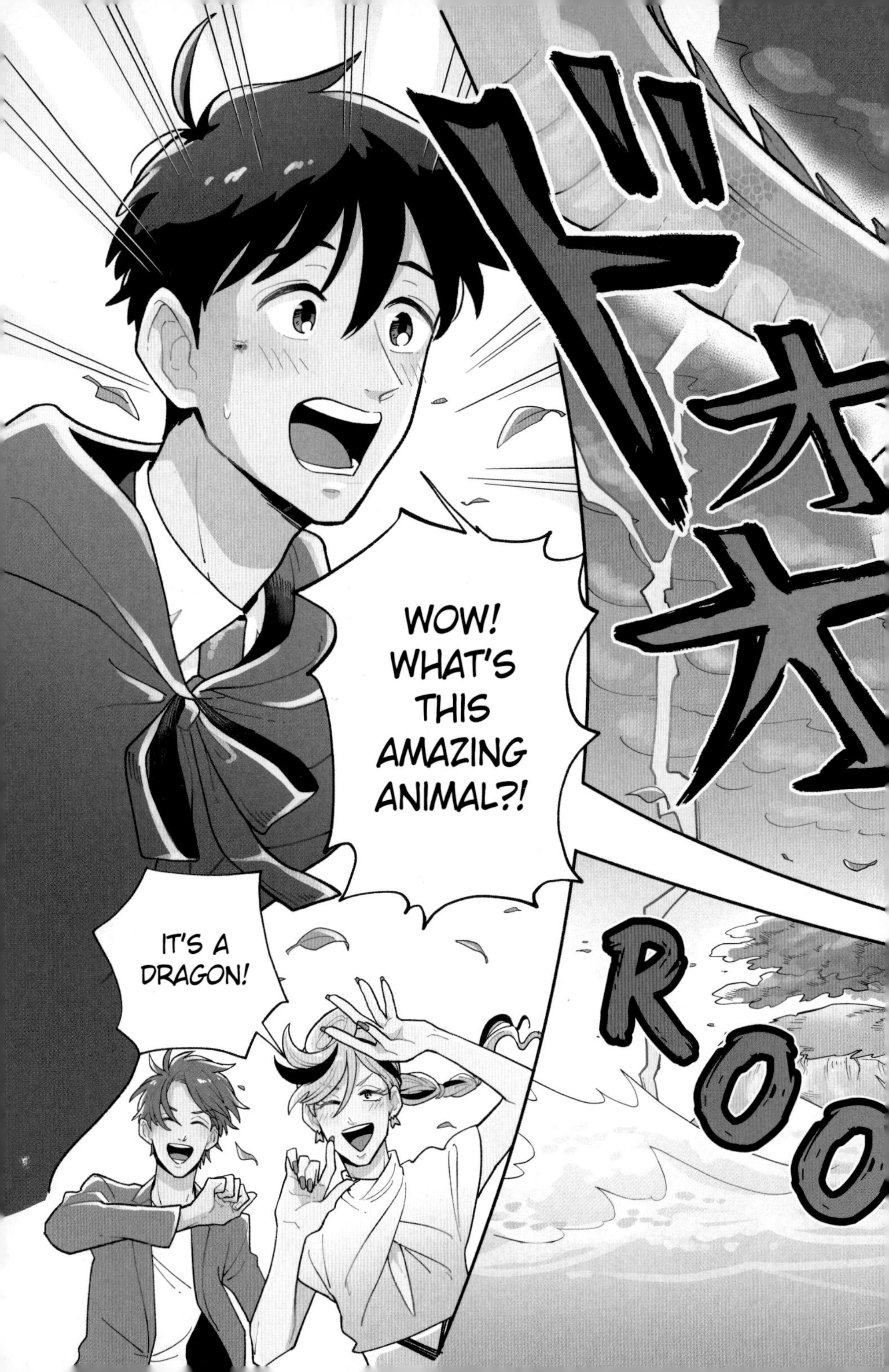
ROO
WOW! WHAT'S THIS AMAZING ANIMAL?!
IT'S A DRAGON!

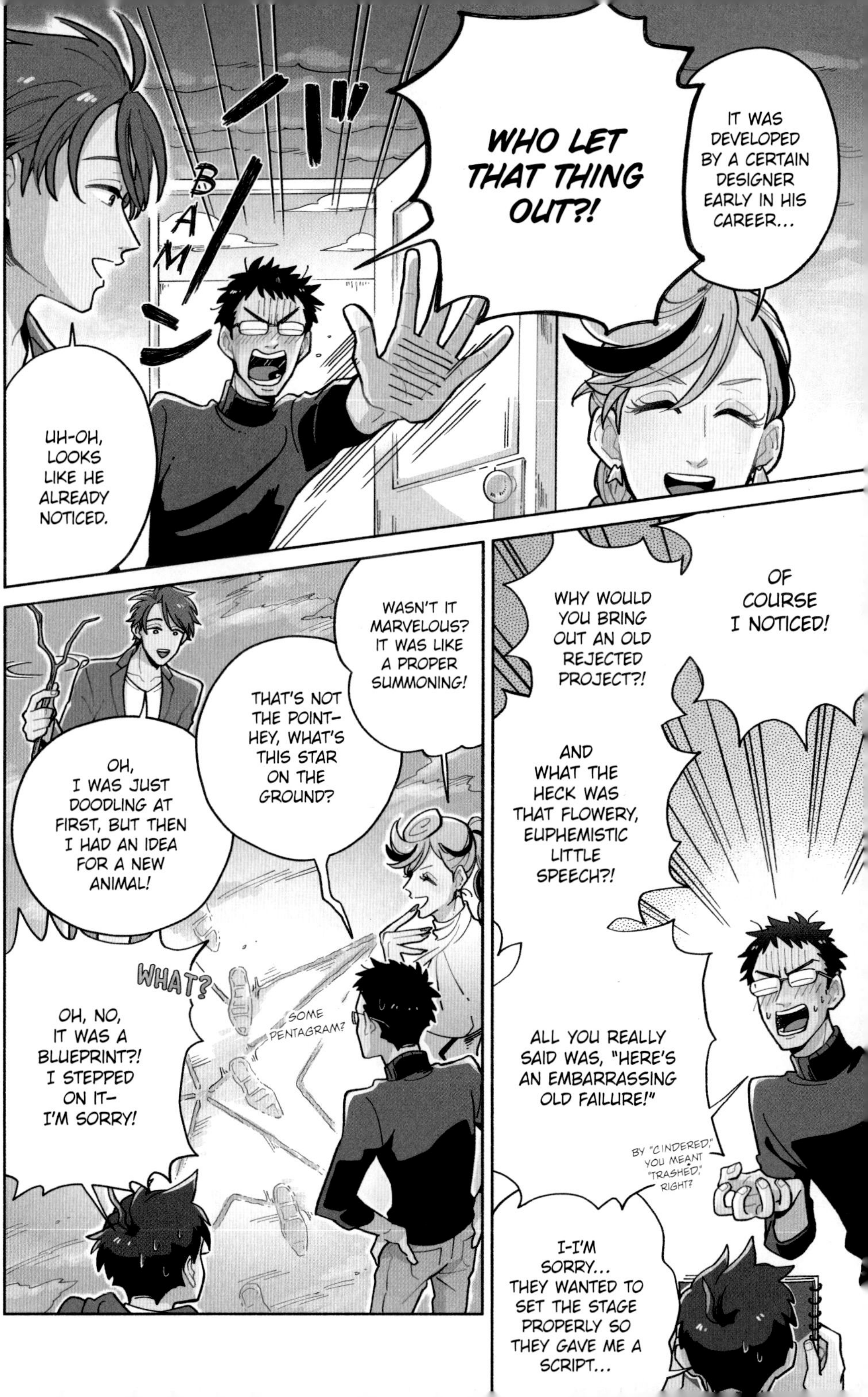
IT WAS DEVELOPED BY A CERTAIN DESIGNER EARLY IN HIS CAREER…
WHO LET THAT THING OUT?!
BAM
UH-OH, LOOKS LIKE HE ALREADY NOTICED.
OF COURSE I NOTICED!
WHY WOULD YOU BRING OUT AN OLD REJECTED PROJECT?!
AND WHAT THE HECK WAS THAT FLOWERY, EUPHEMISTIC LITTLE SPEECH?!
ALL YOU REALLY SAID WAS, "HERE'S AN EMBARRASSING OLD FAILURE!"
BY "CINDERED," YOU MEANT "TRASHED," RIGHT?
I-I'M SORRY… THEY WANTED TO SET THE STAGE PROPERLY SO THEY GAVE ME A SCRIPT…
WASN'T IT MARVELOUS? IT WAS LIKE A PROPER SUMMONING!
THAT'S NOT THE POINT— HEY, WHAT'S THIS STAR ON THE GROUND?
OH, I WAS JUST DOODLING AT FIRST, BUT THEN I HAD AN IDEA FOR A NEW ANIMAL!
WHAT?
SOME PENTAGRAM?
OH, NO, IT WAS A BLUEPRINT?! I STEPPED ON IT— I'M SORRY!

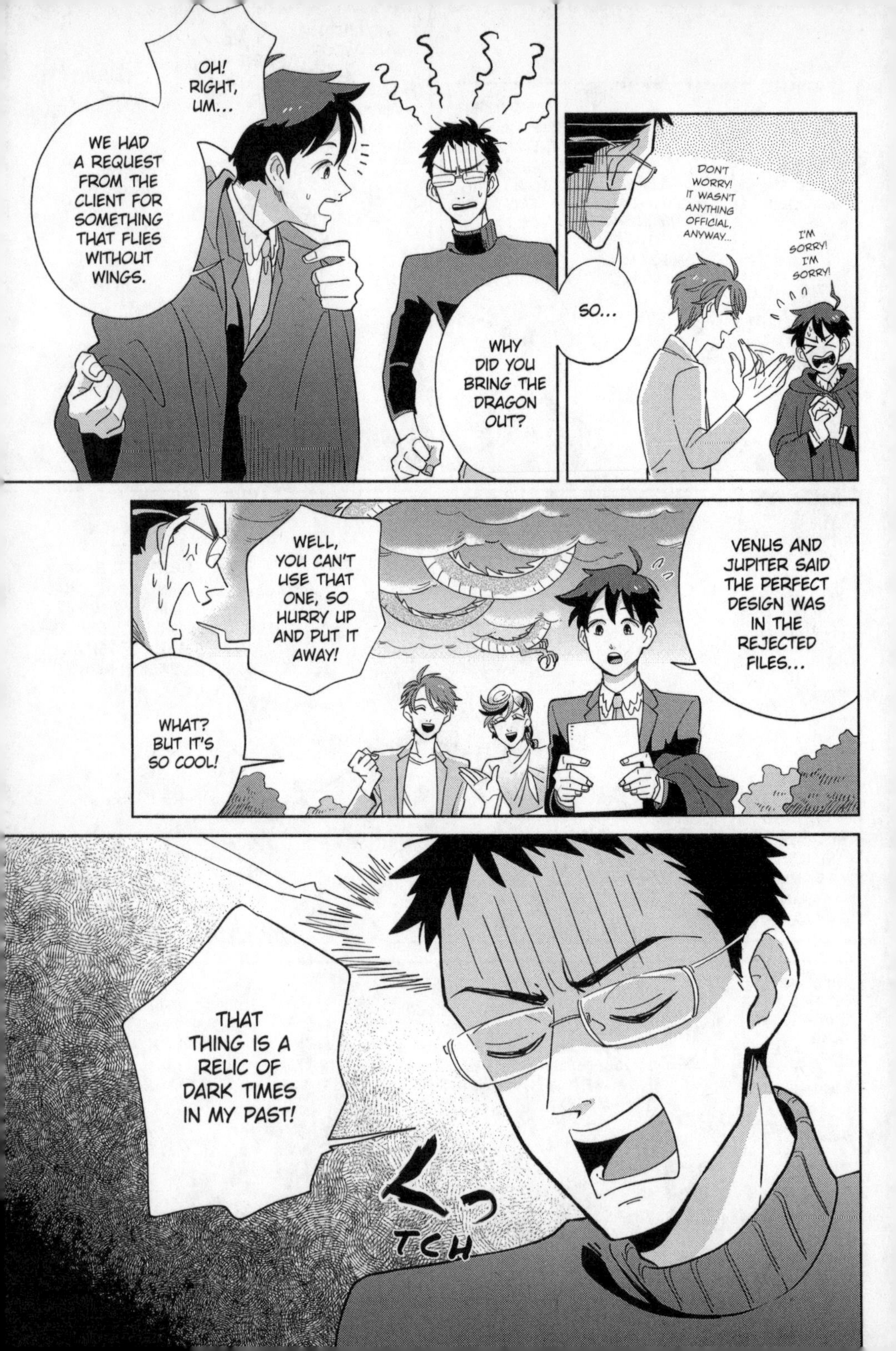

DON'T WORRY! IT WASN'T ANYTHING OFFICIAL, ANYWAY...
I'M SORRY! I'M SORRY!
SO...
WHY DID YOU BRING THE DRAGON OUT?
OH! RIGHT, UM...
WE HAD A REQUEST FROM THE CLIENT FOR SOMETHING THAT FLIES WITHOUT WINGS.
VENUS AND JUPITER SAID THE PERFECT DESIGN WAS IN THE REJECTED FILES...
WELL, YOU CAN'T USE THAT ONE, SO HURRY UP AND PUT IT AWAY!
WHAT? BUT IT'S SO COOL!
THAT THING IS A RELIC OF DARK TIMES IN MY PAST!
TCH

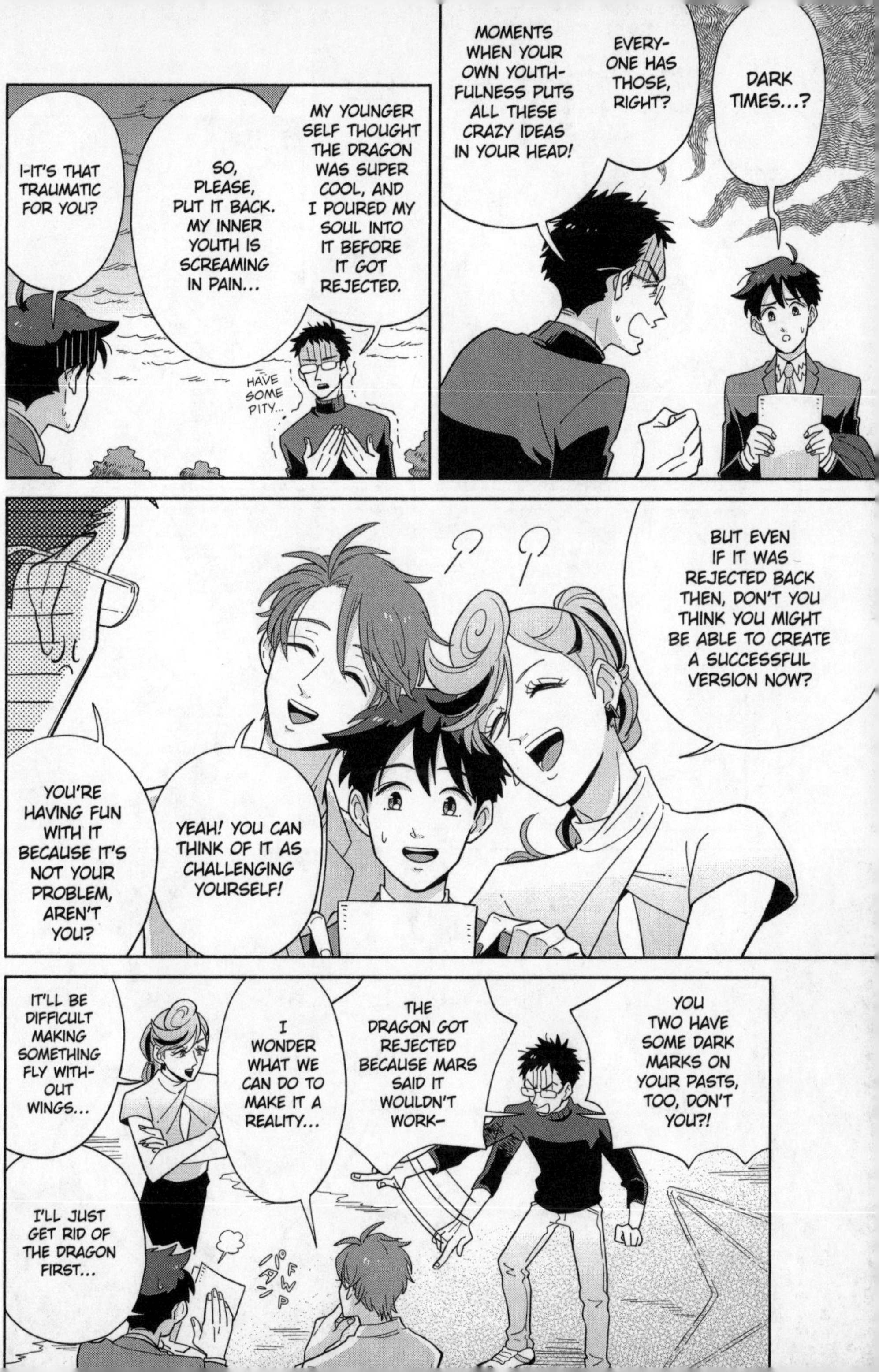
DARK TIMES...?
EVERY-ONE HAS THOSE, RIGHT?
MOMENTS WHEN YOUR OWN YOUTH-FULNESS PUTS ALL THESE CRAZY IDEAS IN YOUR HEAD!
MY YOUNGER SELF THOUGHT THE DRAGON WAS SUPER COOL, AND I POURED MY SOUL INTO IT BEFORE IT GOT REJECTED.
SO, PLEASE, PUT IT BACK. MY INNER YOUTH IS SCREAMING IN PAIN...
HAVE SOME PITY...
I-IT'S THAT TRAUMATIC FOR YOU?
BUT EVEN IF IT WAS REJECTED BACK THEN, DON'T YOU THINK YOU MIGHT BE ABLE TO CREATE A SUCCESSFUL VERSION NOW?
YEAH! YOU CAN THINK OF IT AS CHALLENGING YOURSELF!
YOU'RE HAVING FUN WITH IT BECAUSE IT'S NOT YOUR PROBLEM, AREN'T YOU?
YOU TWO HAVE SOME DARK MARKS ON YOUR PASTS, TOO, DON'T YOU?!
THE DRAGON GOT REJECTED BECAUSE MARS SAID IT WOULDN'T WORK-
I WONDER WHAT WE CAN DO TO MAKE IT A REALITY...
IT'LL BE DIFFICULT MAKING SOMETHING FLY WITH-OUT WINGS...
I'LL JUST GET RID OF THE DRAGON FIRST...

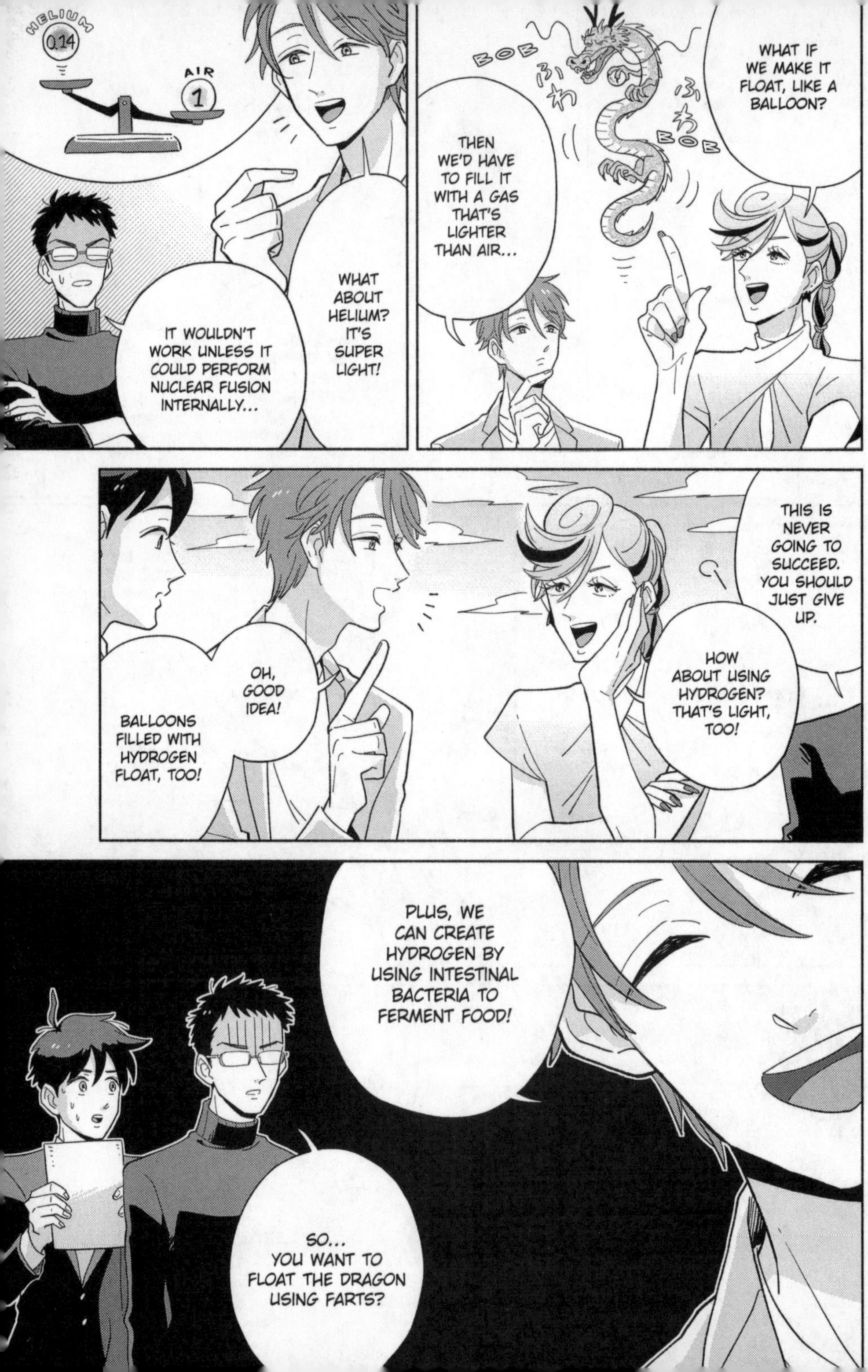
WHAT IF WE MAKE IT FLOAT, LIKE A BALLOON?
BOB
ふわ
ふわ
BOB
THEN WE'D HAVE TO FILL IT WITH A GAS THAT'S LIGHTER THAN AIR...
HELIUM
0.14
AIR
1
WHAT ABOUT HELIUM? IT'S SUPER LIGHT!
IT WOULDN'T WORK UNLESS IT COULD PERFORM NUCLEAR FUSION INTERNALLY...
THIS IS NEVER GOING TO SUCCEED. YOU SHOULD JUST GIVE UP.
HOW ABOUT USING HYDROGEN? THAT'S LIGHT, TOO!
OH, GOOD IDEA!
BALLOONS FILLED WITH HYDROGEN FLOAT, TOO!
PLUS, WE CAN CREATE HYDROGEN BY USING INTESTINAL BACTERIA TO FERMENT FOOD!
SO... YOU WANT TO FLOAT THE DRAGON USING FARTS?

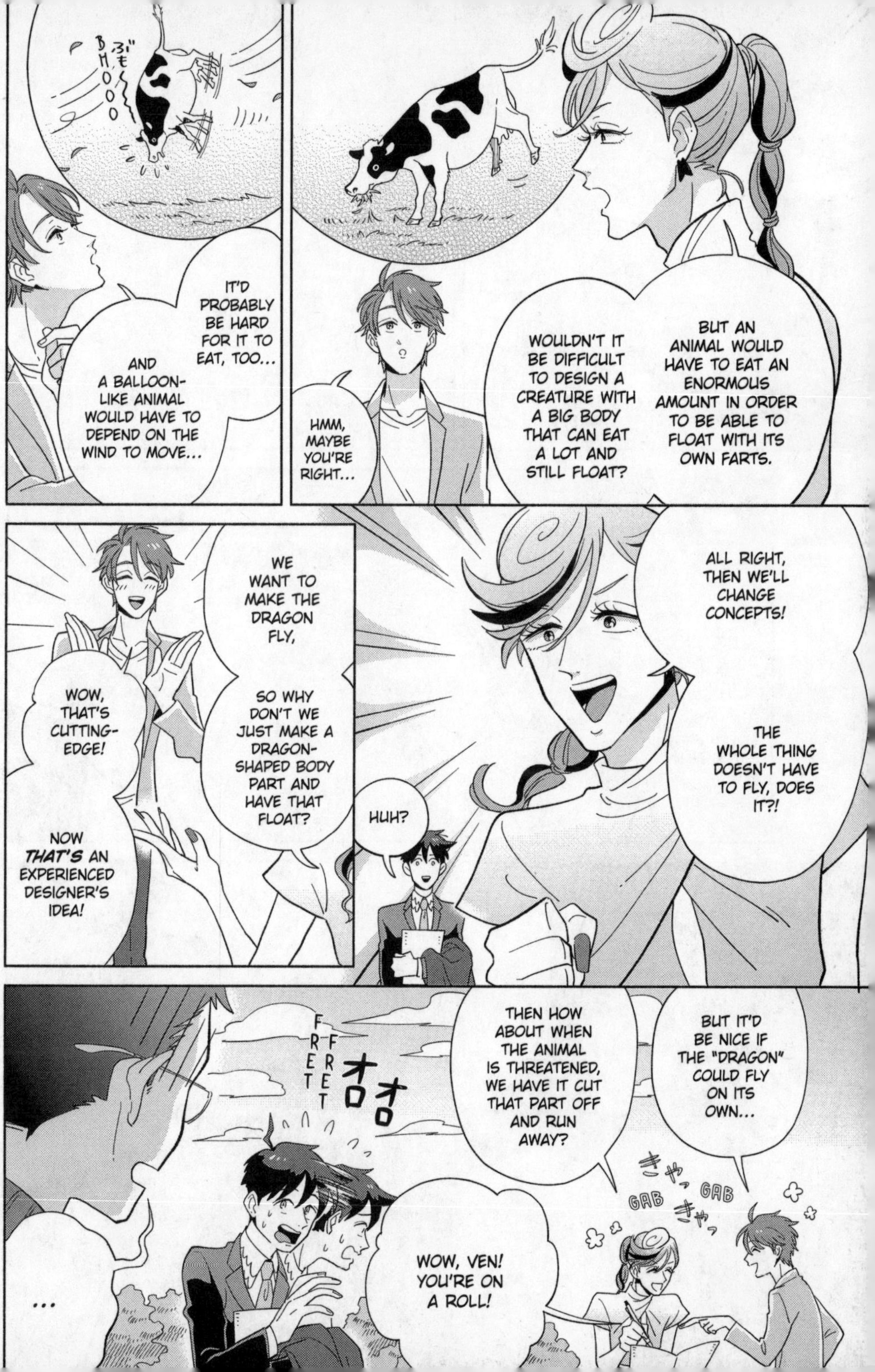
BUT AN ANIMAL WOULD HAVE TO EAT AN ENORMOUS AMOUNT IN ORDER TO BE ABLE TO FLOAT WITH ITS OWN FARTS.
WOULDN'T IT BE DIFFICULT TO DESIGN A CREATURE WITH A BIG BODY THAT CAN EAT A LOT AND STILL FLOAT?
HMM, MAYBE YOU'RE RIGHT...
ぶも～
BMOOO
IT'D PROBABLY BE HARD FOR IT TO EAT, TOO...
AND A BALLOON-LIKE ANIMAL WOULD HAVE TO DEPEND ON THE WIND TO MOVE...
ALL RIGHT, THEN WE'LL CHANGE CONCEPTS!
THE WHOLE THING DOESN'T HAVE TO FLY, DOES IT?!
HUH?
WE WANT TO MAKE THE DRAGON FLY,
SO WHY DON'T WE JUST MAKE A DRAGON-SHAPED BODY PART AND HAVE THAT FLOAT?
WOW, THAT'S CUTTING-EDGE!
NOW *THAT'S* AN EXPERIENCED DESIGNER'S IDEA!
BUT IT'D BE NICE IF THE "DRAGON" COULD FLY ON ITS OWN...
THEN HOW ABOUT WHEN THE ANIMAL IS THREATENED, WE HAVE IT CUT THAT PART OFF AND RUN AWAY?
きゃっ GAB
GAB きゃっ
WOW, VEN! YOU'RE ON A ROLL!
FRET FRET
オロオロ
...

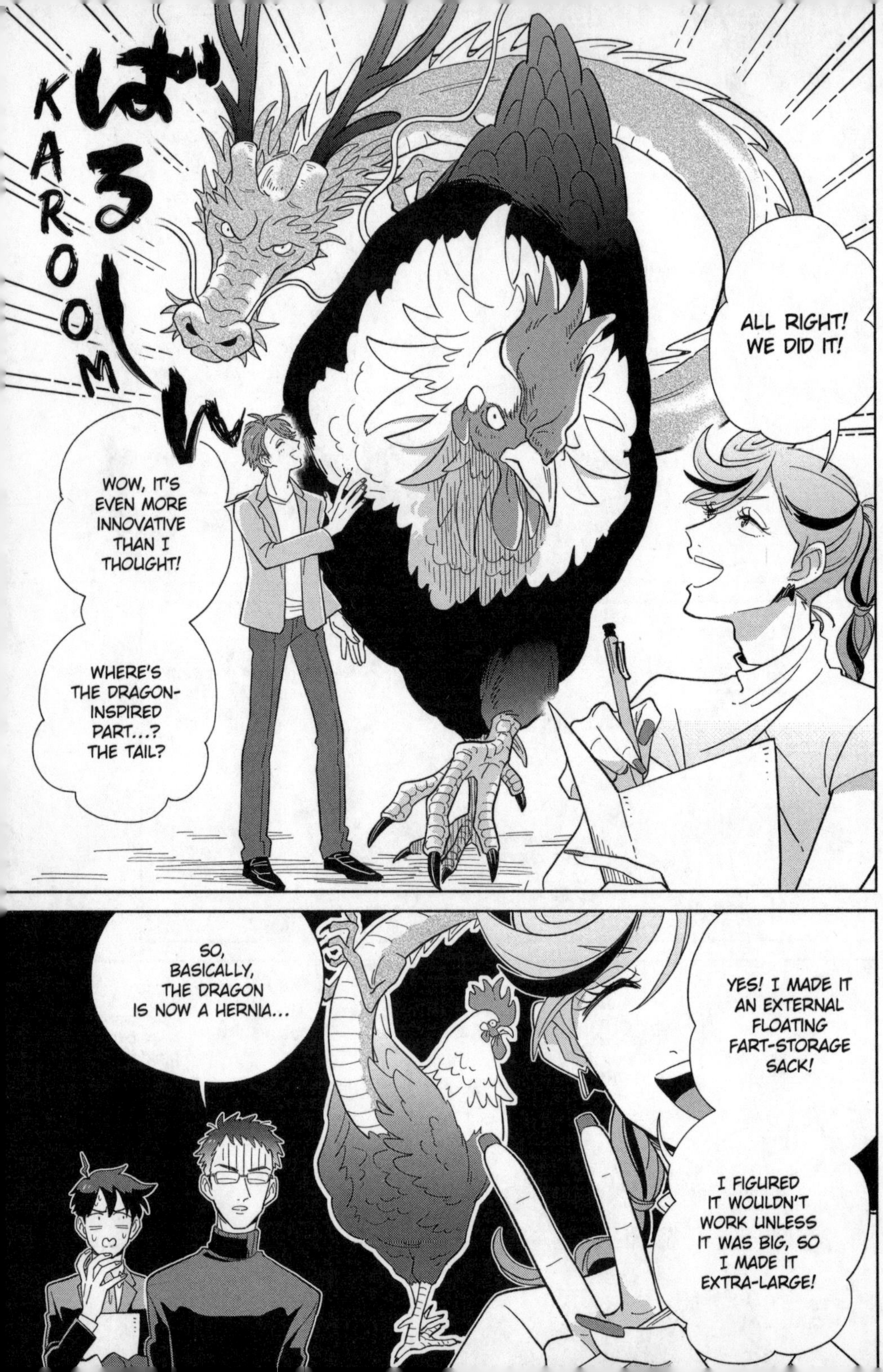

ALL RIGHT! WE DID IT!
ばるーん
KAROOM
WOW, IT'S EVEN MORE INNOVATIVE THAN I THOUGHT!
WHERE'S THE DRAGON-INSPIRED PART...? THE TAIL?
SO, BASICALLY, THE DRAGON IS NOW A HERNIA...
YES! I MADE IT AN EXTERNAL FLOATING FART-STORAGE SACK!
I FIGURED IT WOULDN'T WORK UNLESS IT WAS BIG, SO I MADE IT EXTRA-LARGE!

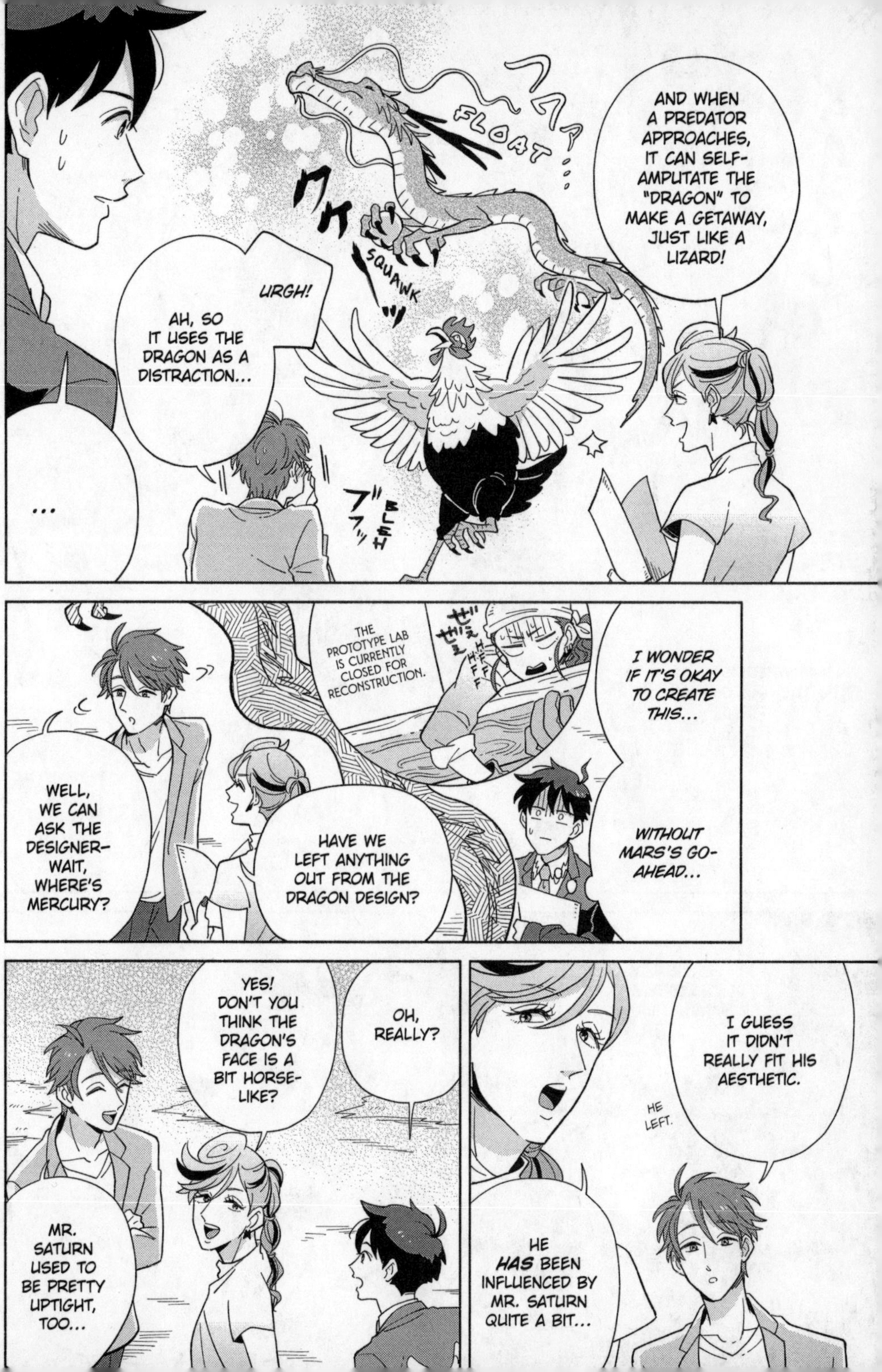
AND WHEN A PREDATOR APPROACHES, IT CAN SELF-AMPUTATE THE "DRAGON" TO MAKE A GETAWAY, JUST LIKE A LIZARD!
FLOAT
SQUAWK
URGH!
AH, SO IT USES THE DRAGON AS A DISTRACTION...
BLEH
...
I WONDER IF IT'S OKAY TO CREATE THIS...
WITHOUT MARS'S GO-AHEAD...
THE PROTOTYPE LAB IS CURRENTLY CLOSED FOR RECONSTRUCTION.
HFF HFF
HAVE WE LEFT ANYTHING OUT FROM THE DRAGON DESIGN?
WELL, WE CAN ASK THE DESIGNER—WAIT, WHERE'S MERCURY?
I GUESS IT DIDN'T REALLY FIT HIS AESTHETIC.
HE LEFT.
HE *HAS* BEEN INFLUENCED BY MR. SATURN QUITE A BIT...
OH, REALLY?
YES! DON'T YOU THINK THE DRAGON'S FACE IS A BIT HORSE-LIKE?
MR. SATURN USED TO BE PRETTY UPTIGHT, TOO...

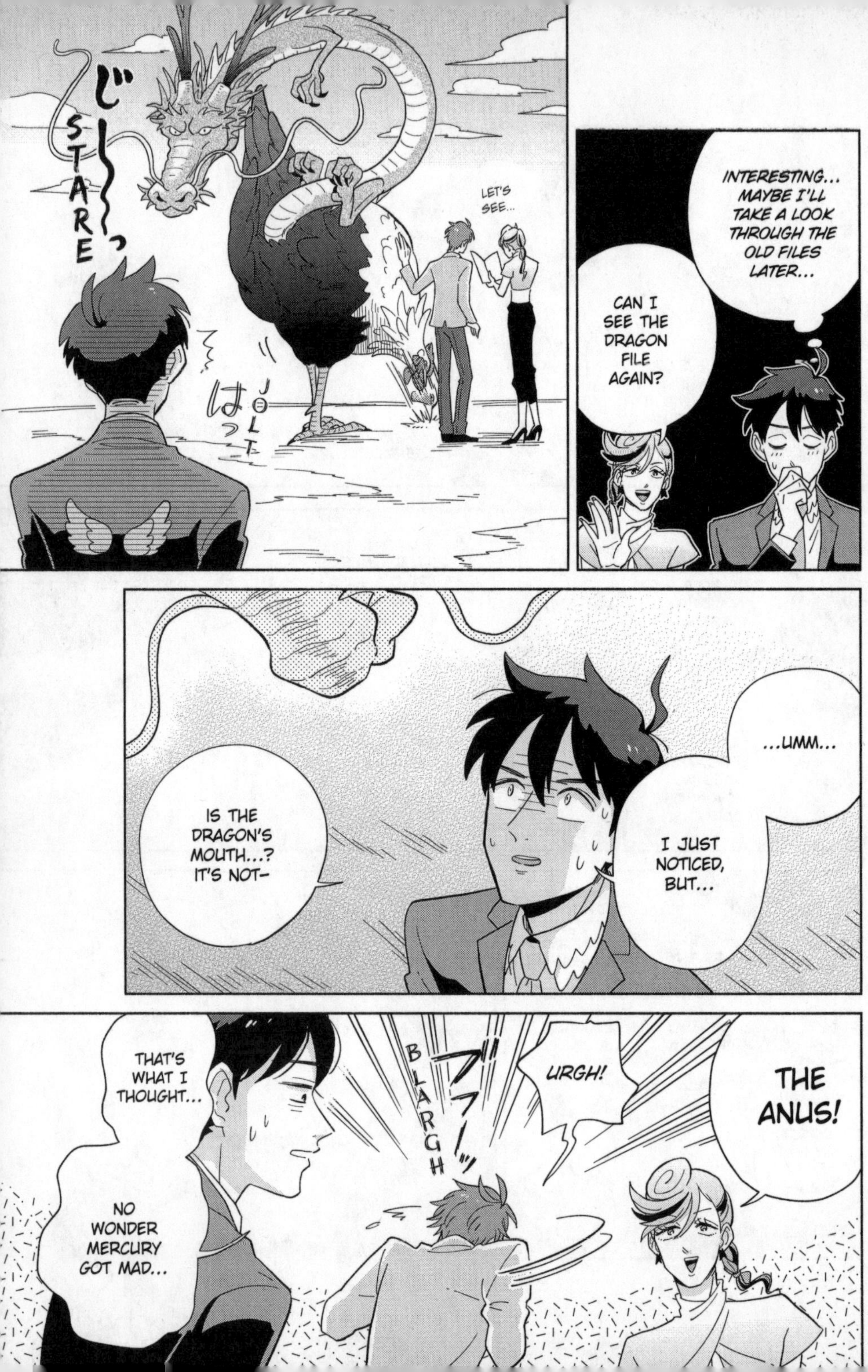
INTERESTING... MAYBE I'LL TAKE A LOOK THROUGH THE OLD FILES LATER...
CAN I SEE THE DRAGON FILE AGAIN?
じーっ
STARE
LET'S SEE...
はっ
JOLT
...UMM...
I JUST NOTICED, BUT...
IS THE DRAGON'S MOUTH...? IT'S NOT-
THE ANUS!
URGH!
BLARGH
THAT'S WHAT I THOUGHT...
NO WONDER MERCURY GOT MAD...

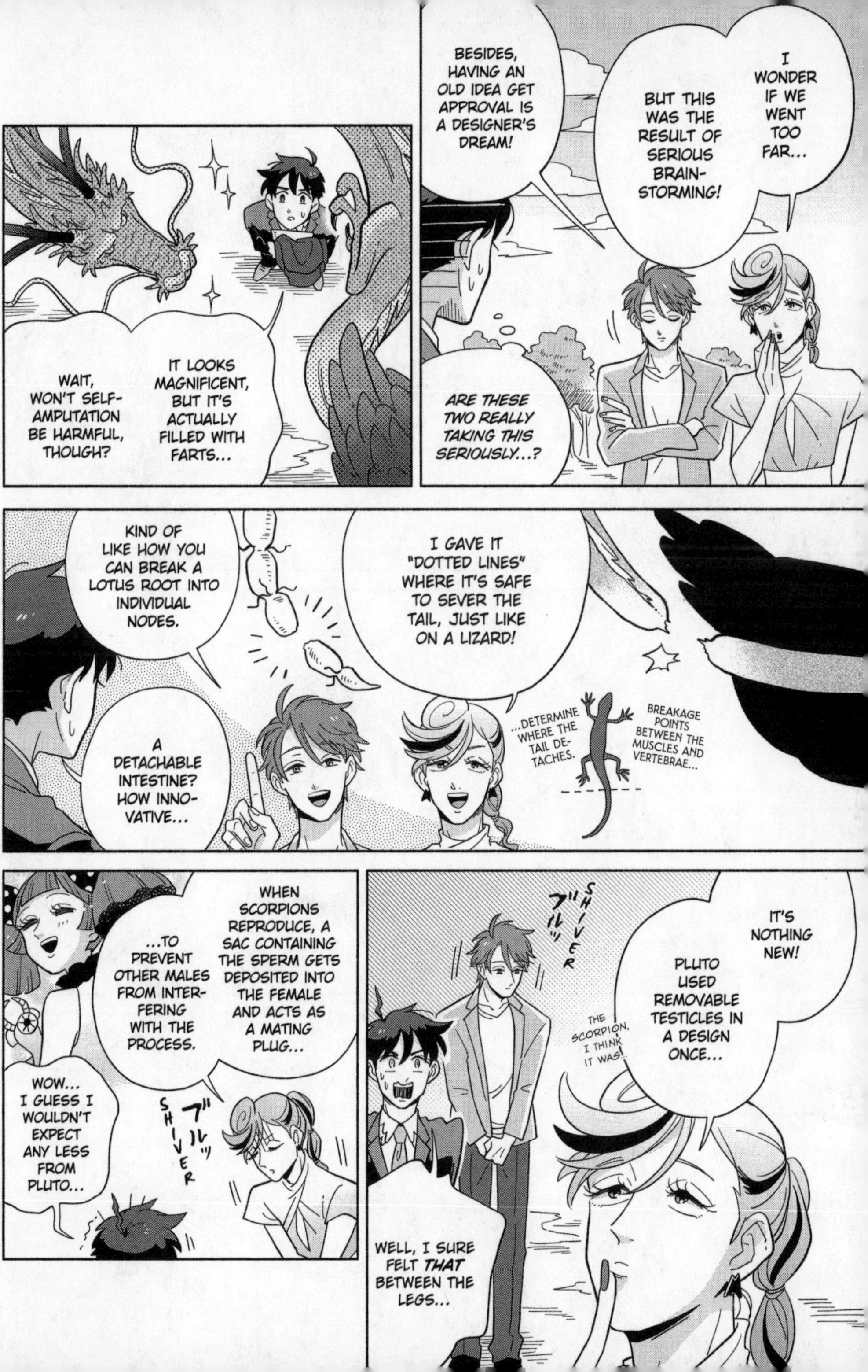
I WONDER IF WE WENT TOO FAR...
BUT THIS WAS THE RESULT OF SERIOUS BRAIN-STORMING!
BESIDES, HAVING AN OLD IDEA GET APPROVAL IS A DESIGNER'S DREAM!
ARE THESE TWO REALLY TAKING THIS SERIOUSLY...?
IT LOOKS MAGNIFICENT, BUT IT'S ACTUALLY FILLED WITH FARTS...
WAIT, WON'T SELF-AMPUTATION BE HARMFUL, THOUGH?
I GAVE IT "DOTTED LINES" WHERE IT'S SAFE TO SEVER THE TAIL, JUST LIKE ON A LIZARD!
BREAKAGE POINTS BETWEEN THE MUSCLES AND VERTEBRAE...
...DETERMINE WHERE THE TAIL DETACHES.
KIND OF LIKE HOW YOU CAN BREAK A LOTUS ROOT INTO INDIVIDUAL NODES.
A DETACHABLE INTESTINE? HOW INNOVATIVE...
IT'S NOTHING NEW!
PLUTO USED REMOVABLE TESTICLES IN A DESIGN ONCE...
THE SCORPION, I THINK IT WAS!
ブルッ SHIVER
WELL, I SURE FELT *THAT* BETWEEN THE LEGS...
WHEN SCORPIONS REPRODUCE, A SAC CONTAINING THE SPERM GETS DEPOSITED INTO THE FEMALE AND ACTS AS A MATING PLUG...
...TO PREVENT OTHER MALES FROM INTER-FERING WITH THE PROCESS.
ブルッ SHIVER
WOW... I GUESS I WOULDN'T EXPECT ANY LESS FROM PLUTO...

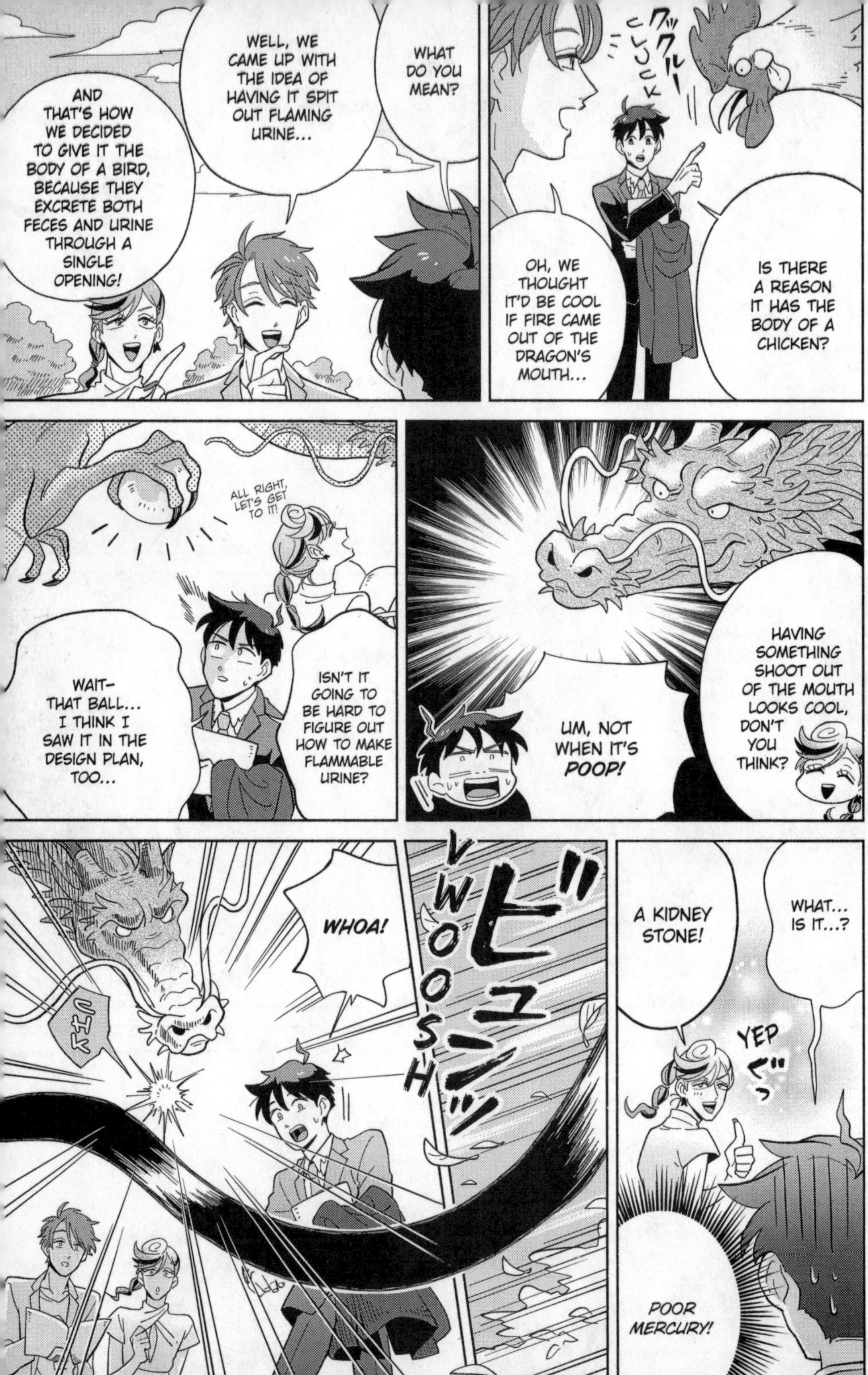
CLUCK
IS THERE A REASON IT HAS THE BODY OF A CHICKEN?
OH, WE THOUGHT IT'D BE COOL IF FIRE CAME OUT OF THE DRAGON'S MOUTH...
WHAT DO YOU MEAN?
WELL, WE CAME UP WITH THE IDEA OF HAVING IT SPIT OUT FLAMING URINE...
AND THAT'S HOW WE DECIDED TO GIVE IT THE BODY OF A BIRD, BECAUSE THEY EXCRETE BOTH FECES AND URINE THROUGH A SINGLE OPENING!
HAVING SOMETHING SHOOT OUT OF THE MOUTH LOOKS COOL, DON'T YOU THINK?
UM, NOT WHEN IT'S *POOP!*
ALL RIGHT, LET'S GET TO IT!
ISN'T IT GOING TO BE HARD TO FIGURE OUT HOW TO MAKE FLAMMABLE URINE?
WAIT- THAT BALL... I THINK I SAW IT IN THE DESIGN PLAN, TOO...
WHAT... IS IT...?
A KIDNEY STONE!
YEP
*POOR MERCURY!*
WHOOSH
*WHOA!*
CHK

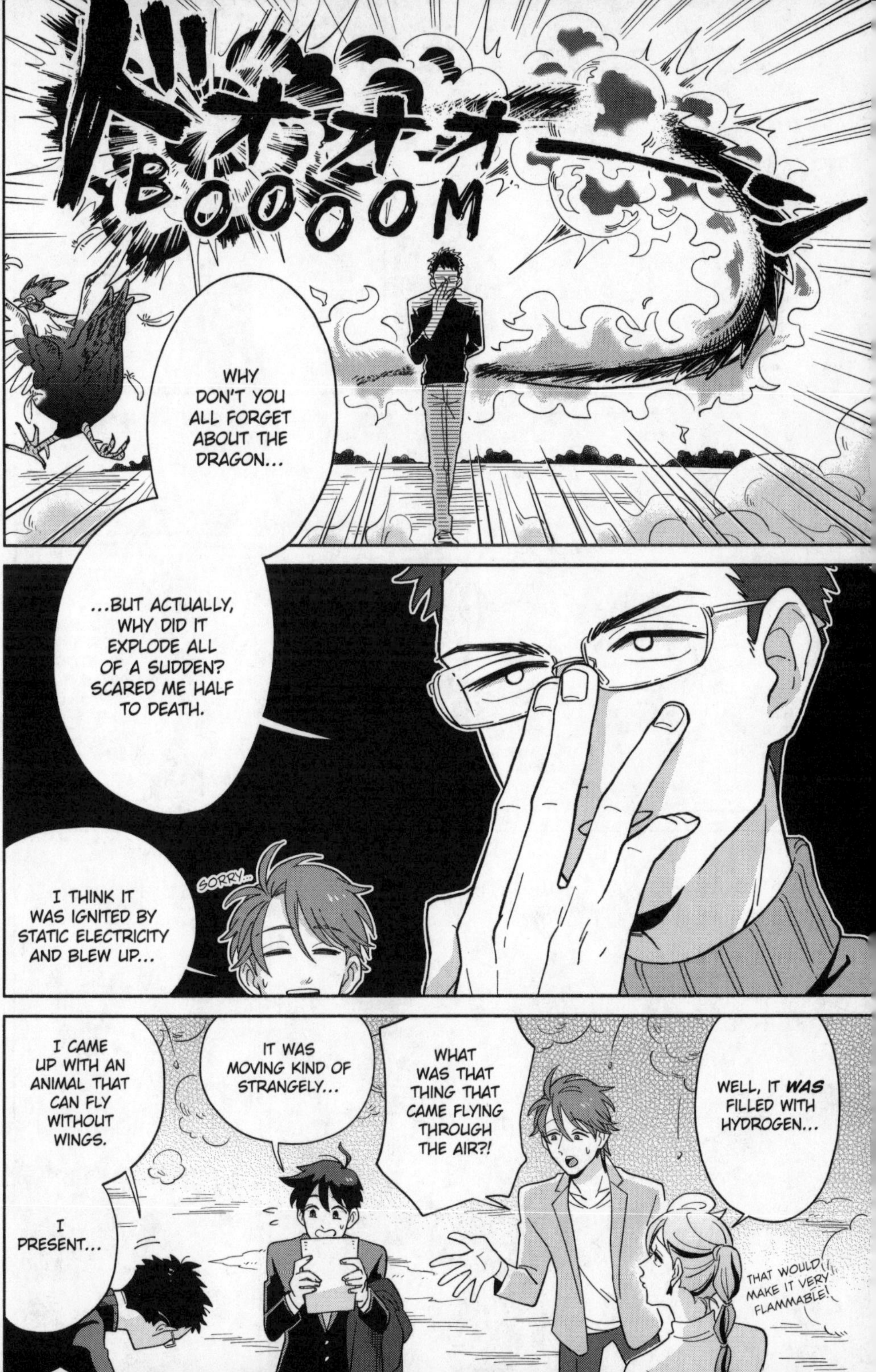
BOOOOM
WHY DON'T YOU ALL FORGET ABOUT THE DRAGON...
...BUT ACTUALLY, WHY DID IT EXPLODE ALL OF A SUDDEN? SCARED ME HALF TO DEATH.
SORRY...
I THINK IT WAS IGNITED BY STATIC ELECTRICITY AND BLEW UP...
WELL, IT *WAS* FILLED WITH HYDROGEN...
THAT WOULD MAKE IT VERY FLAMMABLE!
WHAT WAS THAT THING THAT CAME FLYING THROUGH THE AIR?!
IT WAS MOVING KIND OF STRANGELY...
I CAME UP WITH AN ANIMAL THAT CAN FLY WITHOUT WINGS.
I PRESENT...

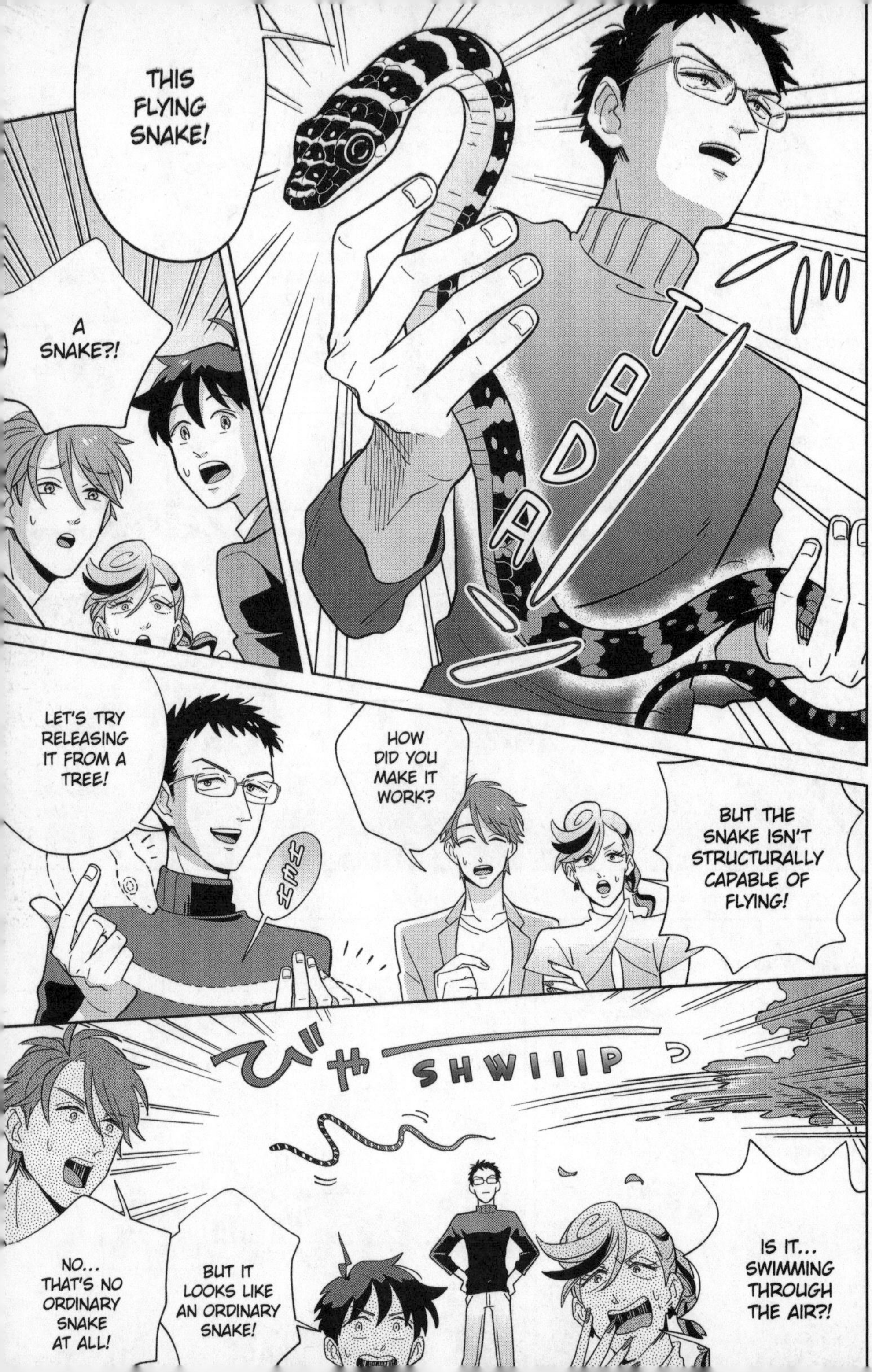
THIS FLYING SNAKE!
TADAA
A SNAKE?!
BUT THE SNAKE ISN'T STRUCTURALLY CAPABLE OF FLYING!
HOW DID YOU MAKE IT WORK?
LET'S TRY RELEASING IT FROM A TREE!
SHWIIIP
IS IT... SWIMMING THROUGH THE AIR?!
BUT IT LOOKS LIKE AN ORDINARY SNAKE!
NO... THAT'S NO ORDINARY SNAKE AT ALL!

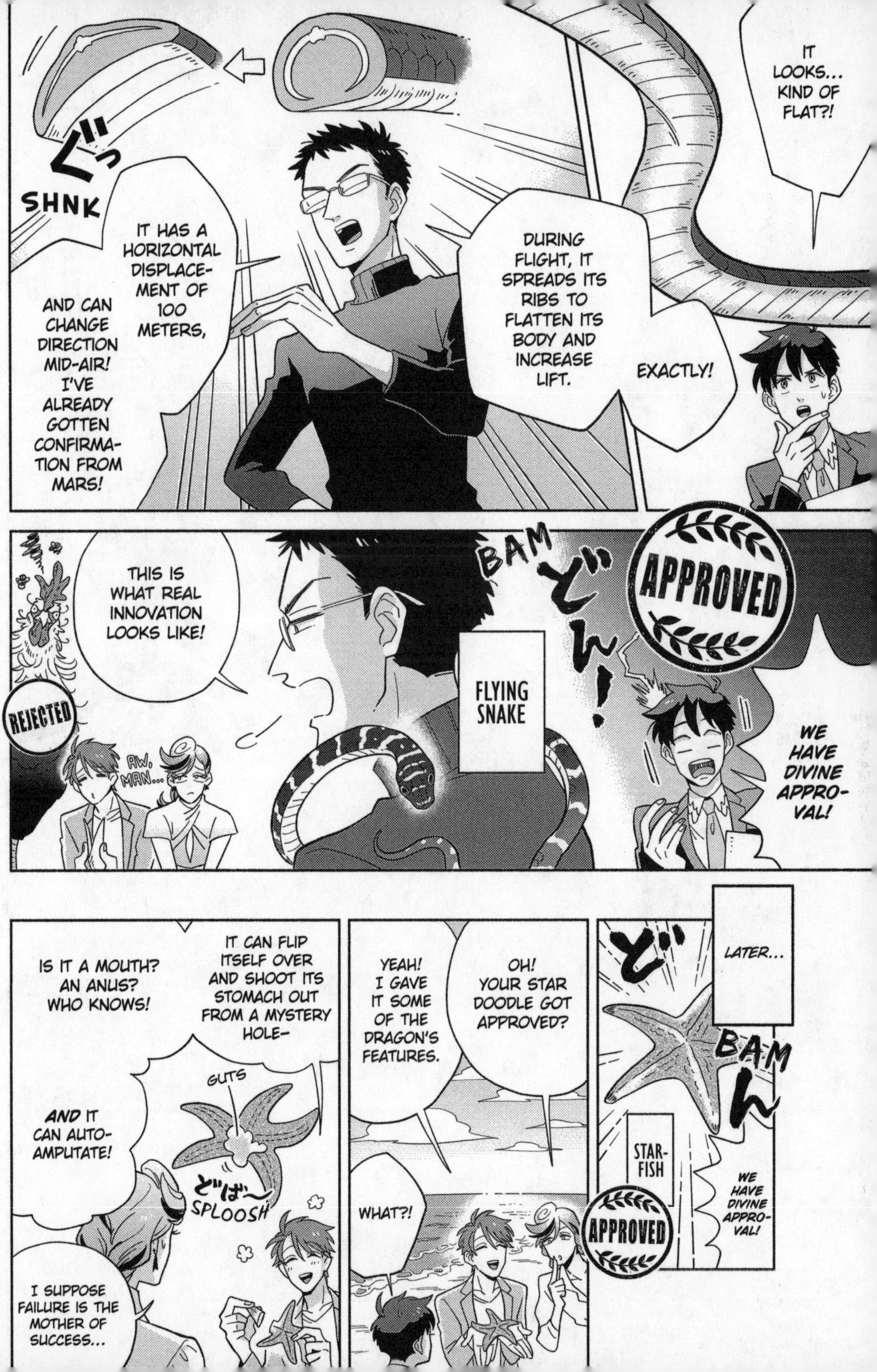
IT LOOKS... KIND OF FLAT?!
EXACTLY!
DURING FLIGHT, IT SPREADS ITS RIBS TO FLATTEN ITS BODY AND INCREASE LIFT.
IT HAS A HORIZONTAL DISPLACEMENT OF 100 METERS,
AND CAN CHANGE DIRECTION MID-AIR! I'VE ALREADY GOTTEN CONFIRMATION FROM MARS!
ぐっ
SHNK
APPROVED
どん!
BAM
WE HAVE DIVINE APPROVAL!
FLYING SNAKE
THIS IS WHAT REAL INNOVATION LOOKS LIKE!
REJECTED
AW, MAN...
LATER...
どん
BAM
STARFISH
WE HAVE DIVINE APPROVAL!
APPROVED
OH! YOUR STAR DOODLE GOT APPROVED?
YEAH! I GAVE IT SOME OF THE DRAGON'S FEATURES.
WHAT?!
IT CAN FLIP ITSELF OVER AND SHOOT ITS STOMACH OUT FROM A MYSTERY HOLE-
IS IT A MOUTH? AN ANUS? WHO KNOWS!
GUTS
どばー
SPLOOSH
AND IT CAN AUTO-AMPUTATE!
I SUPPOSE FAILURE IS THE MOTHER OF SUCCESS...

# THE ENCYCLOPEDIA OF
# REAL ANIMALS 09

| ANIMAL 25 | PARADISE TREE SNAKE |
|---|---|

**THE REAL THING**

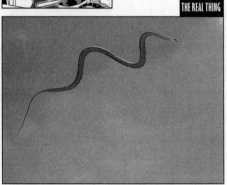

A paradise tree snake gliding through the air in Borneo.
Photo: Photoshot/Aflo

| [Name] | *Chrysopelea paradisi* |
|---|---|
| [Classification] | Class: Reptilia |
| | Order: Squamata |
| | Family: Colubridae |
| | Genus: *Chrysopelea* |
| [Habitat] | South East Asia, including |
| | Thailand and Indonesia |
| [Height] | 100-120 cm (3.3-4 ft) |

There are five different species of flying snake, including the golden tree snake and the banded flying snake, but the one most frequently witnessed flying through the air is the paradise tree snake. These arboreal snakes can't fly into the air from the ground via their own strength, but rather glide through the air by manipulating their movement as they jump from tree to tree. They flare out their ribs and flatten their abdomens out into pseudo-wings that are nearly twice the snakes' normal width to create lift (the component of the aerodynamic forces acting on a flying object that opposes gravity) and allow the reptiles to move through the air in a swimming motion. They have been known to glide approximately 100 meters (328 feet).

Paradise tree snakes are mildly venomous with rear fangs and prey on small amphibians such as frogs and small mammals such as mice. They lay around five eggs at one time.

## SPECIAL ITEM | LZ 129 HINDENBURG

ふわ
BOB
ふわ
BOB

ILLUSTRATION

Hindenburg

One hypothesis puts forth that the 1937 fire was started by an electric spark caused by a buildup of static electricity.

**[Name]** Luftschiff Zeppelin #129 Hindenburg
**[Classification]** Large commercial passenger-carrying rigid airship
**[Completion year]** 1936
**[Length]** 245 m (803 ft)

Like the dragon in this chapter, the Hindenburg airship exploded when the hydrogen that filled it was ignited. One theory points to the ship's outer covering as the source of the initial fire. The resulting explosion became a symbol for the end of the airship era.
In order to make something both hollow and heavy float, the object itself must be very large. The larger the object is, the smaller the surface area to volume ratio.

## ANIMAL 26 | NORTHERN PACIFIC SEASTAR

The most common seastar in Japan, Northern Pacific seastars have no brains and move in a wriggling motion using the nerves throughout their bodies. They can evert their stomachs through the mouths located on the underside of their bodies to hunt and digest prey much larger than their mouths. Their anuses are located on the top sides of their central discs, but they can also excrete waste through their mouths. They are highly regenerative, and as long as a portion of their central disc remains, they can fully regrow themselves from just one arm.

GUTS
どばー
SPLOOSH

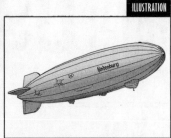

Northern Pacific can evert their stomachs and eat prey such as shellfish.

Photo: Walk Photo
Atelier Ayumu Fukui/Aflo

THE REAL THING

**[Name]** *Asterias amurensis*
**[Classification]** Phylum: Echinodermata
Superclass: Asterozoa
Order: Forcipulatida
Family: Asteriidae
Genus: *Asterias*
**[Habitat]** The coasts of Japan, China, and Russia
**[Length]** 10-20 cm (4-8 in)

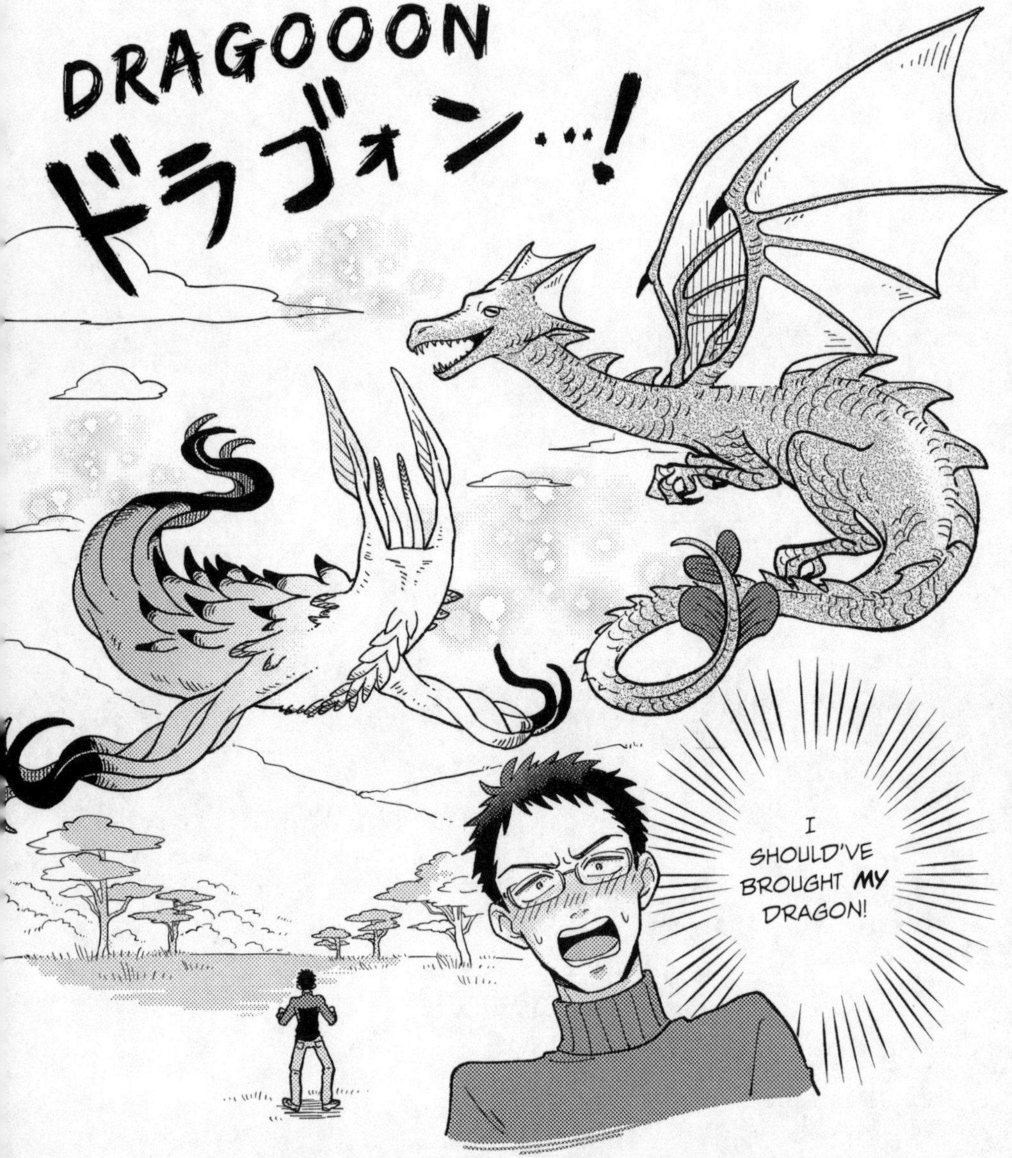
DRAGOOON
ドラゴォン…!
I SHOULD'VE BROUGHT MY DRAGON!

[ I tried drawing the dragons from *Drifting Dragons* and *Witch Hat Atelier*.
A big thank you to Taku Kuwabara and Kamome Shirahama! ]

# HEAVEN'S DESIGN TEAM

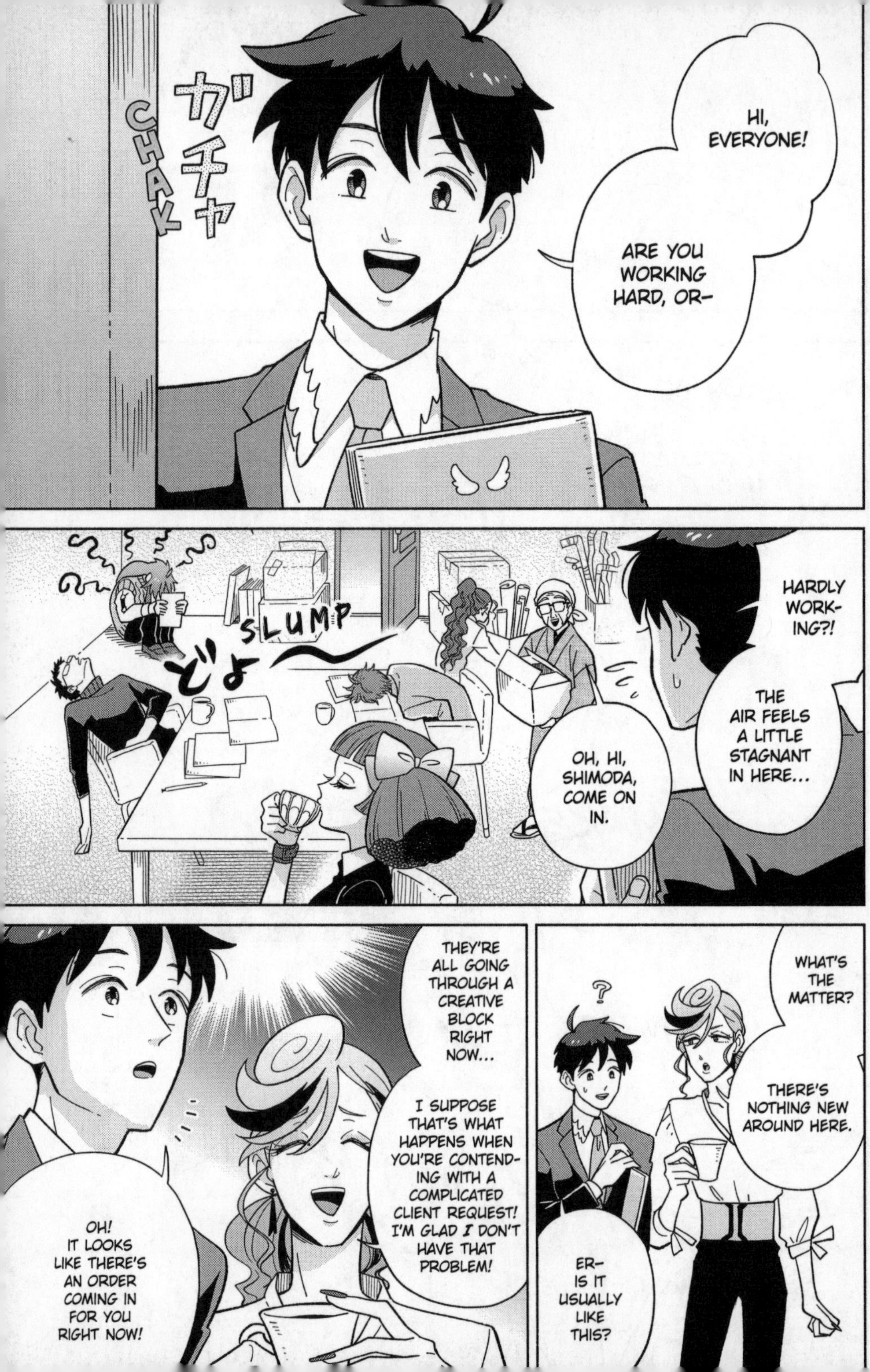
HI, EVERYONE!
ARE YOU WORKING HARD, OR—
ガチャ
CHAK
HARDLY WORKING?!
THE AIR FEELS A LITTLE STAGNANT IN HERE...
OH, HI, SHIMODA, COME ON IN.
SLUMP
どよ
WHAT'S THE MATTER?
THERE'S NOTHING NEW AROUND HERE.
?
ER— IS IT USUALLY LIKE THIS?
THEY'RE ALL GOING THROUGH A CREATIVE BLOCK RIGHT NOW...
I SUPPOSE THAT'S WHAT HAPPENS WHEN YOU'RE CONTENDING WITH A COMPLICATED CLIENT REQUEST! I'M GLAD *I* DON'T HAVE THAT PROBLEM!
OH! IT LOOKS LIKE THERE'S AN ORDER COMING IN FOR YOU RIGHT NOW!

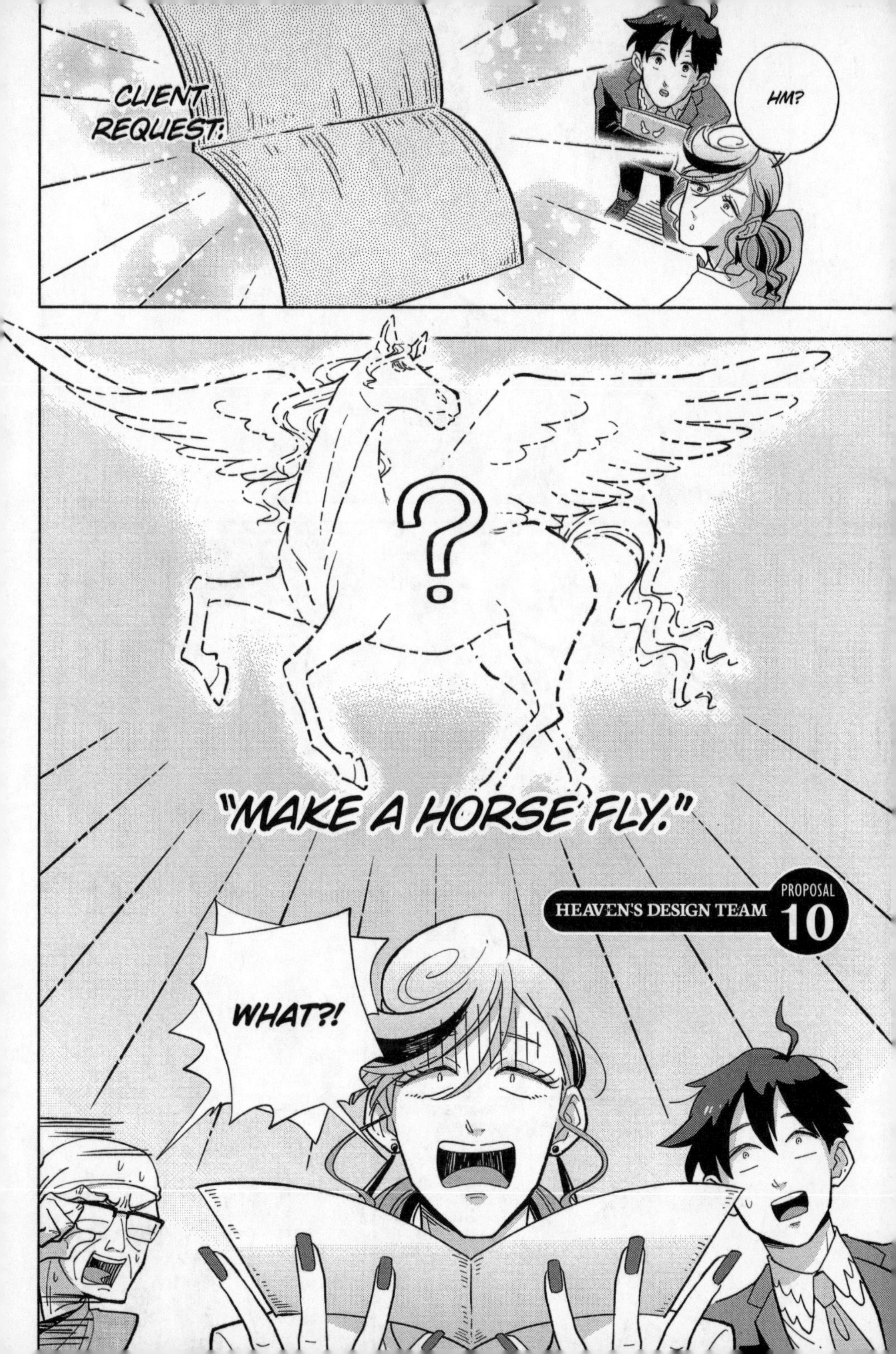
HM?
CLIENT REQUEST:
"MAKE A HORSE FLY."
HEAVEN'S DESIGN TEAM
PROPOSAL
10
WHAT?!

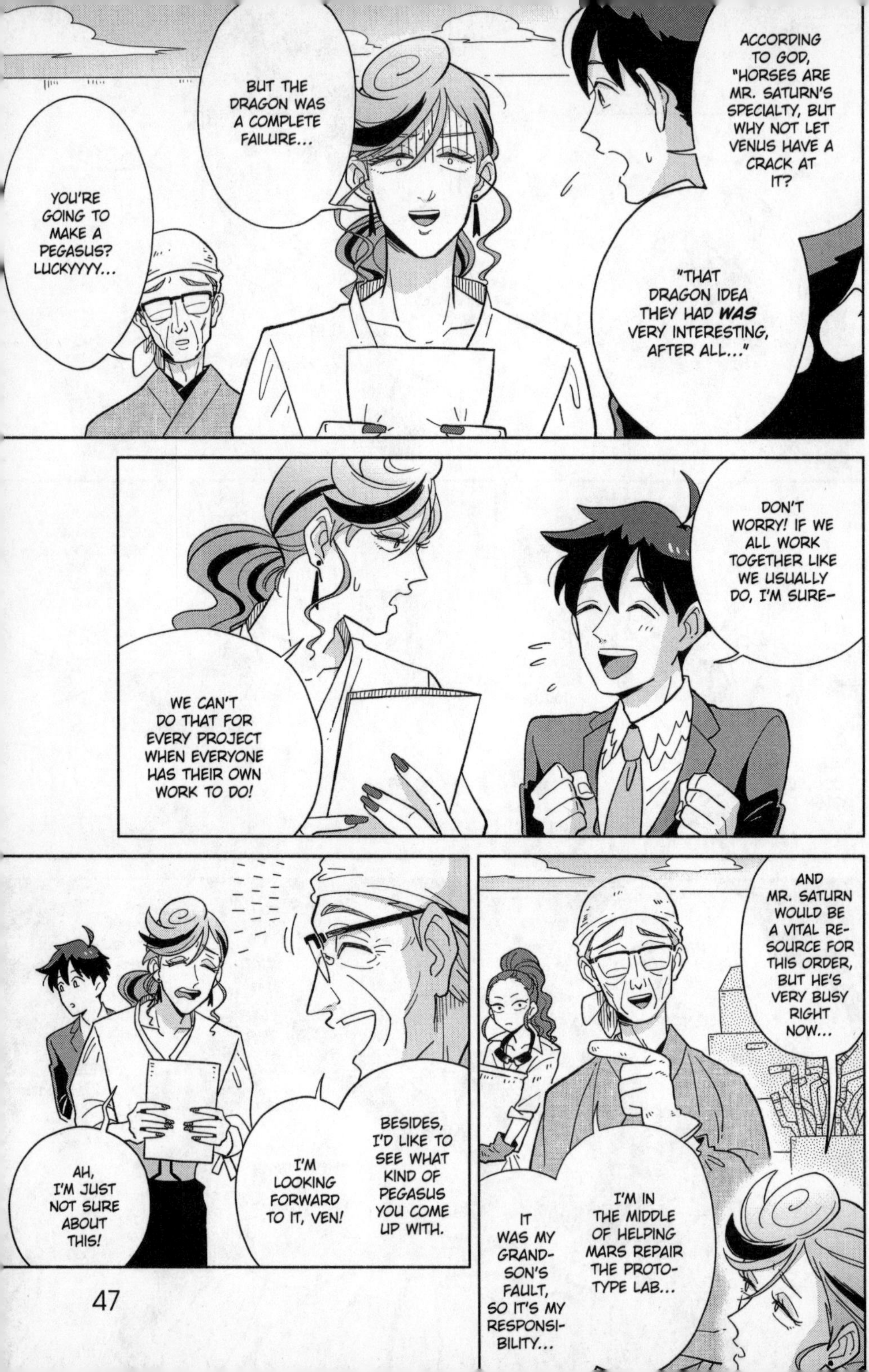
ACCORDING TO GOD, "HORSES ARE MR. SATURN'S SPECIALTY, BUT WHY NOT LET VENUS HAVE A CRACK AT IT?
"THAT DRAGON IDEA THEY HAD **WAS** VERY INTERESTING, AFTER ALL..."
BUT THE DRAGON WAS A COMPLETE FAILURE...
YOU'RE GOING TO MAKE A PEGASUS? LUCKYYYY...
DON'T WORRY! IF WE ALL WORK TOGETHER LIKE WE USUALLY DO, I'M SURE-
WE CAN'T DO THAT FOR EVERY PROJECT WHEN EVERYONE HAS THEIR OWN WORK TO DO!
AND MR. SATURN WOULD BE A VITAL RE-SOURCE FOR THIS ORDER, BUT HE'S VERY BUSY RIGHT NOW...
I'M IN THE MIDDLE OF HELPING MARS REPAIR THE PROTO-TYPE LAB...
IT WAS MY GRAND-SON'S FAULT, SO IT'S MY RESPONSI-BILITY...
BESIDES, I'D LIKE TO SEE WHAT KIND OF PEGASUS YOU COME UP WITH.
I'M LOOKING FORWARD TO IT, VEN!
AH, I'M JUST NOT SURE ABOUT THIS!

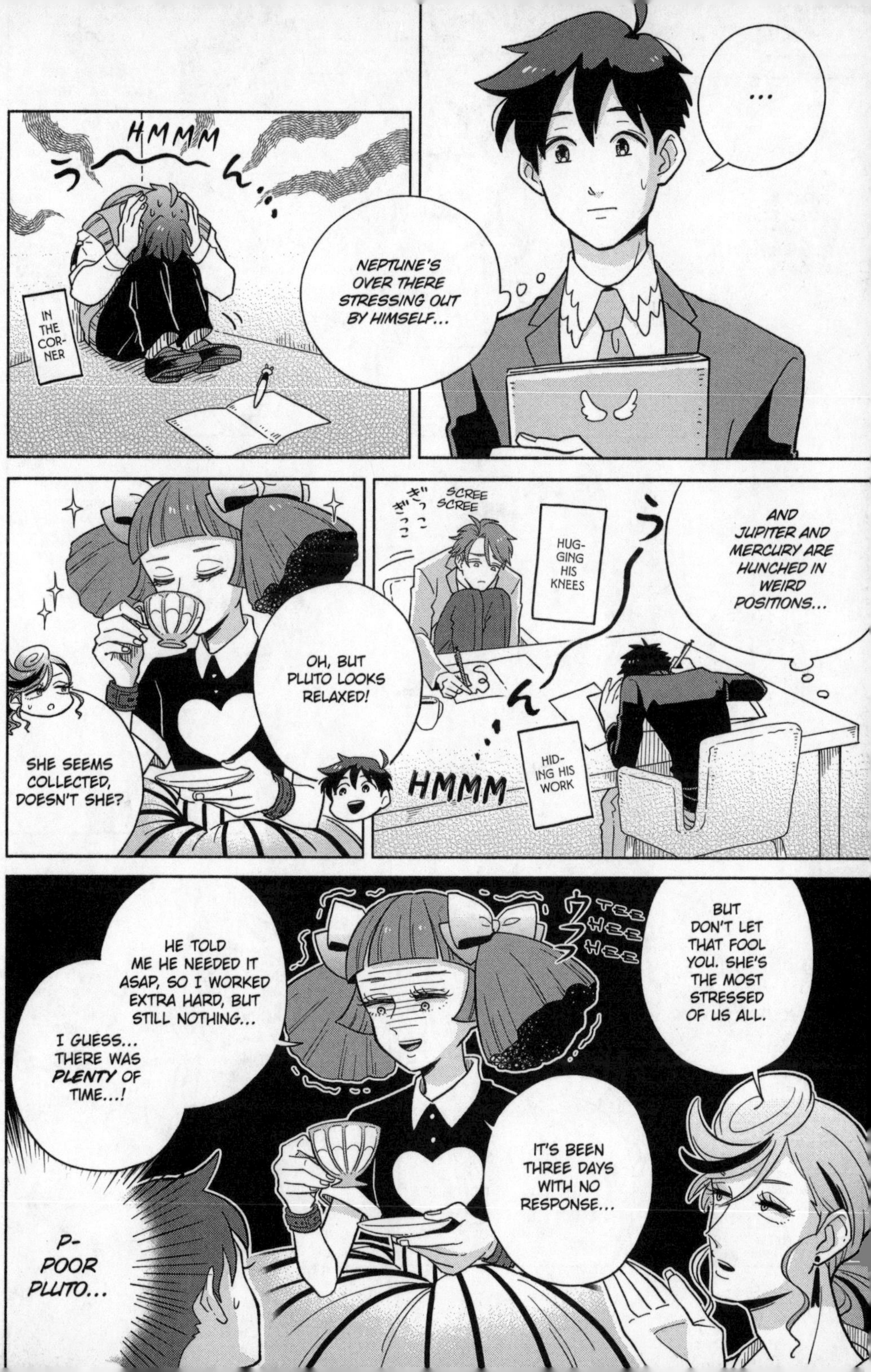
...
NEPTUNE'S OVER THERE STRESSING OUT BY HIMSELF...
う〜ん
HMMM
IN THE CORNER
SCREE SCREE
ぎっこぎっこ
HUGGING HIS KNEES
AND JUPITER AND MERCURY ARE HUNCHED IN WEIRD POSITIONS...
う〜ん
HMMM
HIDING HIS WORK
OH, BUT PLUTO LOOKS RELAXED!
SHE SEEMS COLLECTED, DOESN'T SHE?
BUT DON'T LET THAT FOOL YOU. SHE'S THE MOST STRESSED OF US ALL.
TEE HEE HEE
HE TOLD ME HE NEEDED IT ASAP, SO I WORKED EXTRA HARD, BUT STILL NOTHING...
I GUESS... THERE WAS PLENTY OF TIME...!
IT'S BEEN THREE DAYS WITH NO RESPONSE...
P-POOR PLUTO...

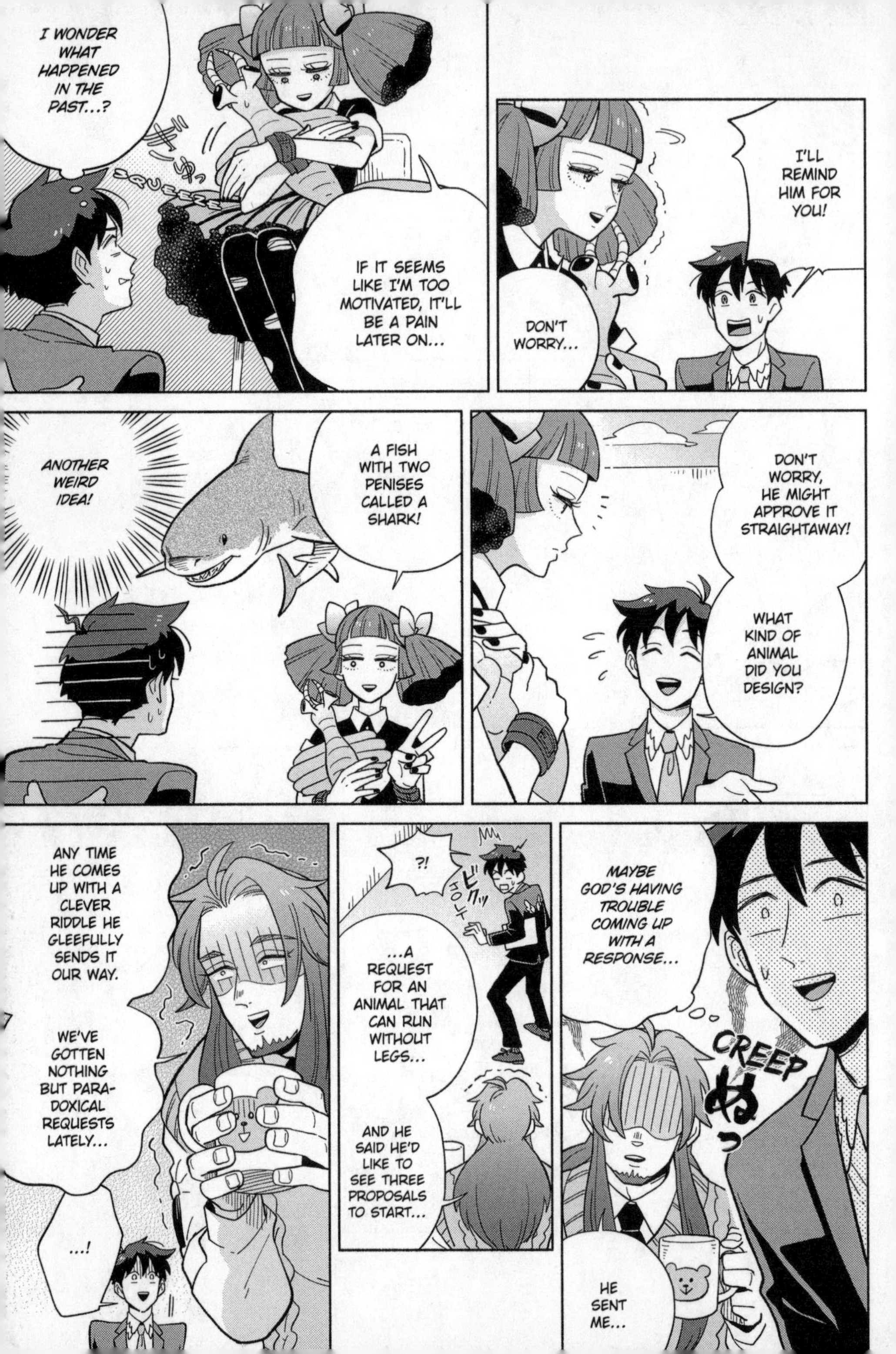
I'LL REMIND HIM FOR YOU!
DON'T WORRY...
IF IT SEEMS LIKE I'M TOO MOTIVATED, IT'LL BE A PAIN LATER ON...
I WONDER WHAT HAPPENED IN THE PAST...?
SQUEEZE
DON'T WORRY, HE MIGHT APPROVE IT STRAIGHTAWAY!
WHAT KIND OF ANIMAL DID YOU DESIGN?
A FISH WITH TWO PENISES CALLED A SHARK!
ANOTHER WEIRD IDEA!
MAYBE GOD'S HAVING TROUBLE COMING UP WITH A RESPONSE...
CREEP
HE SENT ME...
?!
...A REQUEST FOR AN ANIMAL THAT CAN RUN WITHOUT LEGS...
AND HE SAID HE'D LIKE TO SEE THREE PROPOSALS TO START...
ANY TIME HE COMES UP WITH A CLEVER RIDDLE HE GLEEFULLY SENDS IT OUR WAY.
WE'VE GOTTEN NOTHING BUT PARA-DOXICAL REQUESTS LATELY...
...!

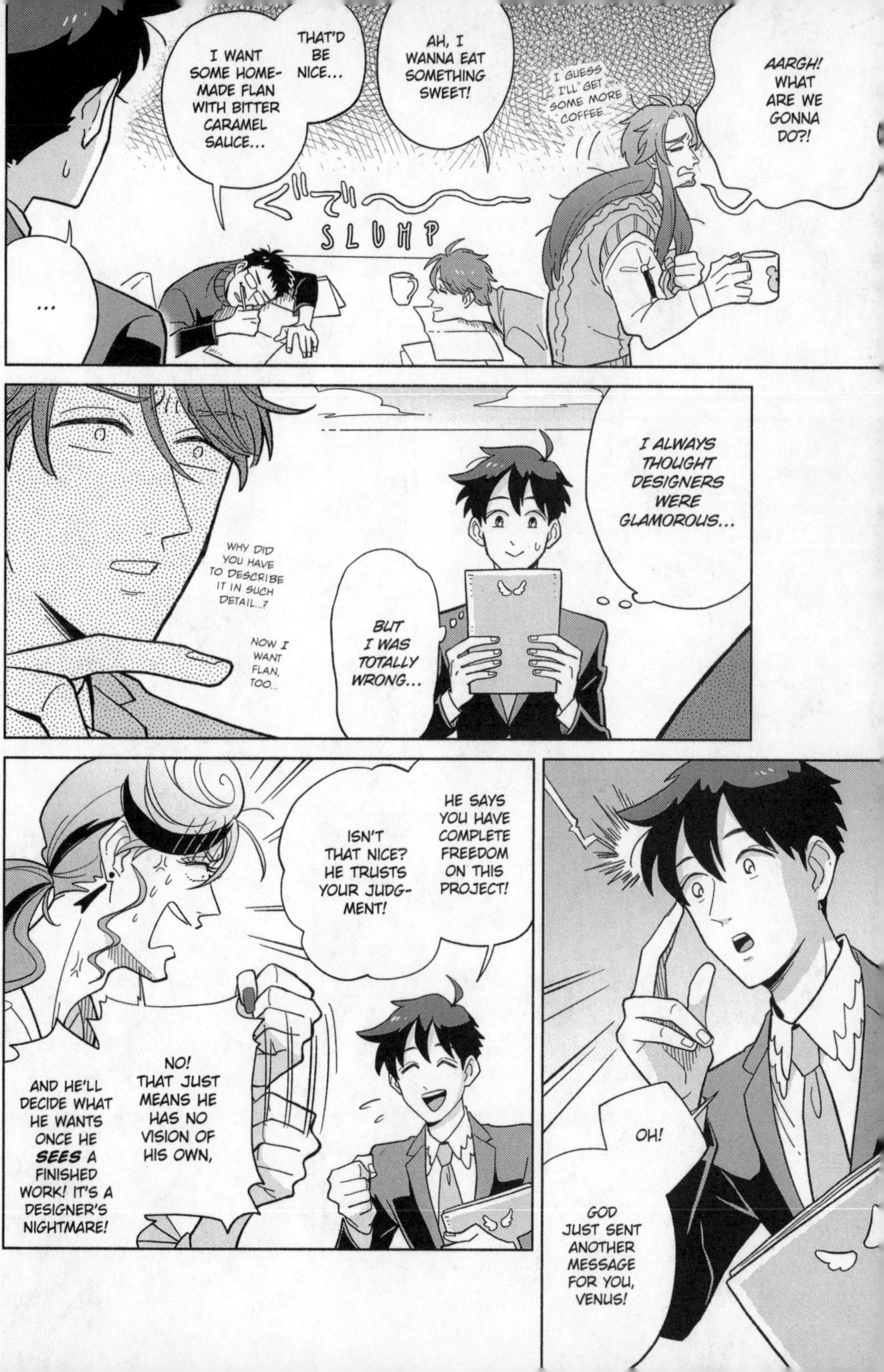
AARGH! WHAT ARE WE GONNA DO?!
I GUESS I'LL GET SOME MORE COFFEE...
AH, I WANNA EAT SOMETHING SWEET!
THAT'D BE NICE...
I WANT SOME HOME-MADE FLAN WITH BITTER CARAMEL SAUCE...
SLUMP
...
I ALWAYS THOUGHT DESIGNERS WERE GLAMOROUS...
BUT I WAS TOTALLY WRONG...
WHY DID YOU HAVE TO DESCRIBE IT IN SUCH DETAIL...?
NOW I WANT FLAN, TOO...
OH!
GOD JUST SENT ANOTHER MESSAGE FOR YOU, VENUS!
HE SAYS YOU HAVE COMPLETE FREEDOM ON THIS PROJECT!
ISN'T THAT NICE? HE TRUSTS YOUR JUDGMENT!
NO! THAT JUST MEANS HE HAS NO VISION OF HIS OWN,
AND HE'LL DECIDE WHAT HE WANTS ONCE HE ***SEES*** A FINISHED WORK! IT'S A DESIGNER'S NIGHTMARE!

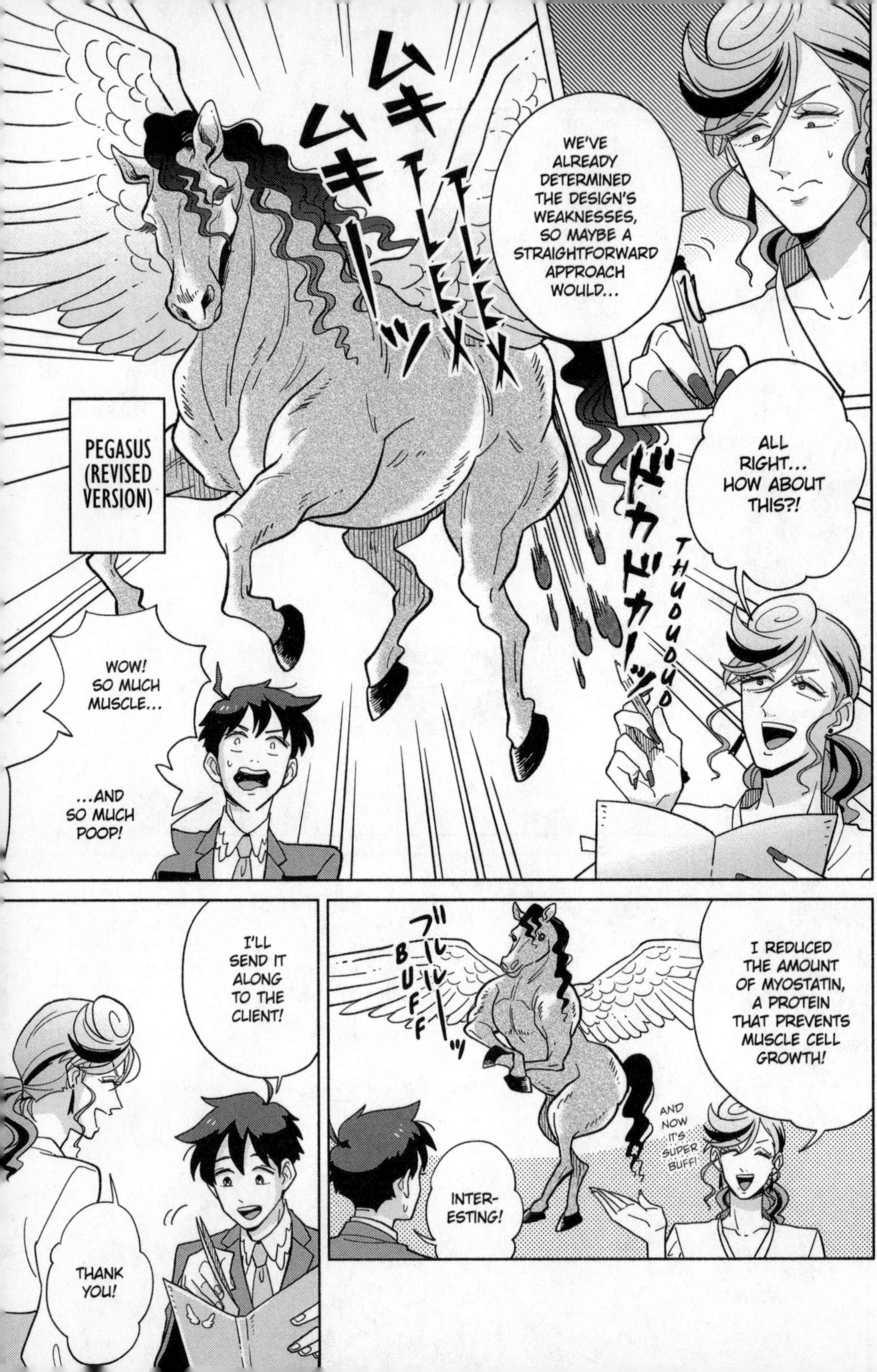
WE'VE ALREADY DETERMINED THE DESIGN'S WEAKNESSES, SO MAYBE A STRAIGHTFORWARD APPROACH WOULD...
ムキムキーッ
FLEX FLEX
ALL RIGHT... HOW ABOUT THIS?!
ドカドカーッ
THUDUDUD
PEGASUS (REVISED VERSION)
WOW! SO MUCH MUSCLE...
...AND SO MUCH POOP!
I REDUCED THE AMOUNT OF MYOSTATIN, A PROTEIN THAT PREVENTS MUSCLE CELL GROWTH!
AND NOW IT'S SUPER BUFF!
ブルルーッ
BUFF
INTER-ESTING!
I'LL SEND IT ALONG TO THE CLIENT!
THANK YOU!

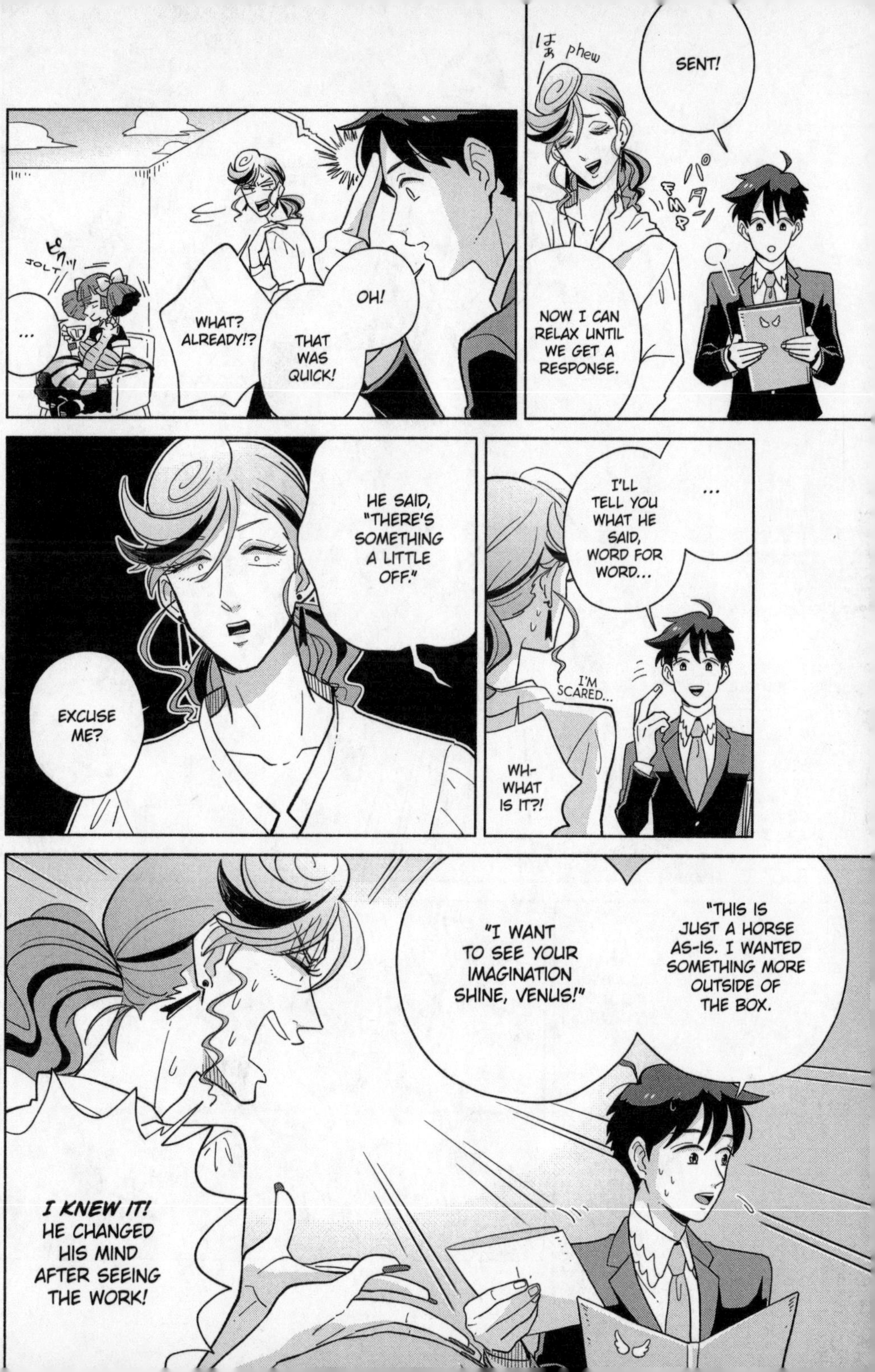
phew
SENT!
NOW I CAN RELAX UNTIL WE GET A RESPONSE.
OH! THAT WAS QUICK!
WHAT? ALREADY!?
JOLT
...
...
I'LL TELL YOU WHAT HE SAID, WORD FOR WORD...
I'M SCARED...
WH- WHAT IS IT?!
HE SAID, "THERE'S SOMETHING A LITTLE OFF."
EXCUSE ME?
"THIS IS JUST A HORSE AS-IS. I WANTED SOMETHING MORE OUTSIDE OF THE BOX.
"I WANT TO SEE YOUR IMAGINATION SHINE, VENUS!"
I KNEW IT! HE CHANGED HIS MIND AFTER SEEING THE WORK!

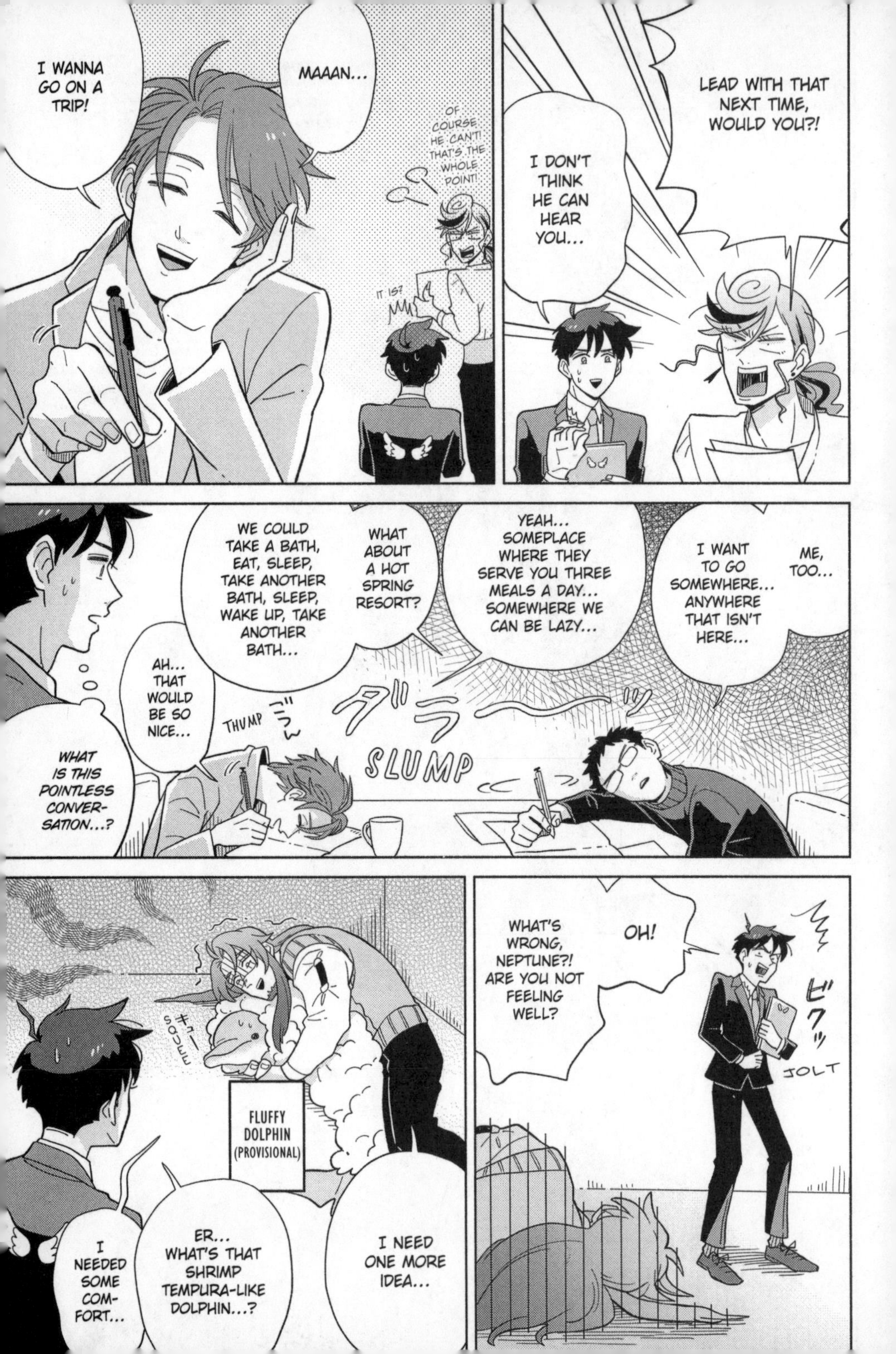

LEAD WITH THAT NEXT TIME, WOULD YOU?!
I DON'T THINK HE CAN HEAR YOU...
MAAAN...
I WANNA GO ON A TRIP!
OF COURSE HE CAN'T! THAT'S THE WHOLE POINT!
IT IS?
ME, TOO...
I WANT TO GO SOMEWHERE... ANYWHERE THAT ISN'T HERE...
YEAH... SOMEPLACE WHERE THEY SERVE YOU THREE MEALS A DAY... SOMEWHERE WE CAN BE LAZY...
WHAT ABOUT A HOT SPRING RESORT?
WE COULD TAKE A BATH, EAT, SLEEP, TAKE ANOTHER BATH, SLEEP, WAKE UP, TAKE ANOTHER BATH...
AH... THAT WOULD BE SO NICE...
THUMP
SLUMP
WHAT IS THIS POINTLESS CONVER-SATION...?
OH!
WHAT'S WRONG, NEPTUNE?! ARE YOU NOT FEELING WELL?
JOLT
SQUEE
FLUFFY DOLPHIN (PROVISIONAL)
I NEED ONE MORE IDEA...
ER... WHAT'S THAT SHRIMP TEMPURA-LIKE DOLPHIN...?
I NEEDED SOME COMFORT...

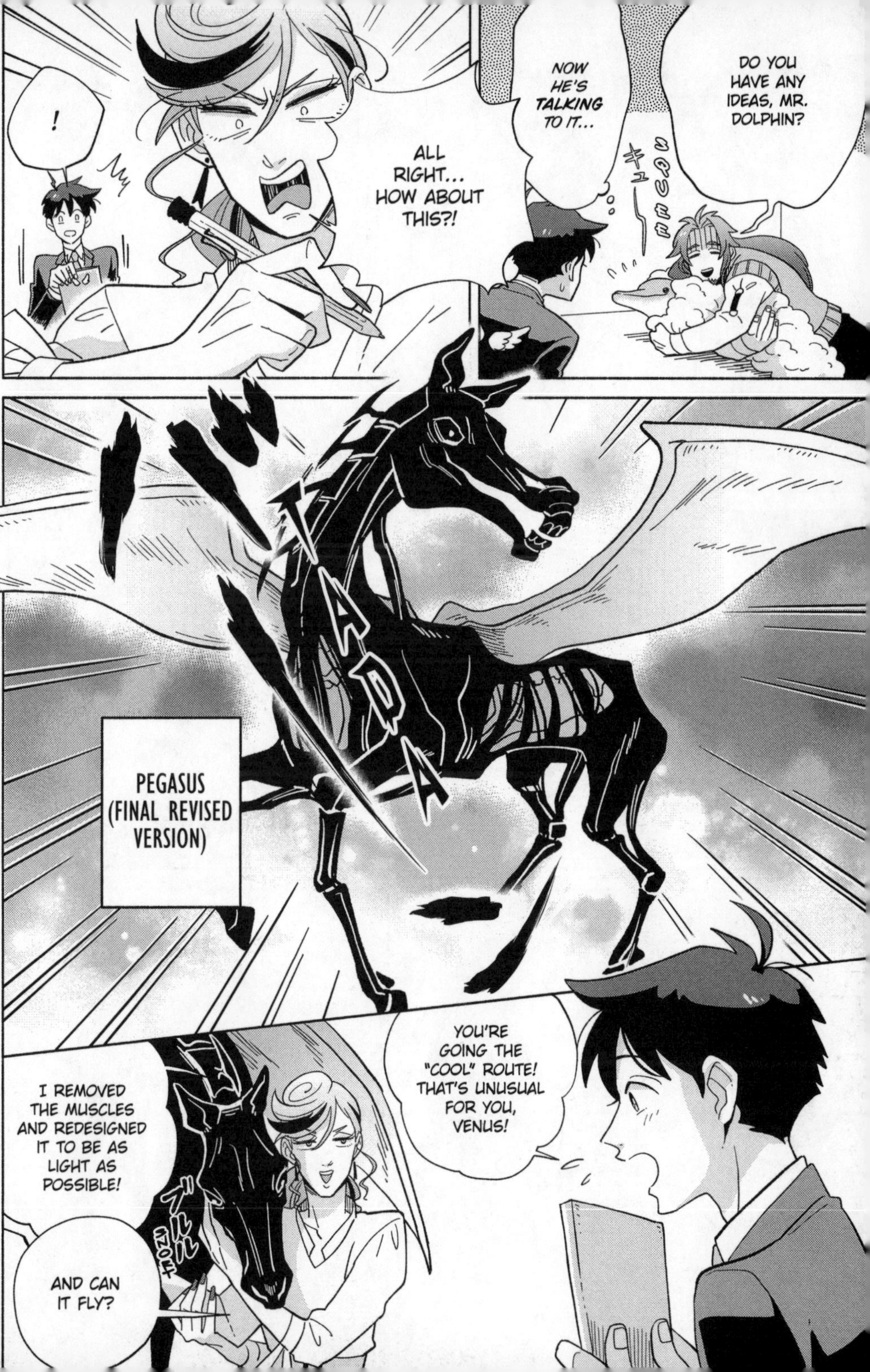
DO YOU HAVE ANY IDEAS, MR. DOLPHIN?
キュー
SQUEE
NOW HE'S *TALKING* TO IT...
ALL RIGHT... HOW ABOUT THIS?!
!
TADA
PEGASUS (FINAL REVISED VERSION)
YOU'RE GOING THE "COOL" ROUTE! THAT'S UNUSUAL FOR YOU, VENUS!
I REMOVED THE MUSCLES AND REDESIGNED IT TO BE AS LIGHT AS POSSIBLE!
ブルル
SNORT
AND CAN IT FLY?

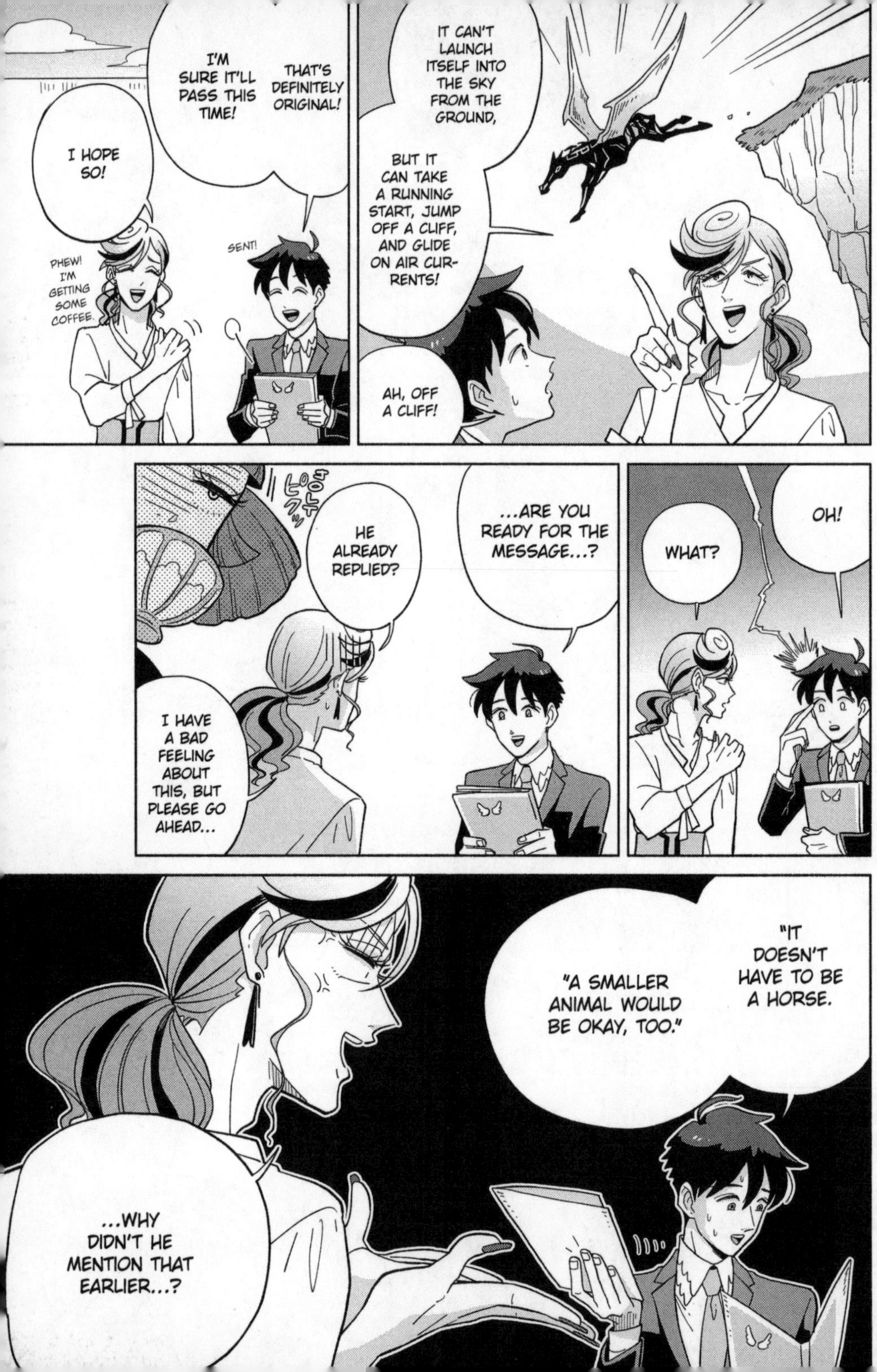
IT CAN'T LAUNCH ITSELF INTO THE SKY FROM THE GROUND,
BUT IT CAN TAKE A RUNNING START, JUMP OFF A CLIFF, AND GLIDE ON AIR CURRENTS!
AH, OFF A CLIFF!
THAT'S DEFINITELY ORIGINAL!
I'M SURE IT'LL PASS THIS TIME!
I HOPE SO!
SENT!
PHEW! I'M GETTING SOME COFFEE.
OH!
WHAT?
...ARE YOU READY FOR THE MESSAGE...?
HE ALREADY REPLIED?
I HAVE A BAD FEELING ABOUT THIS, BUT PLEASE GO AHEAD...
"IT DOESN'T HAVE TO BE A HORSE.
"A SMALLER ANIMAL WOULD BE OKAY, TOO."
...WHY DIDN'T HE MENTION THAT EARLIER...?

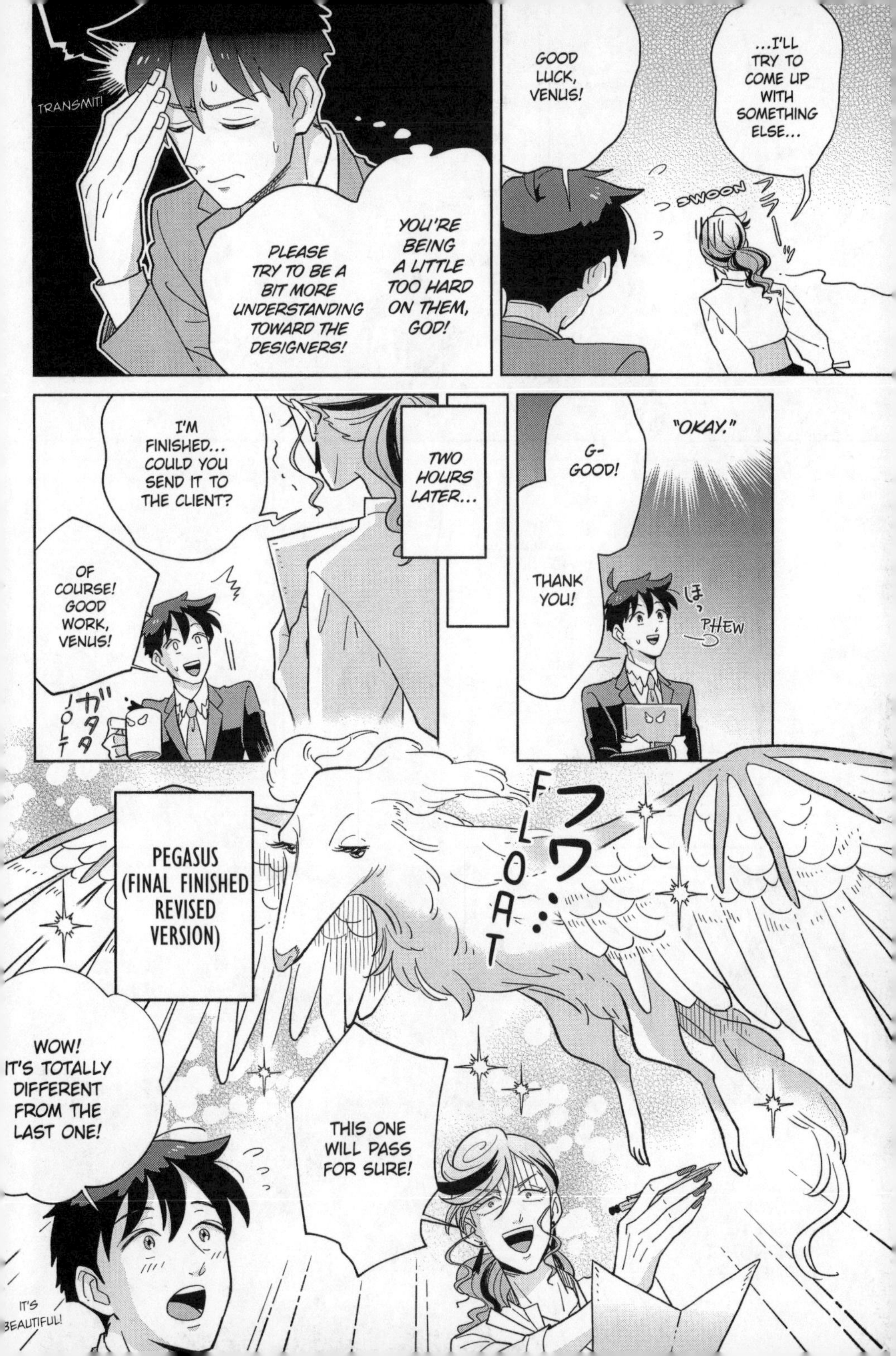
...I'LL TRY TO COME UP WITH SOMETHING ELSE...
GOOD LUCK, VENUS!
フラ～ッ
SWOON
TRANSMIT!
YOU'RE BEING A LITTLE TOO HARD ON THEM, GOD!
PLEASE TRY TO BE A BIT MORE UNDERSTANDING TOWARD THE DESIGNERS!
"OKAY."
G-GOOD!
THANK YOU!
ほっ
PHEW
TWO HOURS LATER...
I'M FINISHED... COULD YOU SEND IT TO THE CLIENT?
OF COURSE! GOOD WORK, VENUS!
ガタタ
JOLT
フワ
FLOAT
PEGASUS (FINAL FINISHED REVISED VERSION)
THIS ONE WILL PASS FOR SURE!
WOW! IT'S TOTALLY DIFFERENT FROM THE LAST ONE!
IT'S BEAUTIFUL!

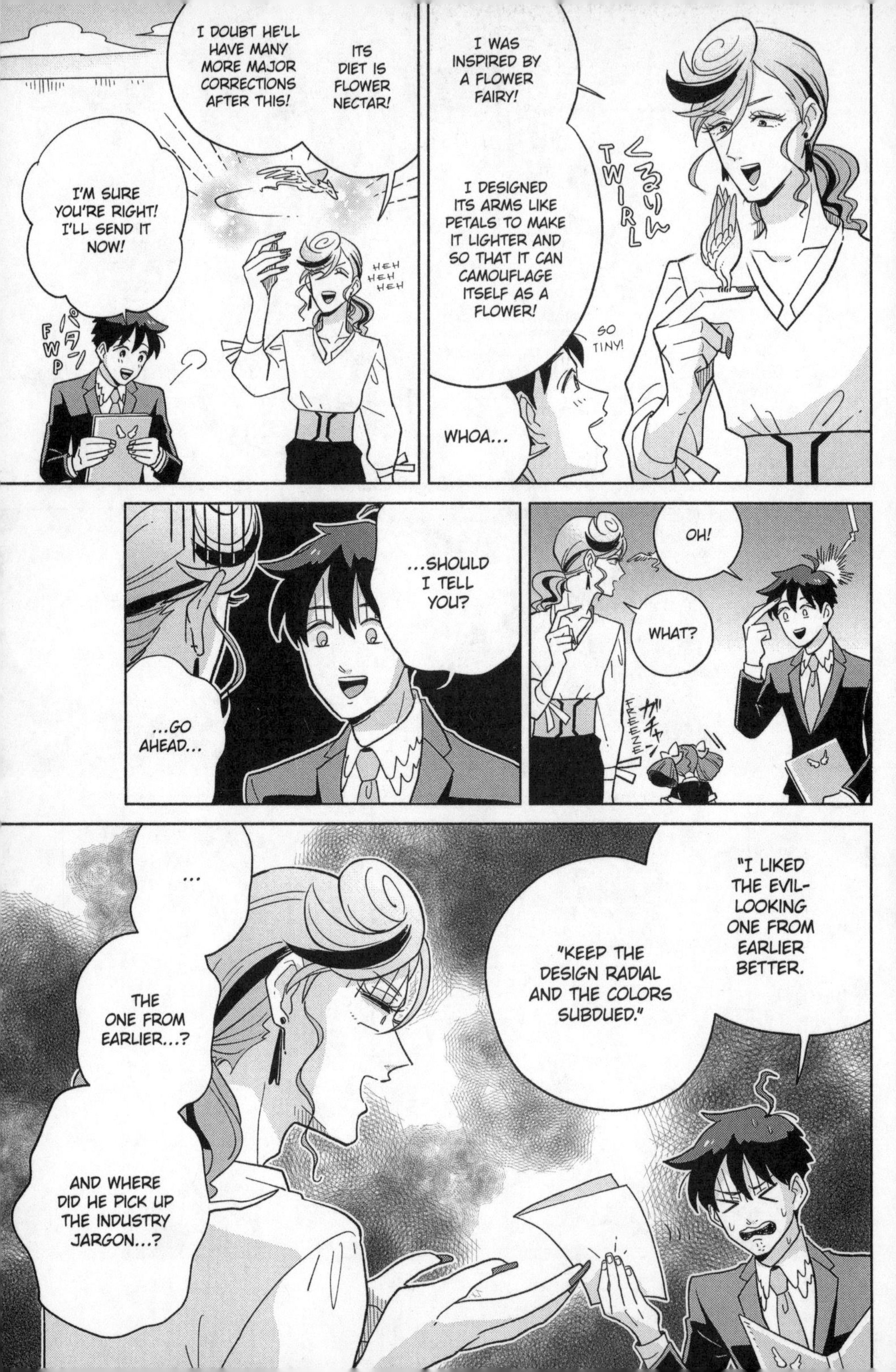
I WAS INSPIRED BY A FLOWER FAIRY!
I DESIGNED ITS ARMS LIKE PETALS TO MAKE IT LIGHTER AND SO THAT IT CAN CAMOUFLAGE ITSELF AS A FLOWER!
くるりん
TWIRL
SO TINY!
WHOA...
ITS DIET IS FLOWER NECTAR!
I DOUBT HE'LL HAVE MANY MORE MAJOR CORRECTIONS AFTER THIS!
HEH HEH HEH
I'M SURE YOU'RE RIGHT! I'LL SEND IT NOW!
パタン
FWP
OH!
WHAT?
ガチャン
FREEZE
...SHOULD I TELL YOU?
...GO AHEAD...
"I LIKED THE EVIL-LOOKING ONE FROM EARLIER BETTER.
"KEEP THE DESIGN RADIAL AND THE COLORS SUBDUED."
...
THE ONE FROM EARLIER...?
AND WHERE DID HE PICK UP THE INDUSTRY JARGON...?

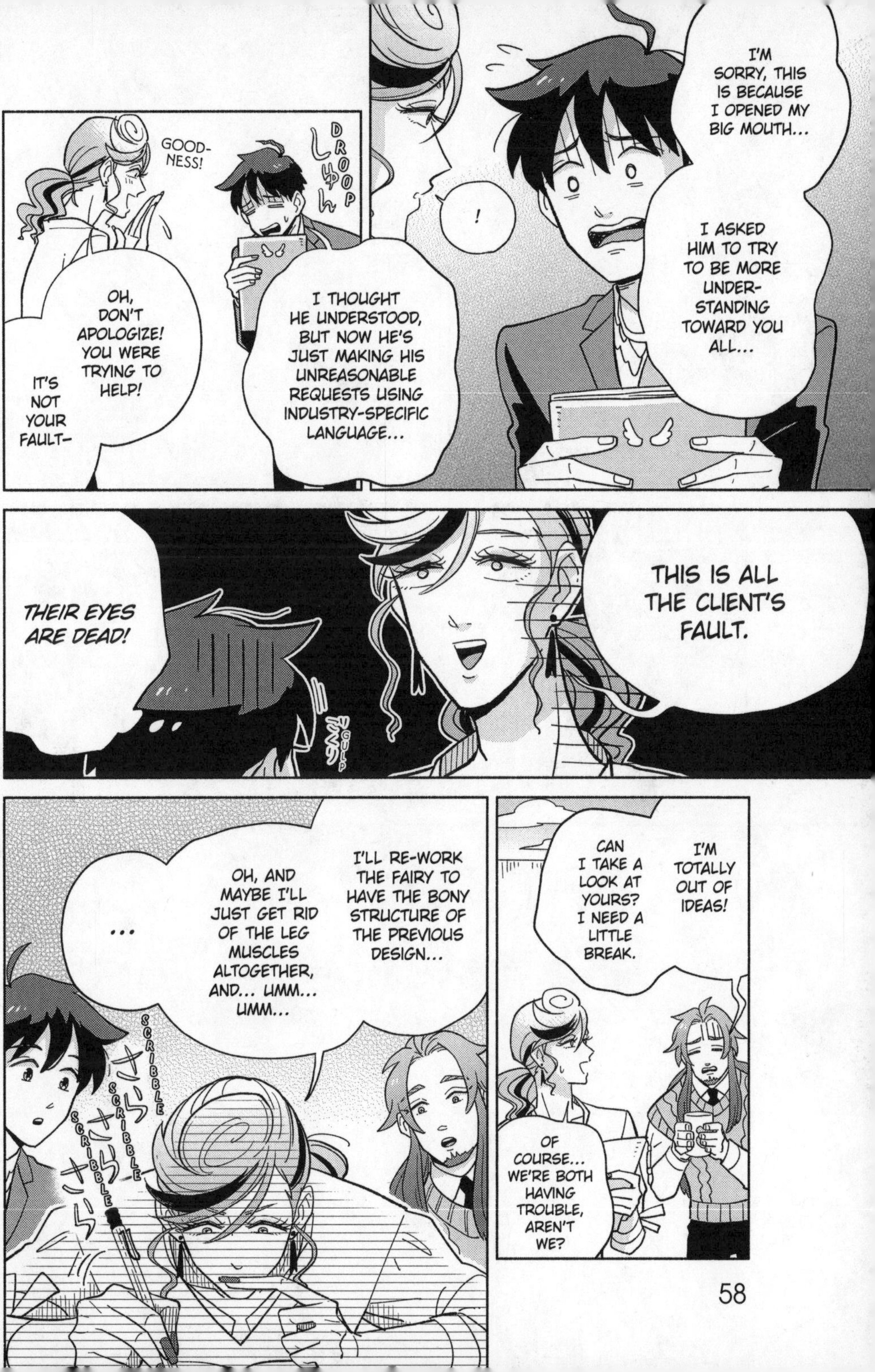

I'M SORRY, THIS IS BECAUSE I OPENED MY BIG MOUTH...
I ASKED HIM TO TRY TO BE MORE UNDER-STANDING TOWARD YOU ALL...
!
DROOP
GOOD-NESS!
I THOUGHT HE UNDERSTOOD, BUT NOW HE'S JUST MAKING HIS UNREASONABLE REQUESTS USING INDUSTRY-SPECIFIC LANGUAGE...
OH, DON'T APOLOGIZE! YOU WERE TRYING TO HELP!
IT'S NOT YOUR FAULT-
THIS IS ALL THE CLIENT'S FAULT.
GULP
THEIR EYES ARE DEAD!
I'M TOTALLY OUT OF IDEAS!
CAN I TAKE A LOOK AT YOURS? I NEED A LITTLE BREAK.
OF COURSE... WE'RE BOTH HAVING TROUBLE, AREN'T WE?
I'LL RE-WORK THE FAIRY TO HAVE THE BONY STRUCTURE OF THE PREVIOUS DESIGN...
OH, AND MAYBE I'LL JUST GET RID OF THE LEG MUSCLES ALTOGETHER, AND... UMM... UMM...
...
SCRIBBLE
SCRIBBLE
SCRIBBLE

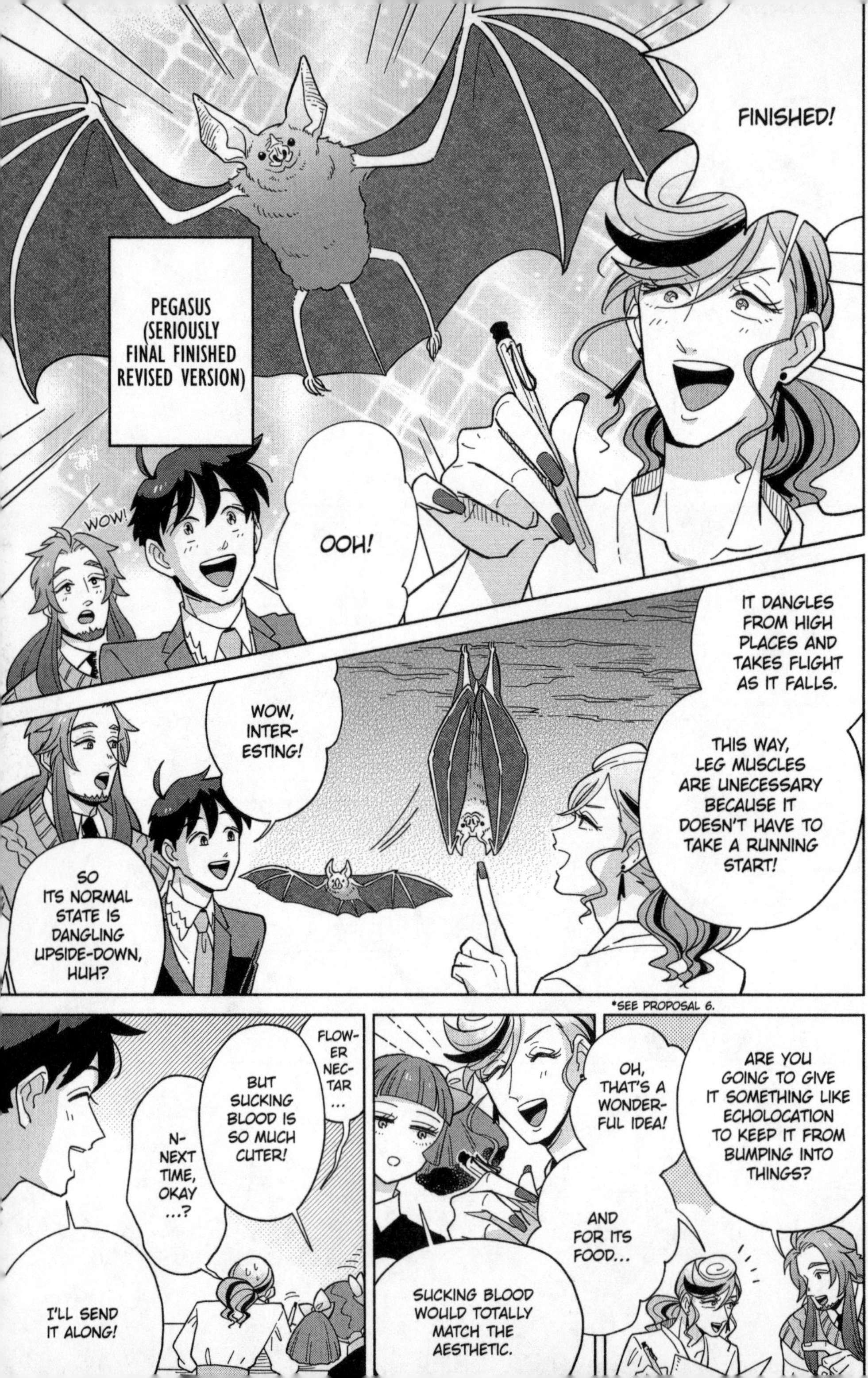
FINISHED!
PEGASUS (SERIOUSLY FINAL FINISHED REVISED VERSION)
OOH!
WOW!
IT DANGLES FROM HIGH PLACES AND TAKES FLIGHT AS IT FALLS.
THIS WAY, LEG MUSCLES ARE UNECESSARY BECAUSE IT DOESN'T HAVE TO TAKE A RUNNING START!
WOW, INTER-ESTING!
SO ITS NORMAL STATE IS DANGLING UPSIDE-DOWN, HUH?
*SEE PROPOSAL 6.
ARE YOU GOING TO GIVE IT SOMETHING LIKE ECHOLOCATION TO KEEP IT FROM BUMPING INTO THINGS?
OH, THAT'S A WONDER-FUL IDEA!
AND FOR ITS FOOD...
SUCKING BLOOD WOULD TOTALLY MATCH THE AESTHETIC.
FLOWER-ER NEC-TAR...
BUT SUCKING BLOOD IS SO MUCH CUTER!
N-NEXT TIME, OKAY...?
I'LL SEND IT ALONG!

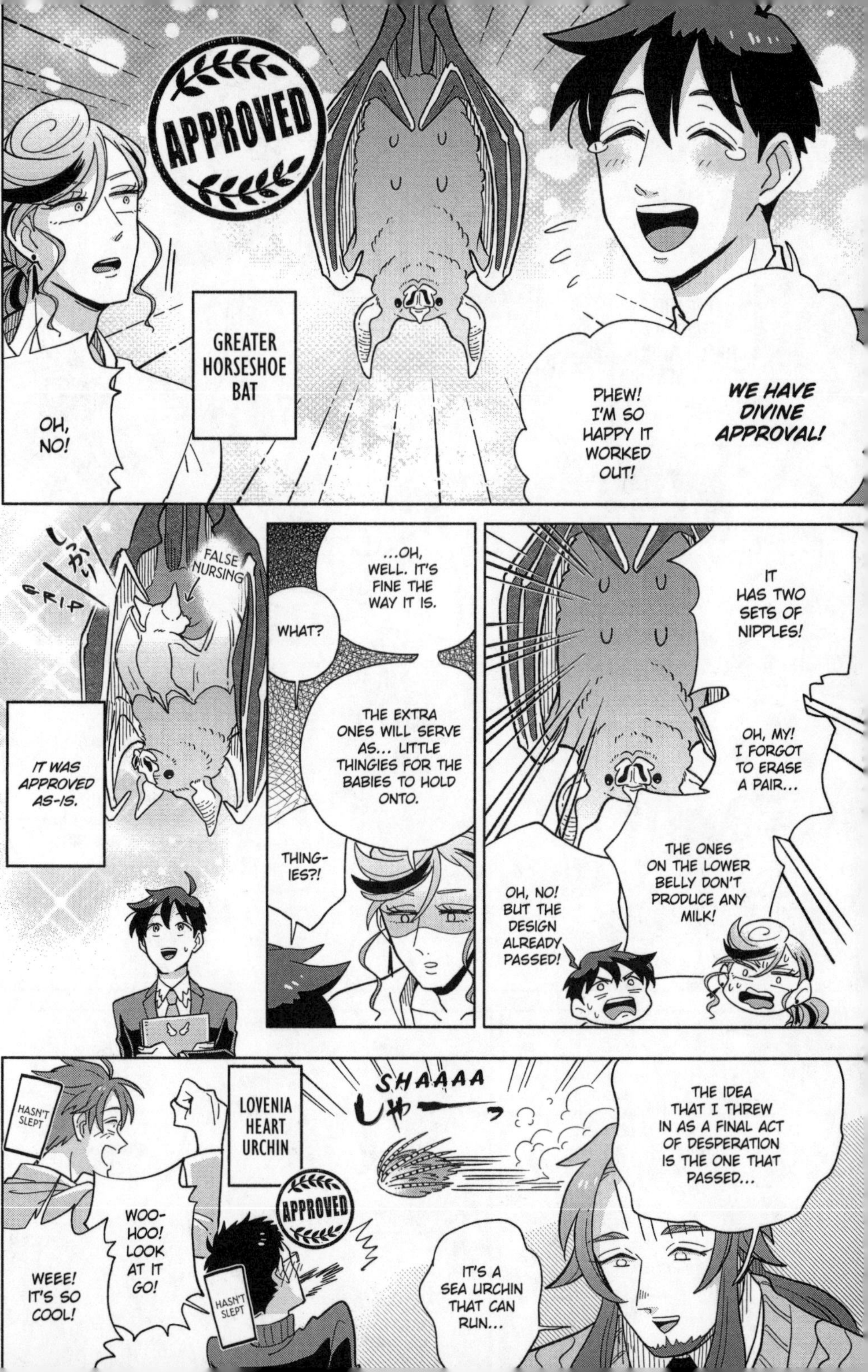
WE HAVE DIVINE APPROVAL!
PHEW! I'M SO HAPPY IT WORKED OUT!
APPROVED
GREATER HORSESHOE BAT
OH, NO!
IT HAS TWO SETS OF NIPPLES!
OH, MY! I FORGOT TO ERASE A PAIR...
THE ONES ON THE LOWER BELLY DON'T PRODUCE ANY MILK!
OH, NO! BUT THE DESIGN ALREADY PASSED!
...OH, WELL. IT'S FINE THE WAY IT IS.
WHAT?
THE EXTRA ONES WILL SERVE AS... LITTLE THINGIES FOR THE BABIES TO HOLD ONTO.
THING-IES?!
しっかり
GRIP
FALSE NURSING
IT WAS APPROVED AS-IS.
THE IDEA THAT I THREW IN AS A FINAL ACT OF DESPERATION IS THE ONE THAT PASSED...
しゃーっ
SHAAAA
LOVENIA HEART URCHIN
APPROVED
IT'S A SEA URCHIN THAT CAN RUN...
WOO-HOO! LOOK AT IT GO!
HASN'T SLEPT
WEEE! IT'S SO COOL!
HASN'T SLEPT

# THE ENCYCLOPEDIA OF REAL ANIMALS 10

| ANIMAL 27 | GREATER HORSESHOE BAT |
|---|---|

THE REAL THING

A greater horseshoe bat in flight inside a cave. The species is common in Japan.

Photo: Science Source/Aflo

Bats are the only mammals capable of flight. The females of certain species, including the greater horseshoe bat, have an extra set of nipples on their pubic area. Young pups wrap their legs around their mothers' necks and clamp their teeth around the false nipple to hold on. While around 70 percent of bats belonging to the Chiroptera order are carnivorous, many species, like the megabat, are nectar-eating. Despite the image of bats as blood-suckers, species like the vampire bat that feed on blood are quite rare. According to modern genetic classification methods (SINE analysis), bats and horses are distantly related. The clade Pegasoferae, which includes bats, horses and other odd-toed ungulates, carnivores, and pangolins, was named after the winged horse Pegasus.

| [Name] | *Rhinolophus ferrumequinum* |
|---|---|
| [Classification] | Class: Mammalia |
| | Order: Chiroptera |
| | Family: Rhinolophidae |
| | Genus: *Rhinolophus* |
| [Habitat] | Northern Africa, Southern Europe, South East Asia, Japan |
| [Size] | 5.5-6.5 cm (2.2-2.6 in) (wing length) |
| | 6-8cm (2.4-3 in) (head to foot) |

# ANIMAL 28 LOVENIA HEART URCHIN

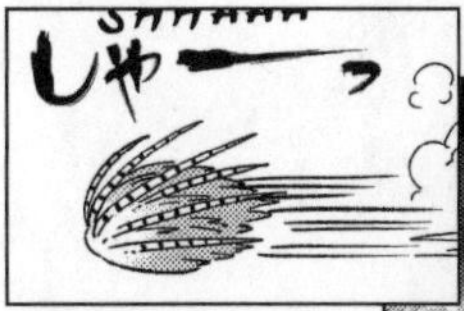
SHAAAAH
しゃーっ

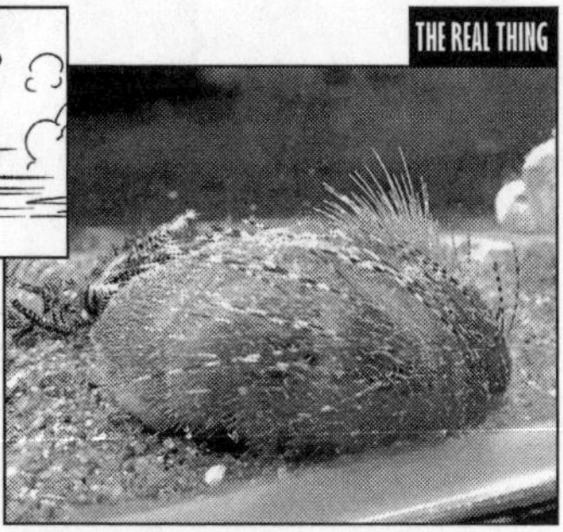
THE REAL THING

Lovenia heart urchins can be found south of the Boso Peninsula and Sagami Bay in Japan, but are extremely rare.
Photo: Toba Aquarium

| | |
|---|---|
| **[Name]** | *Lovenia elongata* |
| **[Classification]** | Phylum: Echinodermata<br>Class: Echinoidea<br>Order: Spatangoida<br>Family: Loveniidae<br>Genus: *Lovenia* |
| **[Habitat]** | Indian Ocean, Western Atlantic Ocean, south of the Boso Peninsula/Sagami Bay |
| **[Length]** | Approximately 10 cm (4 in) |

Normally hidden underneath the sand on the ocean floor, Lovenia heart urchins move along the coasts following tidal movements (and to escape predators, according to some research). They can reach speeds of up to 20 cm (7.9 inches) per second, and are said to be the fastest moving of all sea urchins. They have a row of large spines on either side of their abdomen that they can wave in an alternating motion to achieve high speeds.

# ANIMAL 29 DESIGNER

"Designer" is the generic term for the creatures who are employed in the design field. In their work, they use not only their vision but also take function into consideration to devise new concepts. Because design work is often more commercial than artistic, mediocre client requests result in a large number of disappointing products reaching the market. Achieving commercial success is an important aspect of the job, but there need to be limits. The next time you see a catastrophically designed product, remember this: it's hard out there for a designer.

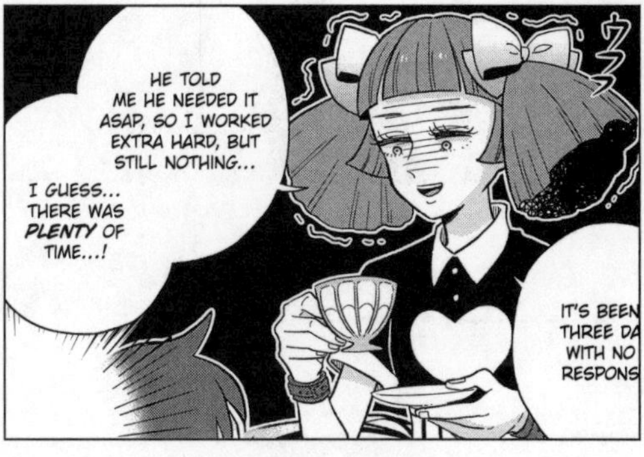
HE TOLD ME HE NEEDED IT ASAP, SO I WORKED EXTRA HARD, BUT STILL NOTHING...
I GUESS... THERE WAS *PLENTY* OF TIME...!
IT'S BEEN THREE DA WITH NO RESPONS

| | |
|---|---|
| **[Name]** | Designer |
| **[Classification]** | Unknown |
| **[Habitat]** | Mainly indoor environments |
| **[Height]** | Approximately 1.5-2 m (5-6.6 ft) |

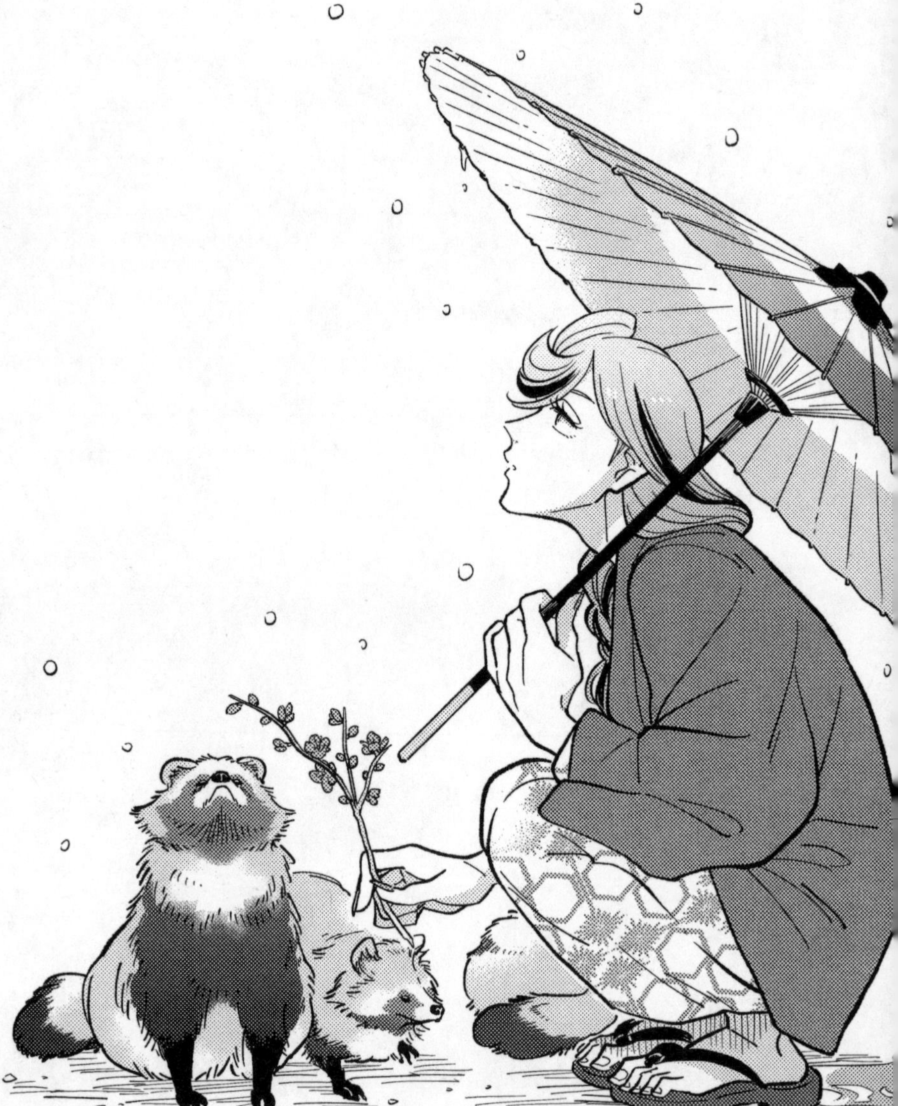

# HEAVEN'S
# DESIGN TEAM

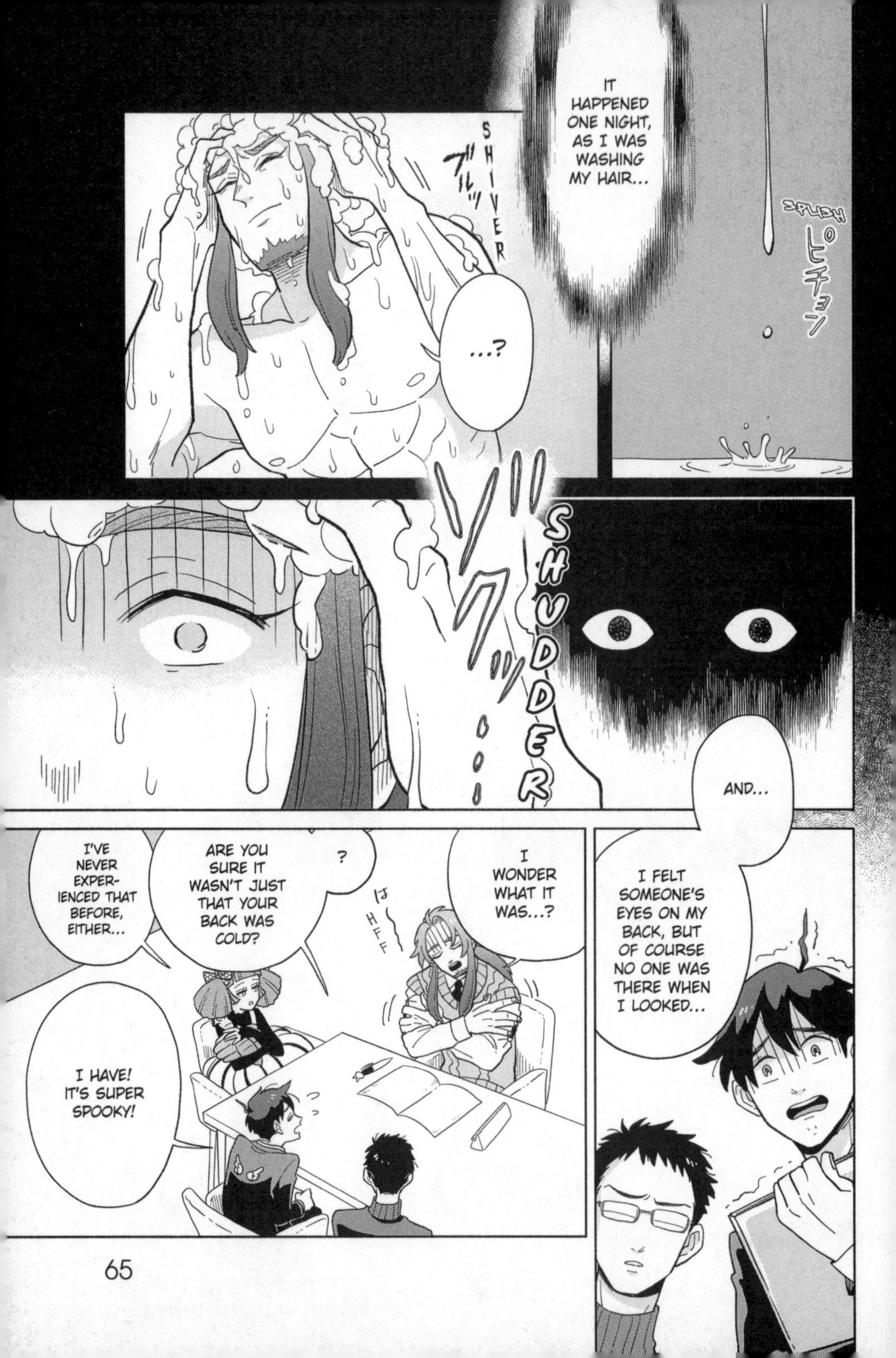
IT HAPPENED ONE NIGHT, AS I WAS WASHING MY HAIR...
SPLISH
ピチョン
SHIVER
ブルッ
...?
SHUDDER
AND...
I FELT SOMEONE'S EYES ON MY BACK, BUT OF COURSE NO ONE WAS THERE WHEN I LOOKED...
I WONDER WHAT IT WAS...?
HFF
?
ARE YOU SURE IT WASN'T JUST THAT YOUR BACK WAS COLD?
I'VE NEVER EXPERIENCED THAT BEFORE, EITHER...
I HAVE! IT'S SUPER SPOOKY!

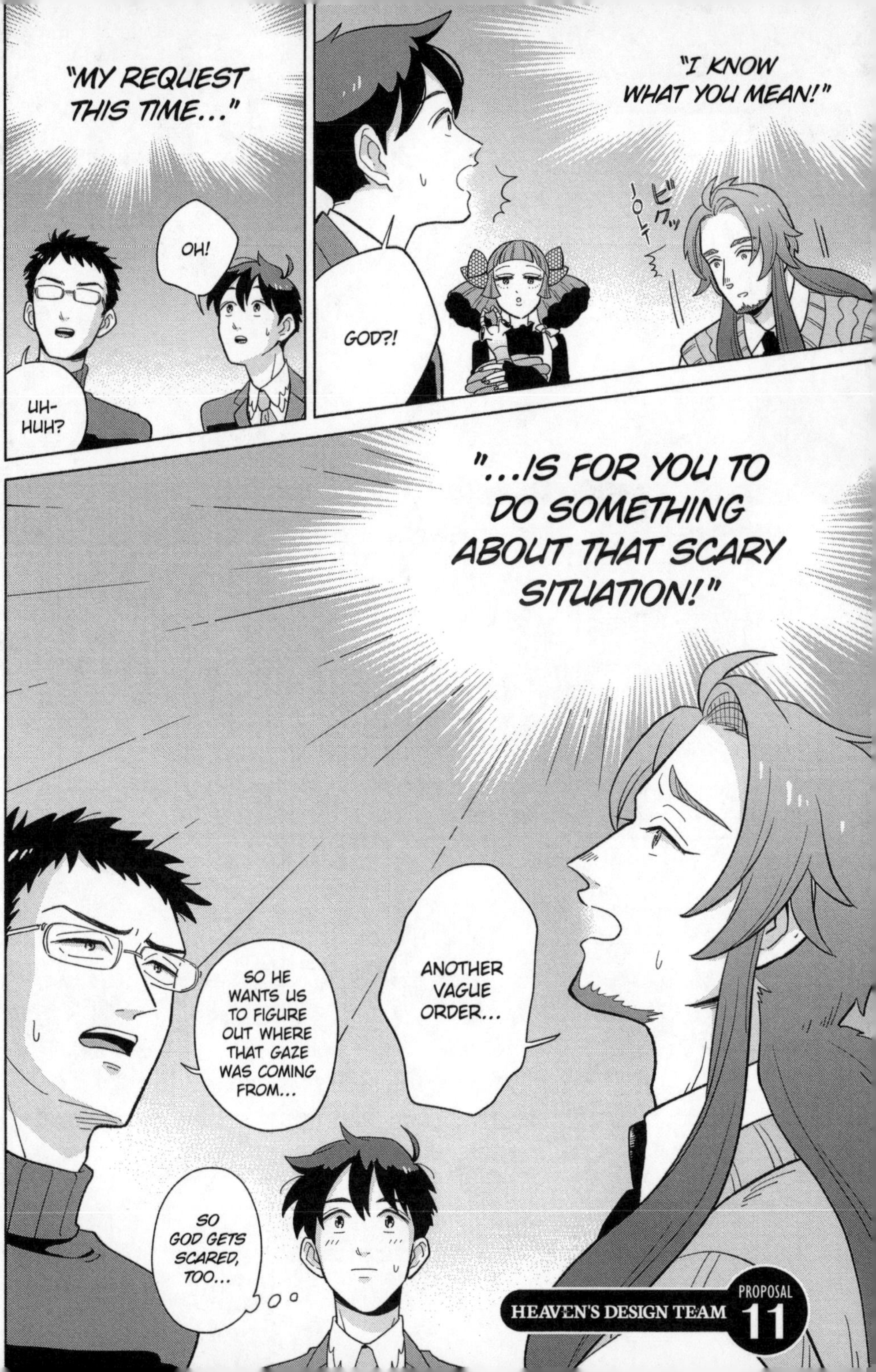
"I KNOW WHAT YOU MEAN!"
ビクッ
GOD?!
"MY REQUEST THIS TIME..."
OH!
UH-HUH?
"...IS FOR YOU TO DO SOMETHING ABOUT THAT SCARY SITUATION!"
ANOTHER VAGUE ORDER...
SO HE WANTS US TO FIGURE OUT WHERE THAT GAZE WAS COMING FROM...
SO GOD GETS SCARED, TOO...
PROPOSAL 11
HEAVEN'S DESIGN TEAM

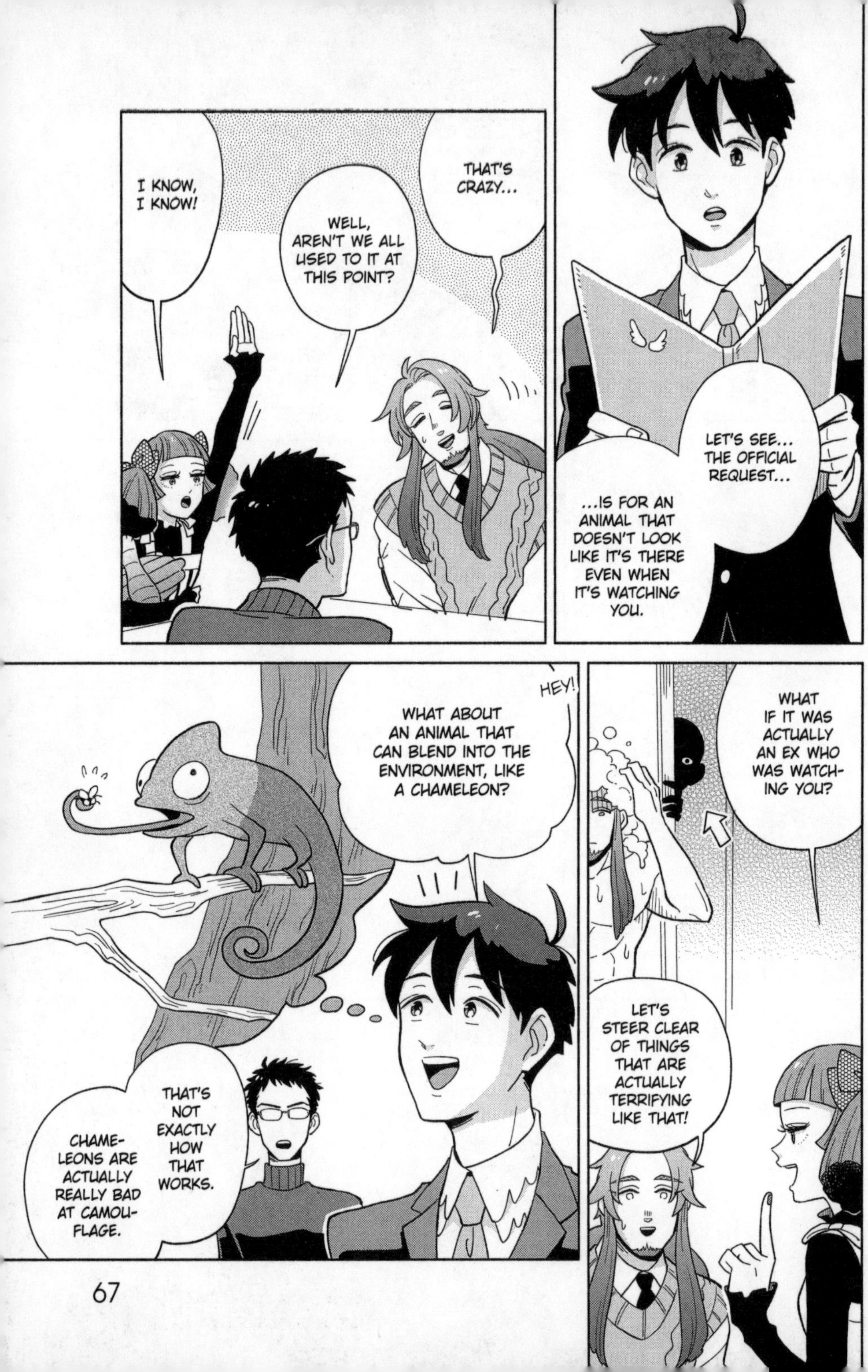
LET'S SEE... THE OFFICIAL REQUEST...
...IS FOR AN ANIMAL THAT DOESN'T LOOK LIKE IT'S THERE EVEN WHEN IT'S WATCHING YOU.
THAT'S CRAZY...
WELL, AREN'T WE ALL USED TO IT AT THIS POINT?
I KNOW, I KNOW!
WHAT IF IT WAS ACTUALLY AN EX WHO WAS WATCHING YOU?
LET'S STEER CLEAR OF THINGS THAT ARE ACTUALLY TERRIFYING LIKE THAT!
HEY!
WHAT ABOUT AN ANIMAL THAT CAN BLEND INTO THE ENVIRONMENT, LIKE A CHAMELEON?
THAT'S NOT EXACTLY HOW THAT WORKS.
CHAME-LEONS ARE ACTUALLY REALLY BAD AT CAMOU-FLAGE.

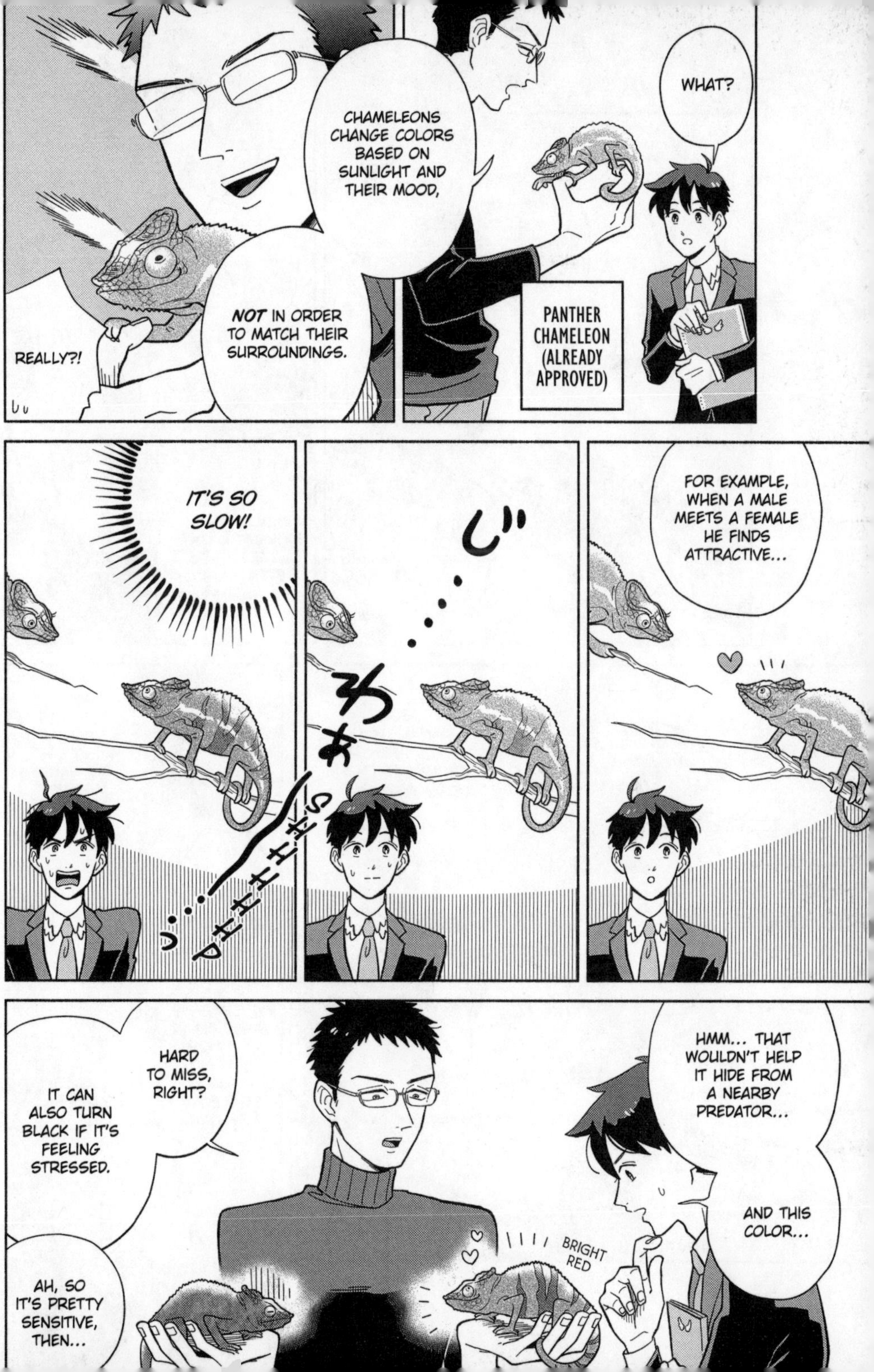
WHAT?
CHAMELEONS CHANGE COLORS BASED ON SUNLIGHT AND THEIR MOOD,
PANTHER CHAMELEON (ALREADY APPROVED)
NOT IN ORDER TO MATCH THEIR SURROUNDINGS.
REALLY?!
FOR EXAMPLE, WHEN A MALE MEETS A FEMALE HE FINDS ATTRACTIVE...
じ...
わぁ
SHHHHHP...
IT'S SO SLOW!
HMM... THAT WOULDN'T HELP IT HIDE FROM A NEARBY PREDATOR...
AND THIS COLOR...
BRIGHT RED
HARD TO MISS, RIGHT?
IT CAN ALSO TURN BLACK IF IT'S FEELING STRESSED.
AH, SO IT'S PRETTY SENSITIVE, THEN...

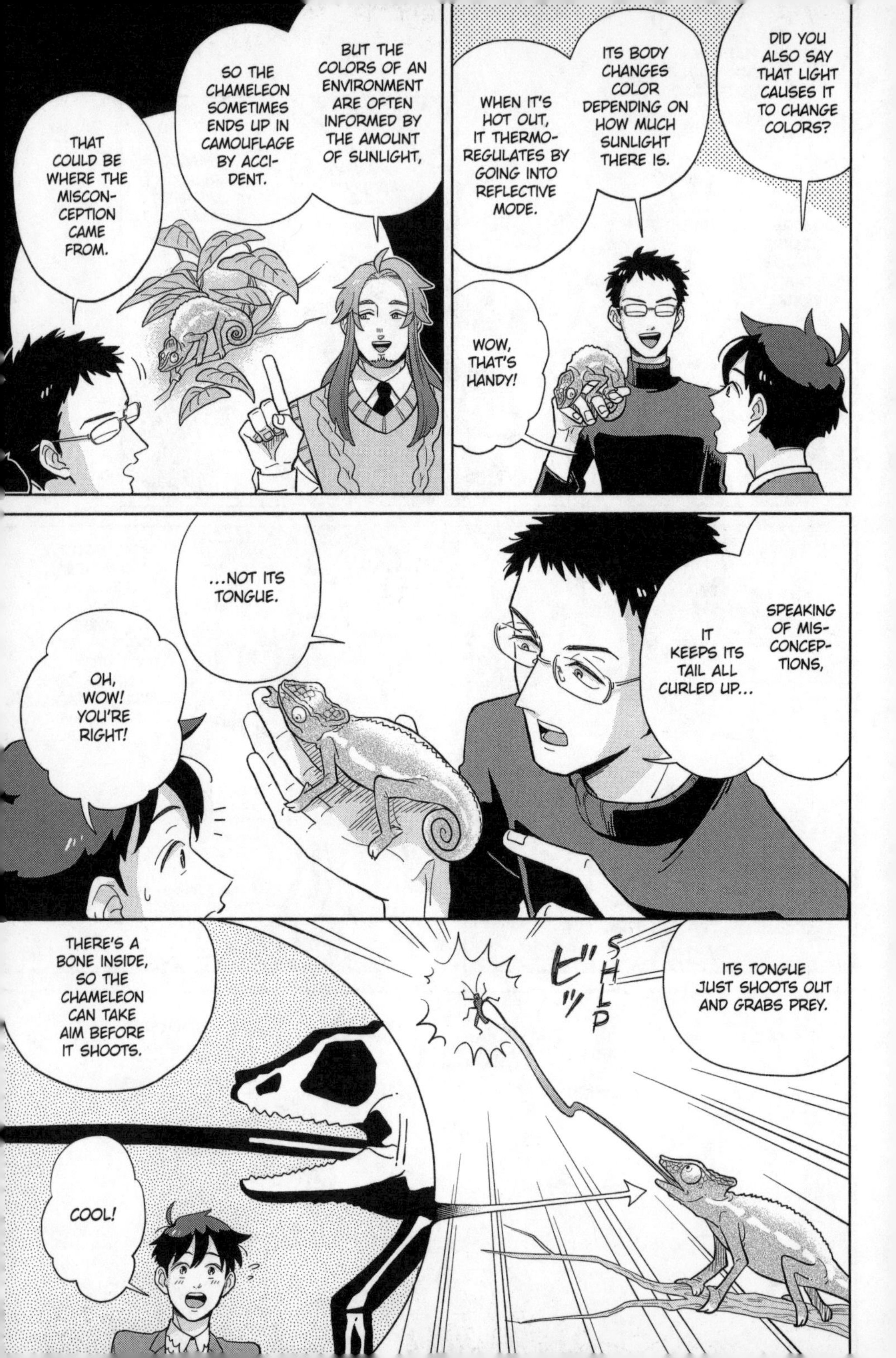
DID YOU ALSO SAY THAT LIGHT CAUSES IT TO CHANGE COLORS?
ITS BODY CHANGES COLOR DEPENDING ON HOW MUCH SUNLIGHT THERE IS.
WHEN IT'S HOT OUT, IT THERMOREGULATES BY GOING INTO REFLECTIVE MODE.
WOW, THAT'S HANDY!
BUT THE COLORS OF AN ENVIRONMENT ARE OFTEN INFORMED BY THE AMOUNT OF SUNLIGHT,
SO THE CHAMELEON SOMETIMES ENDS UP IN CAMOUFLAGE BY ACCIDENT.
THAT COULD BE WHERE THE MISCONCEPTION CAME FROM.
SPEAKING OF MISCONCEPTIONS,
IT KEEPS ITS TAIL ALL CURLED UP...
...NOT ITS TONGUE.
OH, WOW! YOU'RE RIGHT!
ITS TONGUE JUST SHOOTS OUT AND GRABS PREY.
ビッ SHLP
THERE'S A BONE INSIDE, SO THE CHAMELEON CAN TAKE AIM BEFORE IT SHOOTS.
COOL!

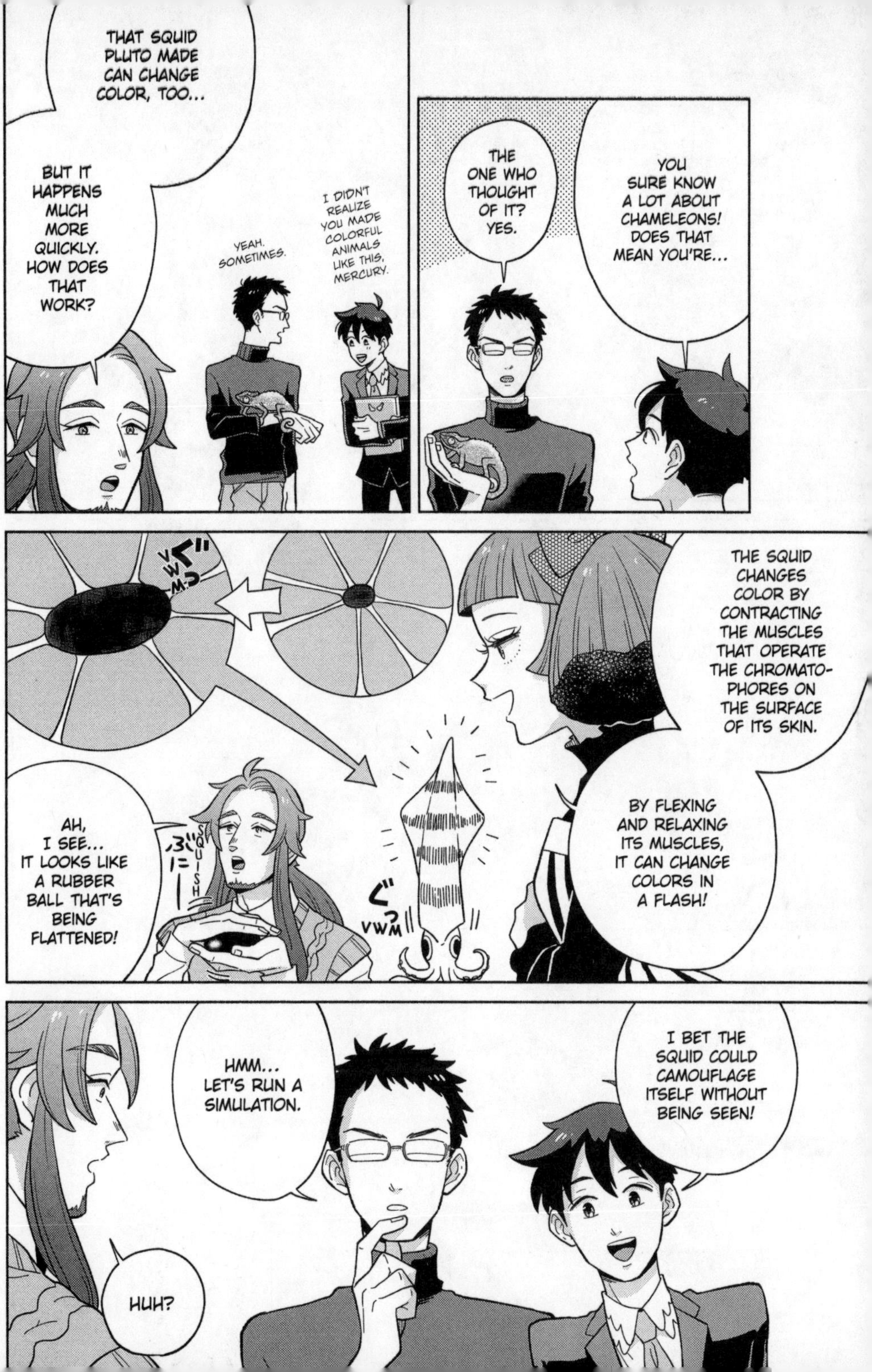
YOU SURE KNOW A LOT ABOUT CHAMELEONS! DOES THAT MEAN YOU'RE...
THE ONE WHO THOUGHT OF IT? YES.
I DIDN'T REALIZE YOU MADE COLORFUL ANIMALS LIKE THIS, MERCURY.
YEAH. SOMETIMES.
THAT SQUID PLUTO MADE CAN CHANGE COLOR, TOO...
BUT IT HAPPENS MUCH MORE QUICKLY. HOW DOES THAT WORK?
THE SQUID CHANGES COLOR BY CONTRACTING THE MUSCLES THAT OPERATE THE CHROMATO-PHORES ON THE SURFACE OF ITS SKIN.
VWM
BY FLEXING AND RELAXING ITS MUSCLES, IT CAN CHANGE COLORS IN A FLASH!
VWM
SQUISH
AH, I SEE... IT LOOKS LIKE A RUBBER BALL THAT'S BEING FLATTENED!
I BET THE SQUID COULD CAMOUFLAGE ITSELF WITHOUT BEING SEEN!
HMM... LET'S RUN A SIMULATION.
HUH?

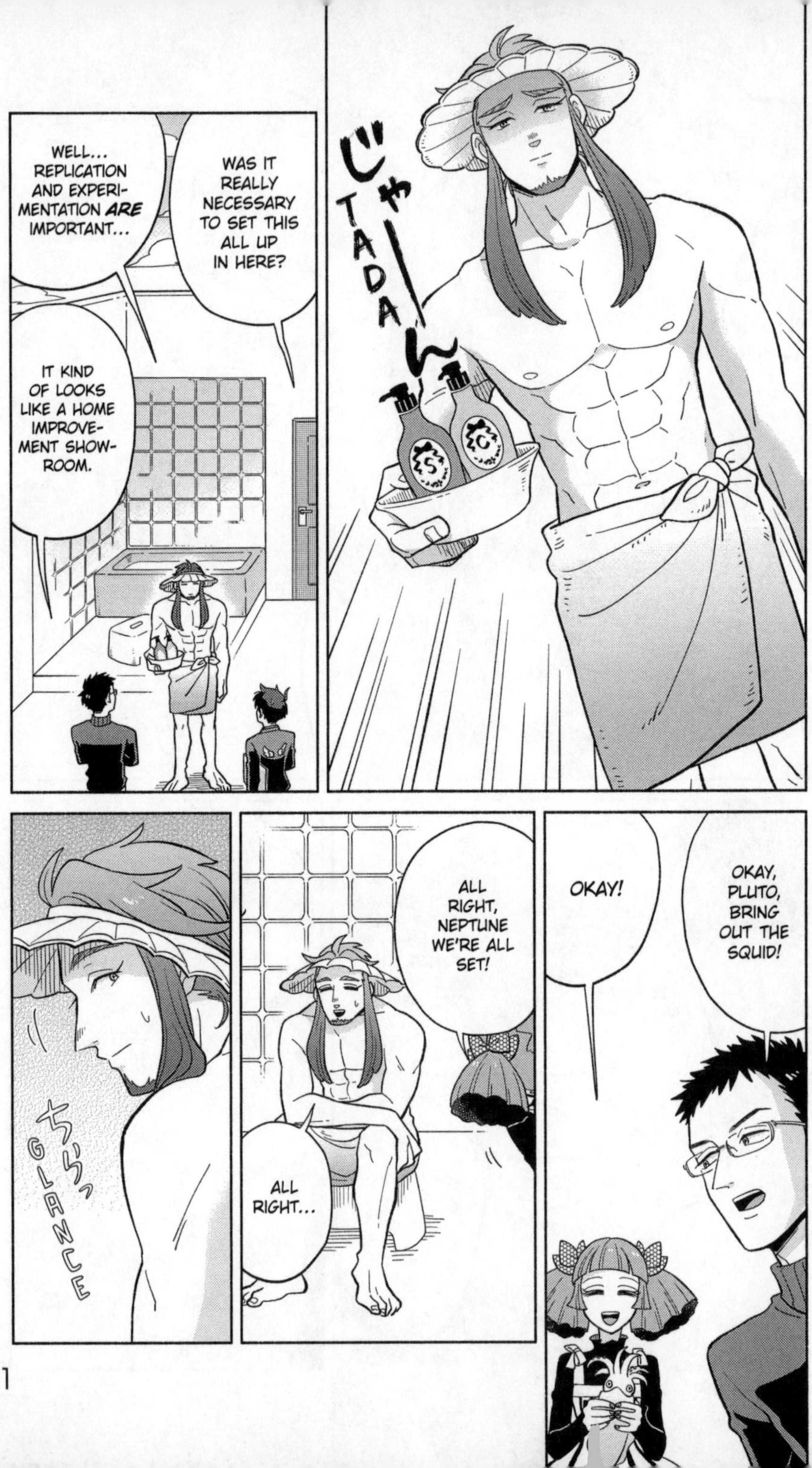
じゃーん
TADA
WAS IT REALLY NECESSARY TO SET THIS ALL UP IN HERE?
WELL... REPLICATION AND EXPERI-MENTATION *ARE* IMPORTANT...
IT KIND OF LOOKS LIKE A HOME IMPROVE-MENT SHOW-ROOM.
OKAY, PLUTO, BRING OUT THE SQUID!
OKAY!
ALL RIGHT, NEPTUNE WE'RE ALL SET!
ALL RIGHT...
ちらっ
GLANCE

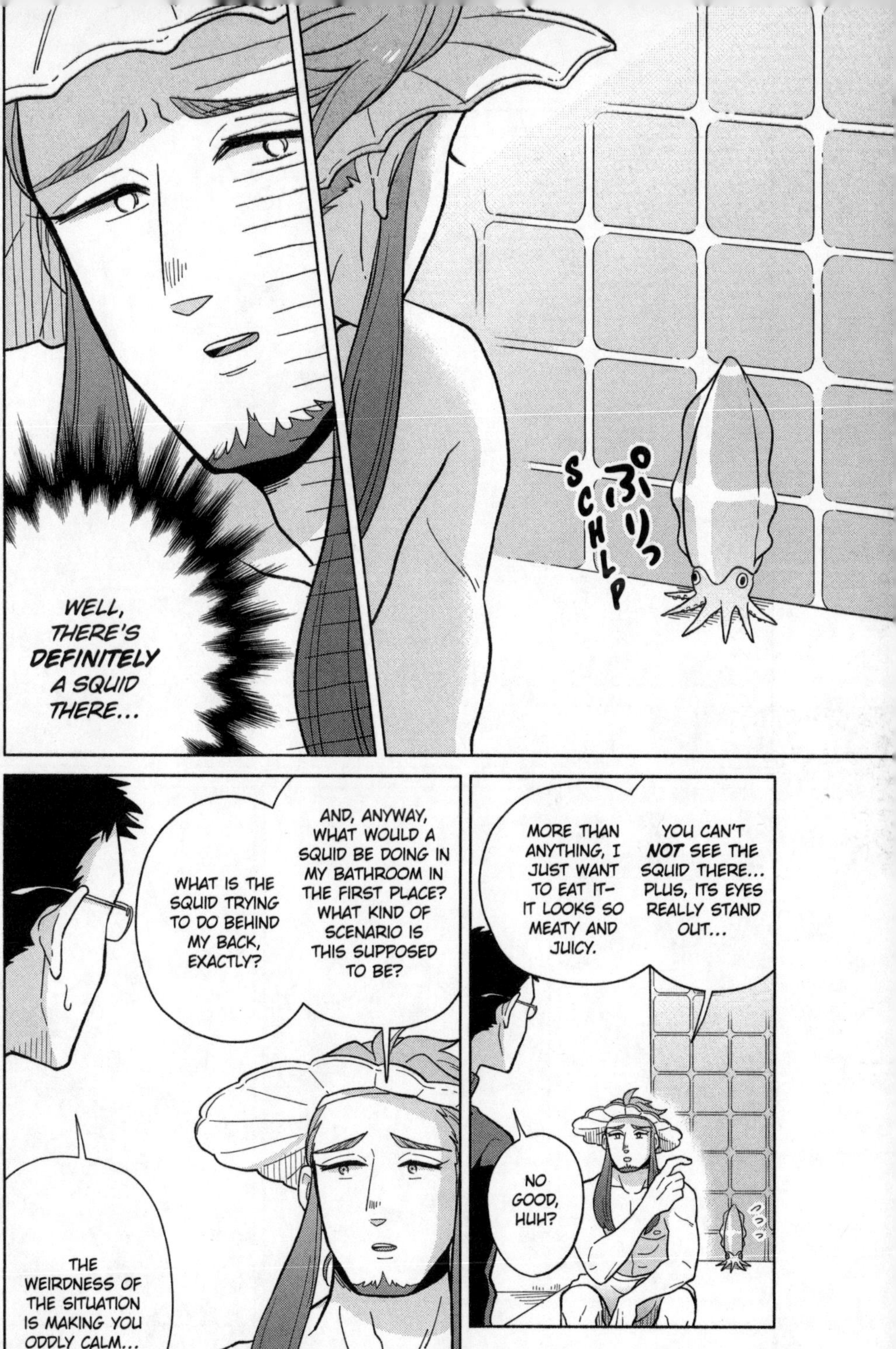
SCHLP
ぷりっ
WELL, THERE'S *DEFINITELY* A SQUID THERE...
YOU CAN'T *NOT* SEE THE SQUID THERE... PLUS, ITS EYES REALLY STAND OUT...
MORE THAN ANYTHING, I JUST WANT TO EAT IT— IT LOOKS SO MEATY AND JUICY.
NO GOOD, HUH?
AND, ANYWAY, WHAT WOULD A SQUID BE DOING IN MY BATHROOM IN THE FIRST PLACE? WHAT KIND OF SCENARIO IS THIS SUPPOSED TO BE?
WHAT IS THE SQUID TRYING TO DO BEHIND MY BACK, EXACTLY?
THE WEIRDNESS OF THE SITUATION IS MAKING YOU ODDLY CALM...

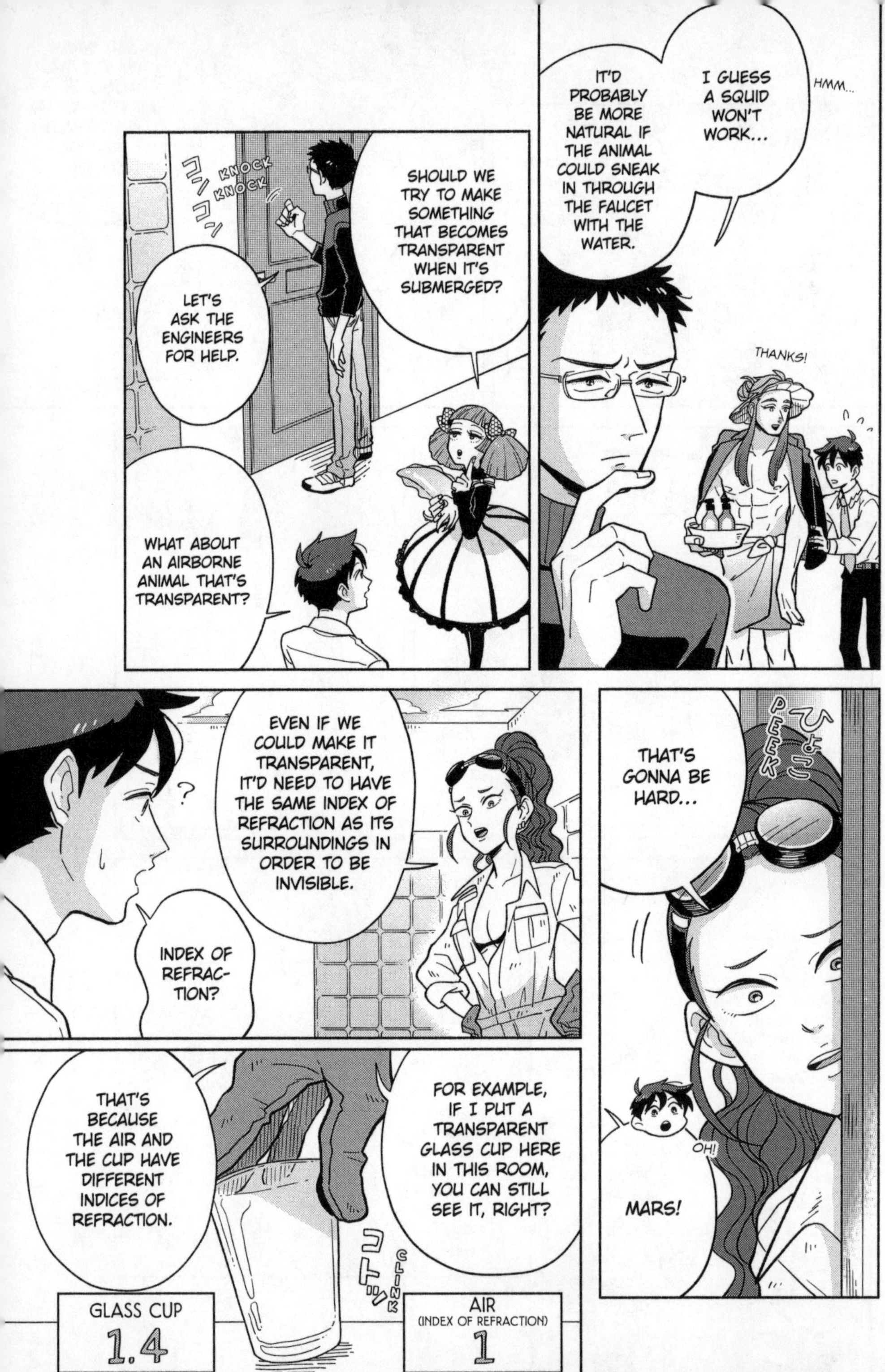
HMM...
I GUESS A SQUID WON'T WORK...
IT'D PROBABLY BE MORE NATURAL IF THE ANIMAL COULD SNEAK IN THROUGH THE FAUCET WITH THE WATER.
THANKS!
SHOULD WE TRY TO MAKE SOMETHING THAT BECOMES TRANSPARENT WHEN IT'S SUBMERGED?
コンコン KNOCK KNOCK
LET'S ASK THE ENGINEERS FOR HELP.
WHAT ABOUT AN AIRBORNE ANIMAL THAT'S TRANSPARENT?
ひょこ PEEK
THAT'S GONNA BE HARD...
OH!
MARS!
EVEN IF WE COULD MAKE IT TRANSPARENT, IT'D NEED TO HAVE THE SAME INDEX OF REFRACTION AS ITS SURROUNDINGS IN ORDER TO BE INVISIBLE.
?
INDEX OF REFRAC-TION?
FOR EXAMPLE, IF I PUT A TRANSPARENT GLASS CUP HERE IN THIS ROOM, YOU CAN STILL SEE IT, RIGHT?
THAT'S BECAUSE THE AIR AND THE CUP HAVE DIFFERENT INDICES OF REFRACTION.
コトッ CLINK
AIR (INDEX OF REFRACTION) 1
GLASS CUP 1.4

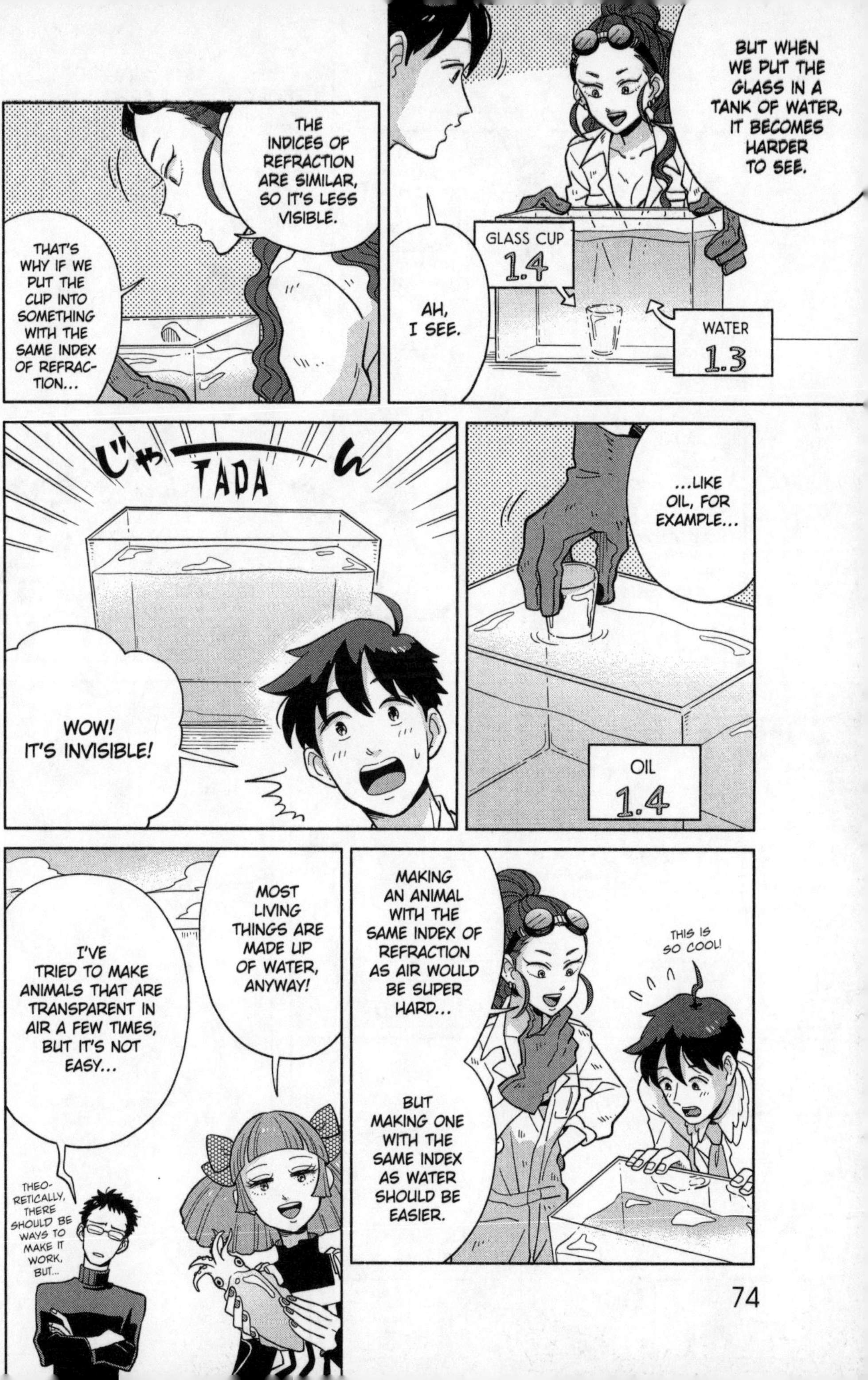
BUT WHEN WE PUT THE GLASS IN A TANK OF WATER, IT BECOMES HARDER TO SEE.
GLASS CUP 1.4
WATER 1.3
AH, I SEE.
THE INDICES OF REFRACTION ARE SIMILAR, SO IT'S LESS VISIBLE.
THAT'S WHY IF WE PUT THE CUP INTO SOMETHING WITH THE SAME INDEX OF REFRAC-TION...
...LIKE OIL, FOR EXAMPLE...
OIL 1.4
じゃーん TADA
WOW! IT'S INVISIBLE!
MAKING AN ANIMAL WITH THE SAME INDEX OF REFRACTION AS AIR WOULD BE SUPER HARD...
THIS IS SO COOL!
BUT MAKING ONE WITH THE SAME INDEX AS WATER SHOULD BE EASIER.
MOST LIVING THINGS ARE MADE UP OF WATER, ANYWAY!
I'VE TRIED TO MAKE ANIMALS THAT ARE TRANSPARENT IN AIR A FEW TIMES, BUT IT'S NOT EASY...
THEO-RETICALLY, THERE SHOULD BE WAYS TO MAKE IT WORK, BUT...

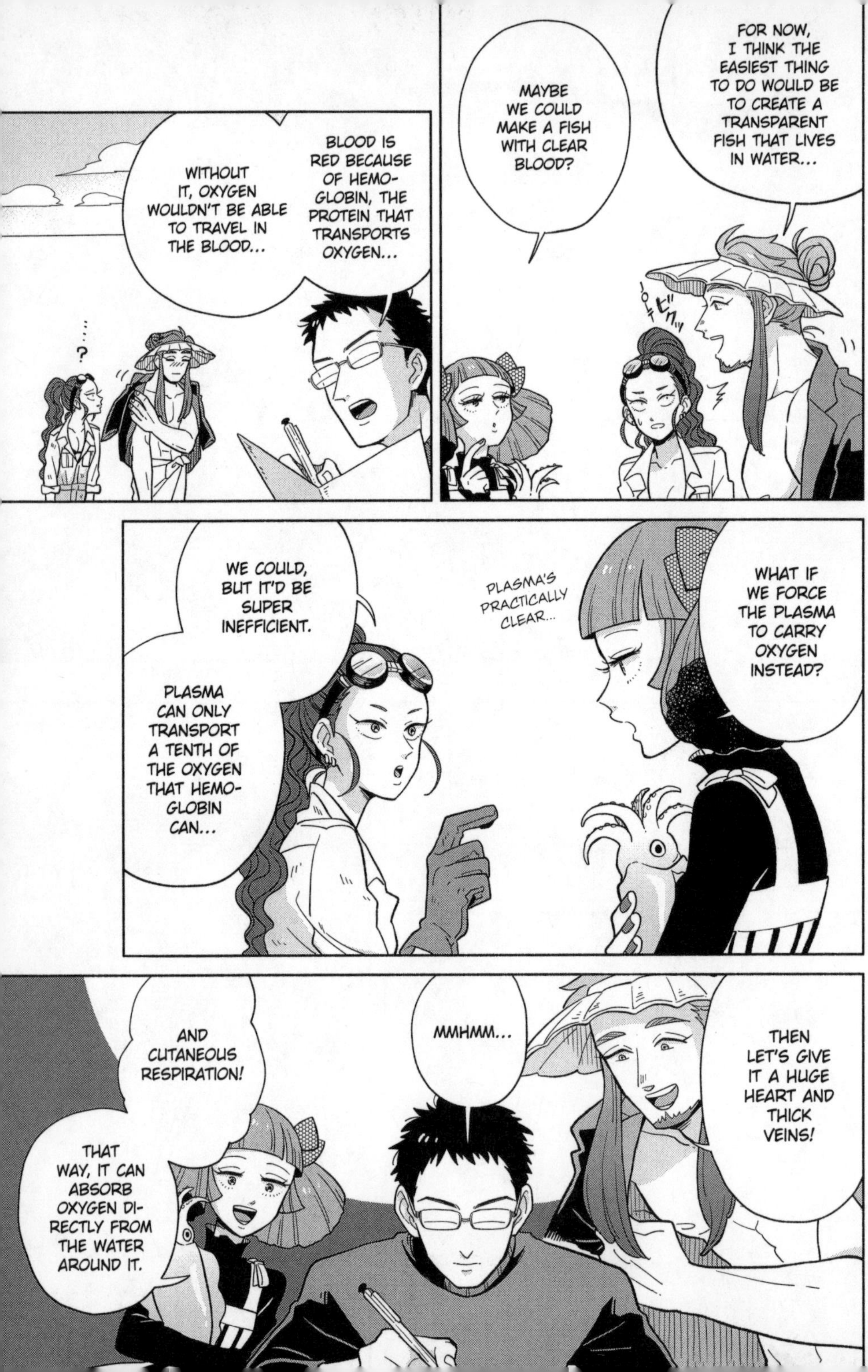
FOR NOW, I THINK THE EASIEST THING TO DO WOULD BE TO CREATE A TRANSPARENT FISH THAT LIVES IN WATER...
MAYBE WE COULD MAKE A FISH WITH CLEAR BLOOD?
BLOOD IS RED BECAUSE OF HEMO-GLOBIN, THE PROTEIN THAT TRANSPORTS OXYGEN...
WITHOUT IT, OXYGEN WOULDN'T BE ABLE TO TRAVEL IN THE BLOOD...
...?
WHAT IF WE FORCE THE PLASMA TO CARRY OXYGEN INSTEAD?
PLASMA'S PRACTICALLY CLEAR...
WE COULD, BUT IT'D BE SUPER INEFFICIENT.
PLASMA CAN ONLY TRANSPORT A TENTH OF THE OXYGEN THAT HEMO-GLOBIN CAN...
THEN LET'S GIVE IT A HUGE HEART AND THICK VEINS!
MMHMM...
AND CUTANEOUS RESPIRATION!
THAT WAY, IT CAN ABSORB OXYGEN DI-RECTLY FROM THE WATER AROUND IT.

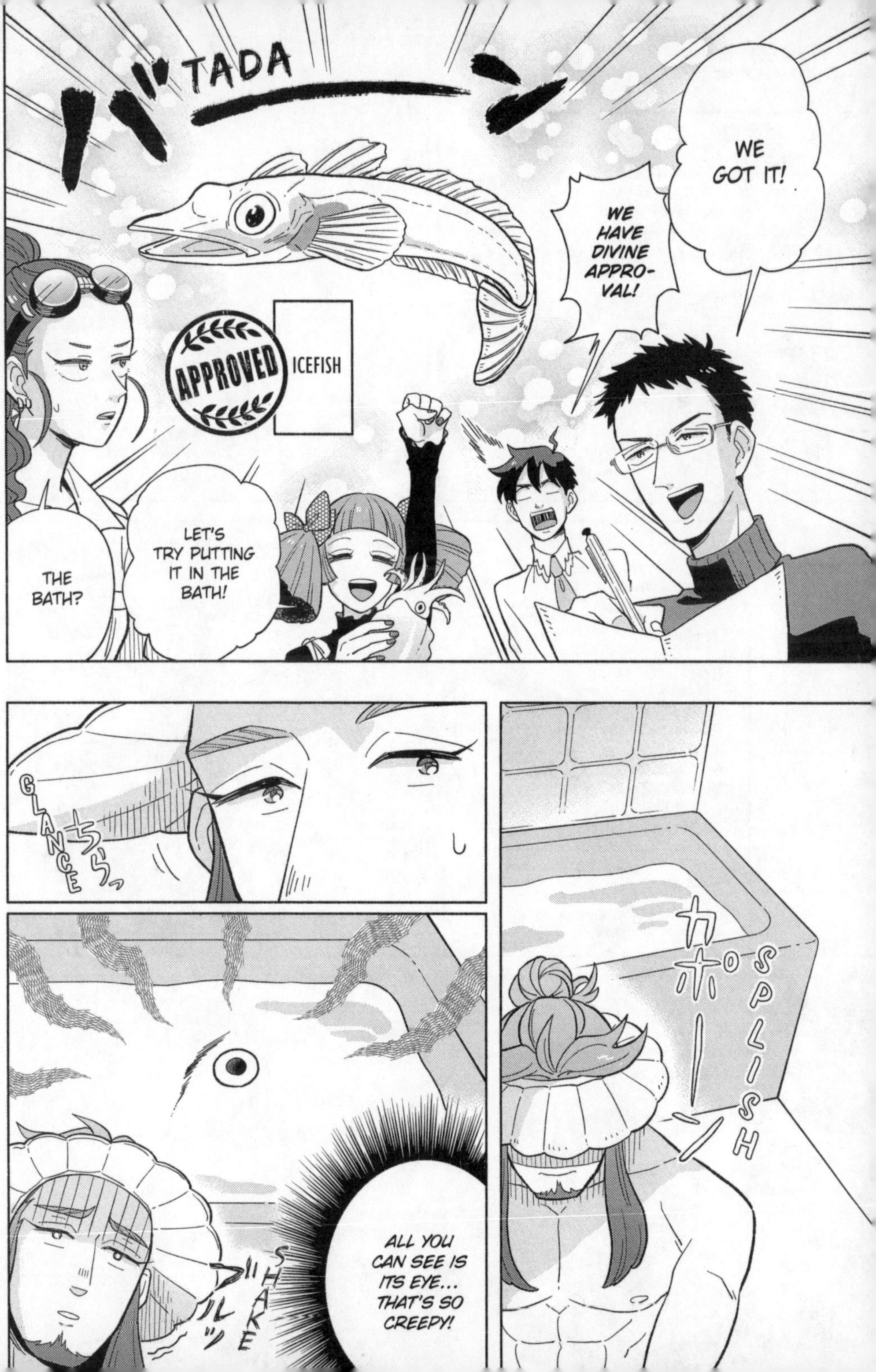
TADA
WE GOT IT!
WE HAVE DIVINE APPROVAL!
APPROVED
ICEFISH
LET'S TRY PUTTING IT IN THE BATH!
THE BATH?
SPLISH
GLANCE
SHAKE
ALL YOU CAN SEE IS ITS EYE... THAT'S SO CREEPY!

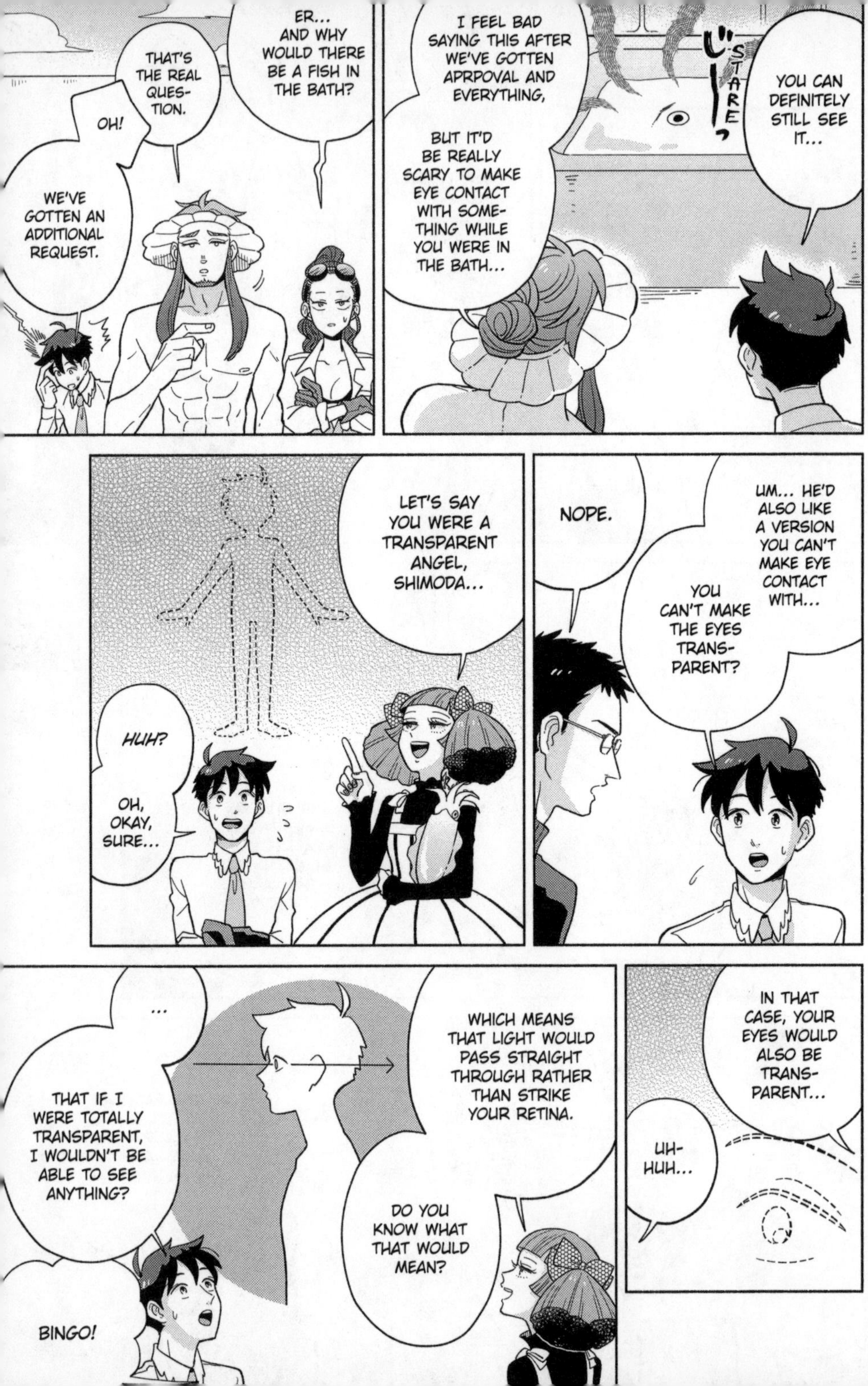
YOU CAN DEFINITELY STILL SEE IT...
STARE
I FEEL BAD SAYING THIS AFTER WE'VE GOTTEN APRPOVAL AND EVERYTHING,
BUT IT'D BE REALLY SCARY TO MAKE EYE CONTACT WITH SOME-THING WHILE YOU WERE IN THE BATH...
ER... AND WHY WOULD THERE BE A FISH IN THE BATH?
THAT'S THE REAL QUES-TION.
OH!
WE'VE GOTTEN AN ADDITIONAL REQUEST.
UM... HE'D ALSO LIKE A VERSION YOU CAN'T MAKE EYE CONTACT WITH...
YOU CAN'T MAKE THE EYES TRANS-PARENT?
NOPE.
LET'S SAY YOU WERE A TRANSPARENT ANGEL, SHIMODA...
HUH?
OH, OKAY, SURE...
IN THAT CASE, YOUR EYES WOULD ALSO BE TRANS-PARENT...
UH-HUH...
WHICH MEANS THAT LIGHT WOULD PASS STRAIGHT THROUGH RATHER THAN STRIKE YOUR RETINA.
...
DO YOU KNOW WHAT THAT WOULD MEAN?
THAT IF I WERE TOTALLY TRANSPARENT, I WOULDN'T BE ABLE TO SEE ANYTHING?
BINGO!

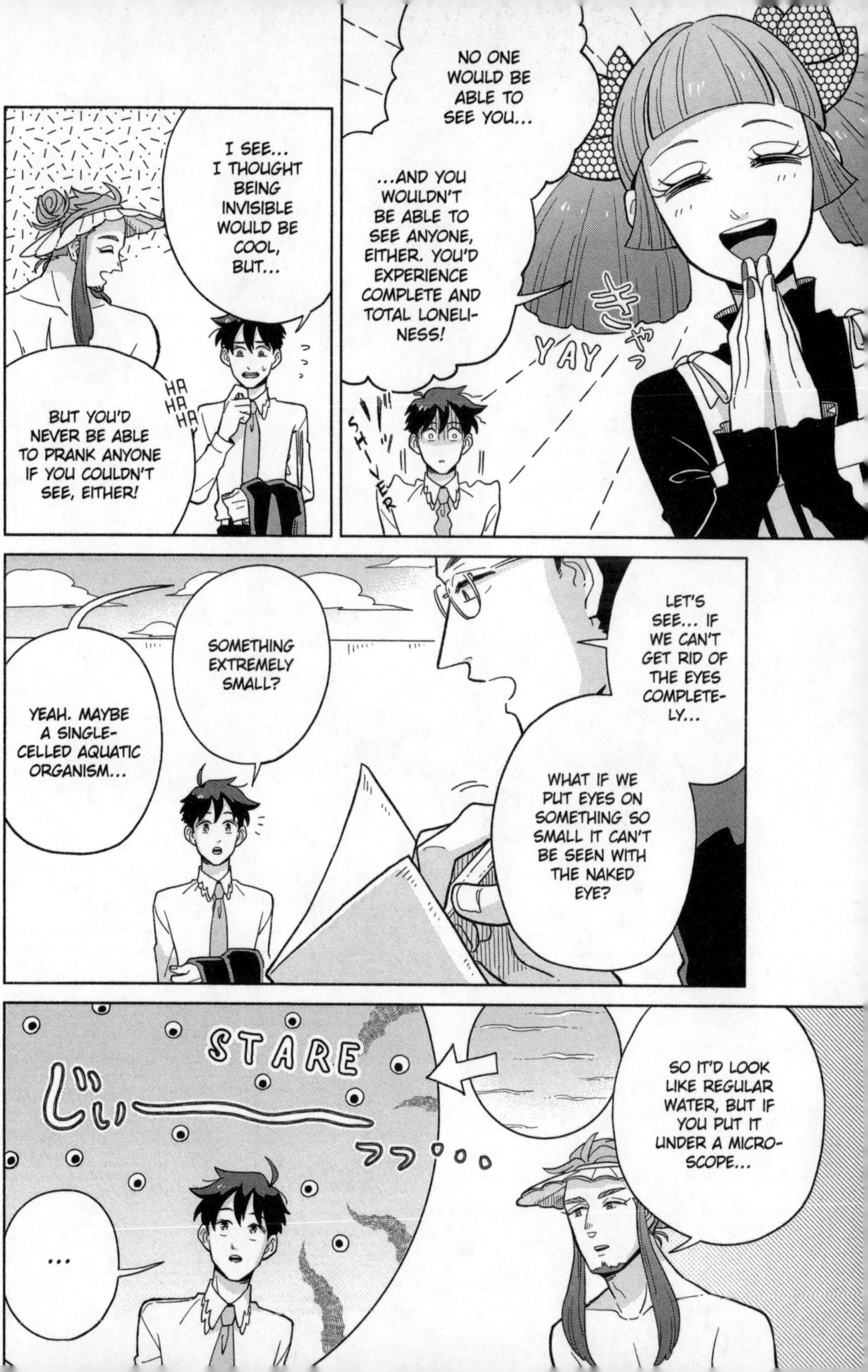

NO ONE WOULD BE ABLE TO SEE YOU...
...AND YOU WOULDN'T BE ABLE TO SEE ANYONE, EITHER. YOU'D EXPERIENCE COMPLETE AND TOTAL LONELI-NESS!
きゃっ
YAY
SHIVER
I SEE... I THOUGHT BEING INVISIBLE WOULD BE COOL, BUT...
HA HA HA HA
BUT YOU'D NEVER BE ABLE TO PRANK ANYONE IF YOU COULDN'T SEE, EITHER!
LET'S SEE... IF WE CAN'T GET RID OF THE EYES COMPLETE-LY...
WHAT IF WE PUT EYES ON SOMETHING SO SMALL IT CAN'T BE SEEN WITH THE NAKED EYE?
SOMETHING EXTREMELY SMALL?
YEAH. MAYBE A SINGLE-CELLED AQUATIC ORGANISM...
SO IT'D LOOK LIKE REGULAR WATER, BUT IF YOU PUT IT UNDER A MICRO-SCOPE...
STARE
じぃーー
...

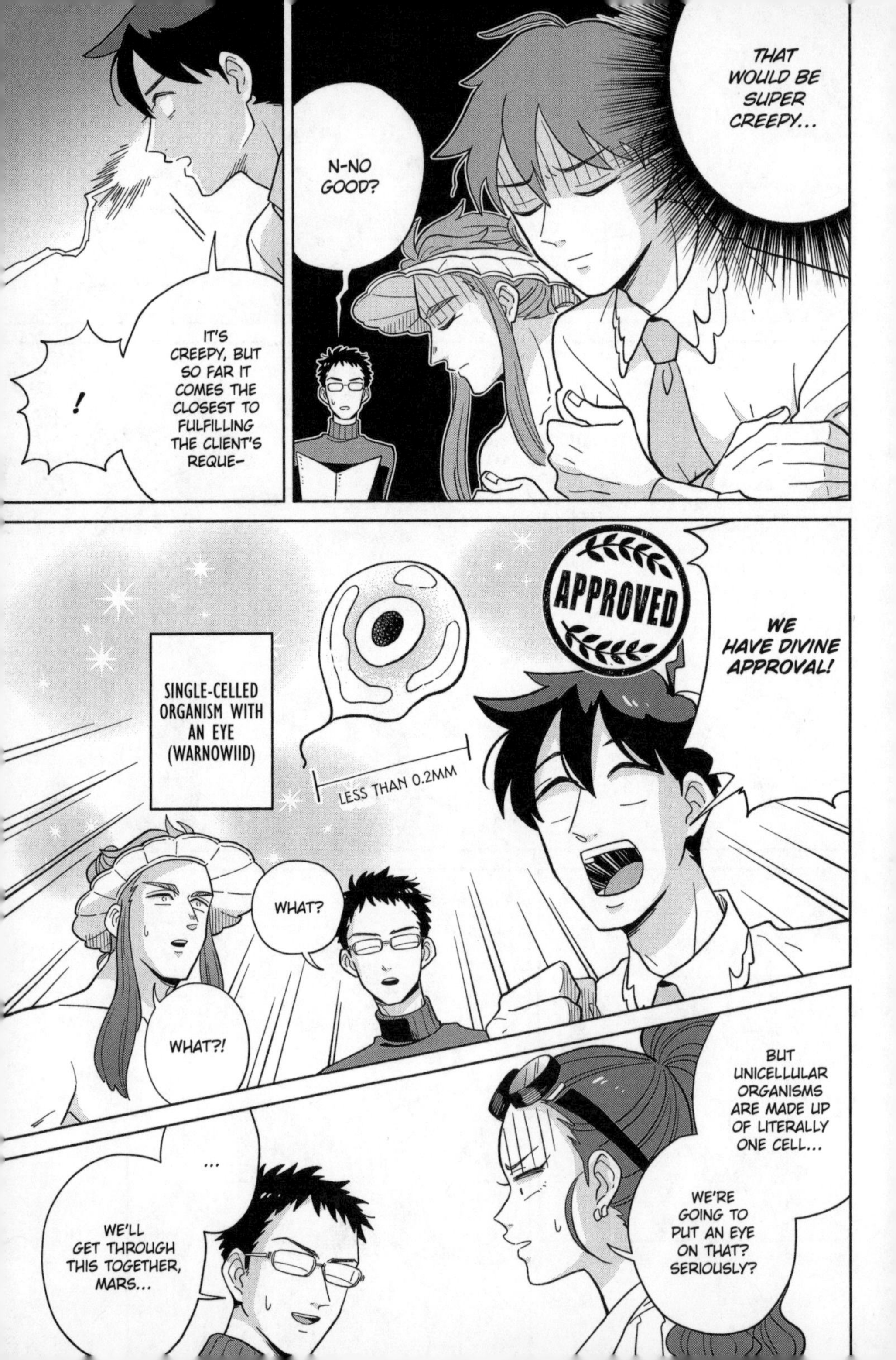
THAT WOULD BE SUPER CREEPY...
N-NO GOOD?
IT'S CREEPY, BUT SO FAR IT COMES THE CLOSEST TO FULFILLING THE CLIENT'S REQUE-
!
APPROVED
WE HAVE DIVINE APPROVAL!
SINGLE-CELLED ORGANISM WITH AN EYE (WARNOWIID)
LESS THAN 0.2MM
WHAT?
WHAT?!
BUT UNICELLULAR ORGANISMS ARE MADE UP OF LITERALLY ONE CELL...
WE'RE GOING TO PUT AN EYE ON THAT? SERIOUSLY?
...
WE'LL GET THROUGH THIS TOGETHER, MARS...

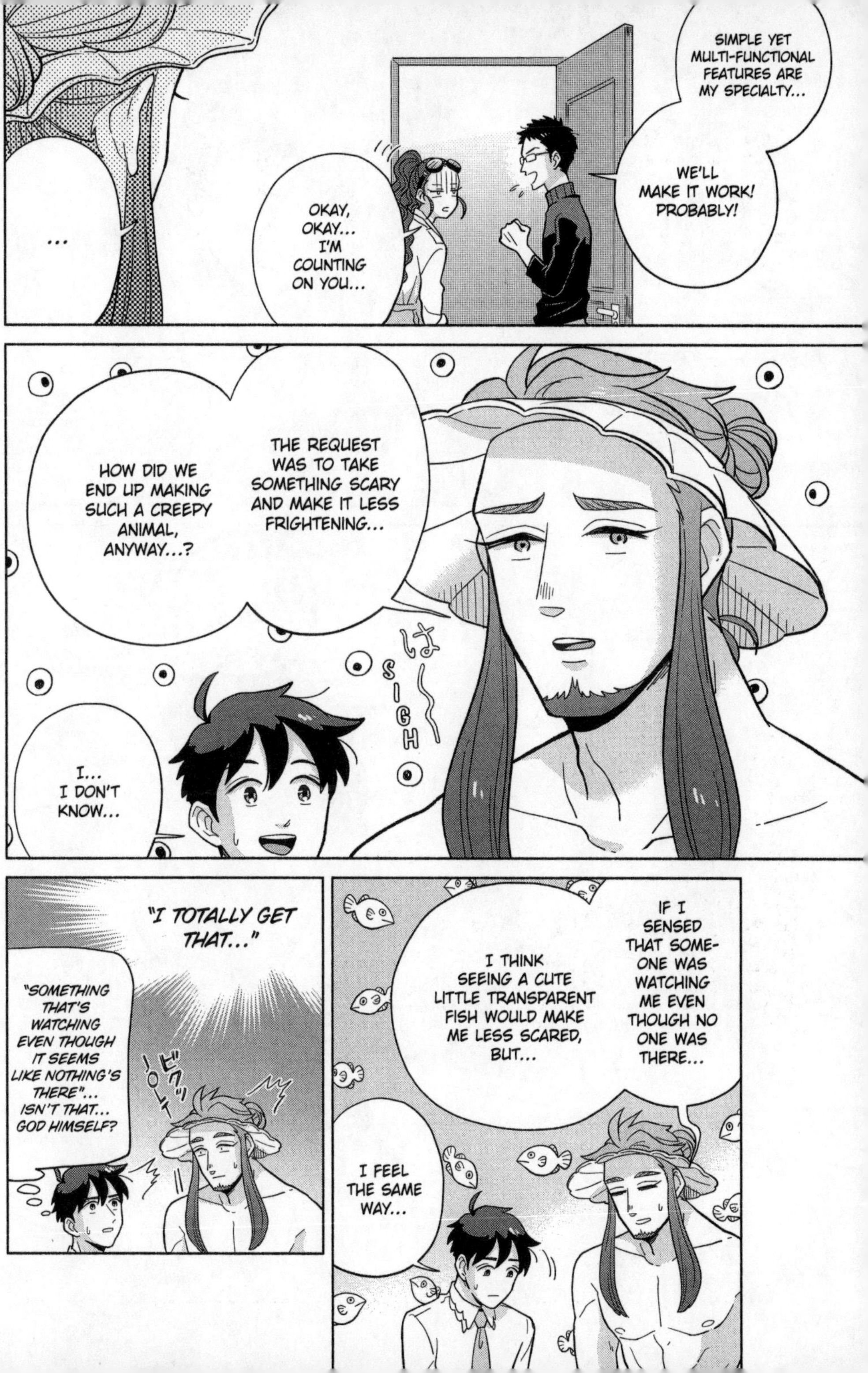
SIMPLE YET MULTI-FUNCTIONAL FEATURES ARE MY SPECIALTY...
WE'LL MAKE IT WORK! PROBABLY!
OKAY, OKAY... I'M COUNTING ON YOU...
...
THE REQUEST WAS TO TAKE SOMETHING SCARY AND MAKE IT LESS FRIGHTENING...
HOW DID WE END UP MAKING SUCH A CREEPY ANIMAL, ANYWAY...?
はー
SIGH
I... I DON'T KNOW...
IF I SENSED THAT SOME-ONE WAS WATCHING ME EVEN THOUGH NO ONE WAS THERE...
I THINK SEEING A CUTE LITTLE TRANSPARENT FISH WOULD MAKE ME LESS SCARED, BUT...
I FEEL THE SAME WAY...
"I TOTALLY GET THAT..."
"SOMETHING THAT'S WATCHING EVEN THOUGH IT SEEMS LIKE NOTHING'S THERE"... ISN'T THAT... GOD HIMSELF?
ビクッ

# THE ENCYCLOPEDIA OF REAL ANIMALS 11

## ANIMAL 30 ICEFISH

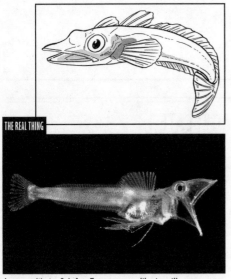

THE REAL THING

A crocodile icefish fry. Even organs, like its gills, are transparent.

Photo: Science Photo Library/Aflo

Icefish fry belonging to the Channichthyidae family live in the extremely cold temperatures of the Southern Ocean and are almost completely transparent. This is because their blood contains almost no hemoglobin, the red proteins inside red blood cells that transport oxygen. So how does their blood carry oxygen?
The oxygen is transported by plasma, and to circulate it throughout their bodies, icefish pump large amounts of low-viscosity blood through their thick veins. Icefish are also helped by the fact that the waters of the Southern Ocean are rich in oxygen. As icefish reach maturity, their cells begin to take on color and they are no longer transparent. In 2011, Tokyo Sea Life Park began holding the only captive icefish in the world. The ocellated icefish female successfully spawned in 2013.

| | |
|---|---|
| **[Name]** | Icefish |
| **[Classification]** | Class: Actinopterygii<br>Order: Perciformes<br>Family: Channichthyidae |
| **[Habitat]** | Southern Ocean around Antarctica and southern South America |
| **[Length]** | Approximately 30 cm (12 in) |

| # PANTHER CHAMELEON

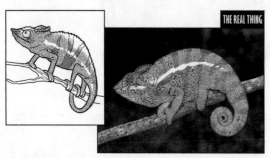

THE REAL THING

A male panther chameleon in Madagascar. His tongue isn't curled, but his tail is coiled in a neat spiral.

Photo: Photoshot/Aflo

Panther chameleons change color depending mainly on sexual attraction, stress, temperature, and light, and the camouflage effect they're famous for is minimal. Their eyes move independently from each other, and allow the chameleon to see in multiple directions without moving their bodies. Their tongues, which extend longer than the length of their abdomens to capture prey, are supported by a bone at their base.

[Name]              *Furcifer pardalis*
[Classification]    Class: Reptilia
                    Order: Squamata
                    Family: Chamaeleonidae
                    Genus: *Furcifer*
[Habitat]           Madagascar
[Length]            30-50 cm (1-1.6 ft)

---

| # TYPE OF DINOFLAGELLATE

Dinoflagellates are a type of unicellular (made up of just one cell) plankton. Recent research found that a certain variety, known as warnowiids, have ocelloids, which are structures containing components analogous to eye structures including the cornea, lens, and retina. Within the ocelloid, a mitochondria serves as the retina, while a melanosome serves as the cornea.

Certain dinoflagellates are photosynthetic but can also move independently. Many protists like these cannot be classified by the rule, "If it moves, it's an animal; if it photosynthesizes, it's a plant."

LESS THAN 0.2MM

[Name]              Warnowia
[Classification]    Phylum: Dinoflagellata
                    Class: Dinophyceae
                    Order: Gymnodiniales
                    Family: Warnowiaceae
[Habitat]           Oceans and waterways
[Length]            Approximately 0.2 mm
                    (0.008 in)

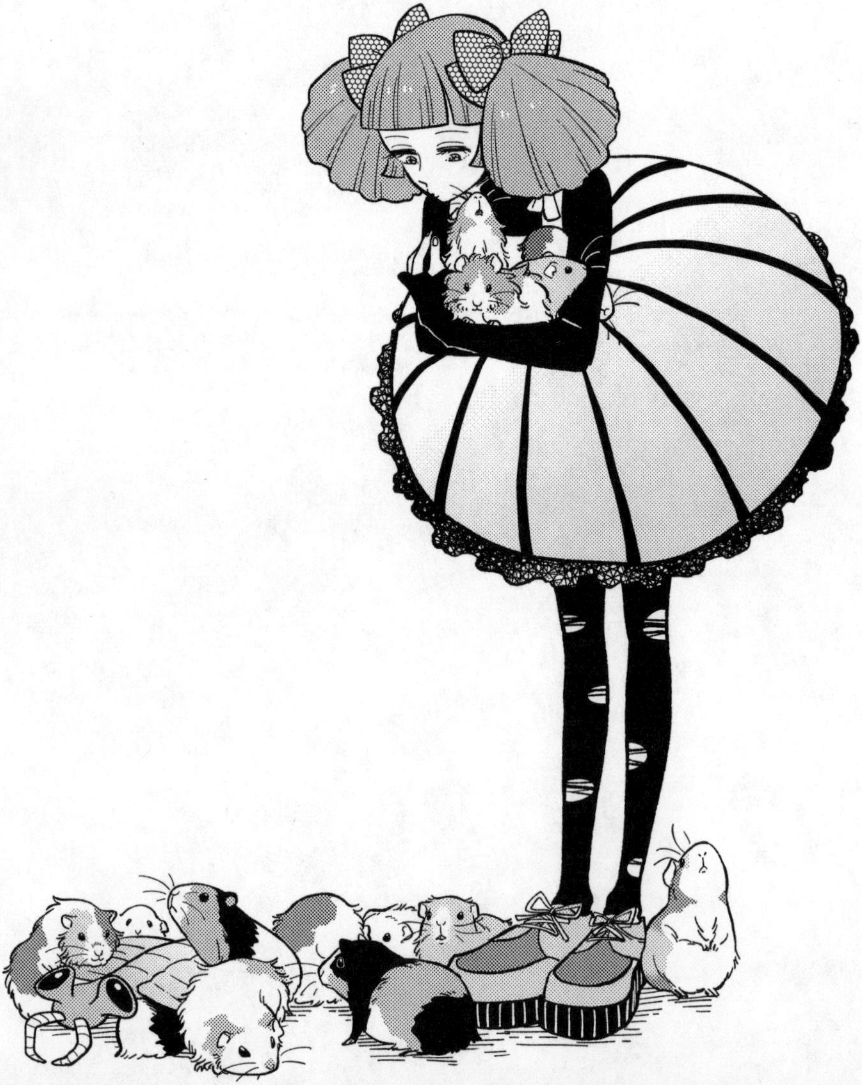

# HEAVEN'S DESIGN TEAM

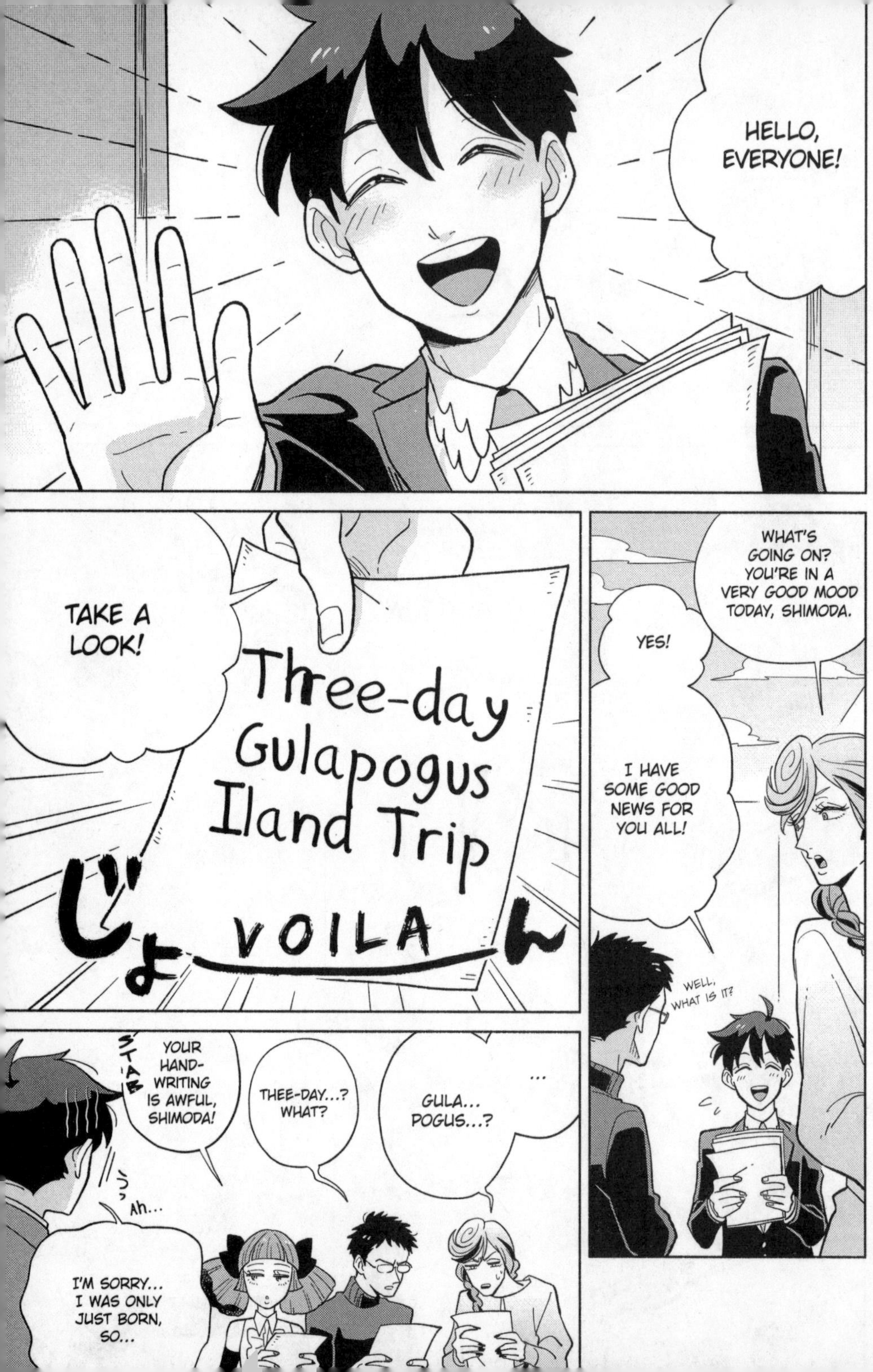
HELLO, EVERYONE!
WHAT'S GOING ON? YOU'RE IN A VERY GOOD MOOD TODAY, SHIMODA.
YES!
I HAVE SOME GOOD NEWS FOR YOU ALL!
WELL, WHAT IS IT?
TAKE A LOOK!
Three-day Gulapogus Iland Trip
VOILA
...
GULA... POGUS...?
THEE-DAY...? WHAT?
YOUR HAND-WRITING IS AWFUL, SHIMODA!
STAB
Ah...
I'M SORRY... I WAS ONLY JUST BORN, SO...

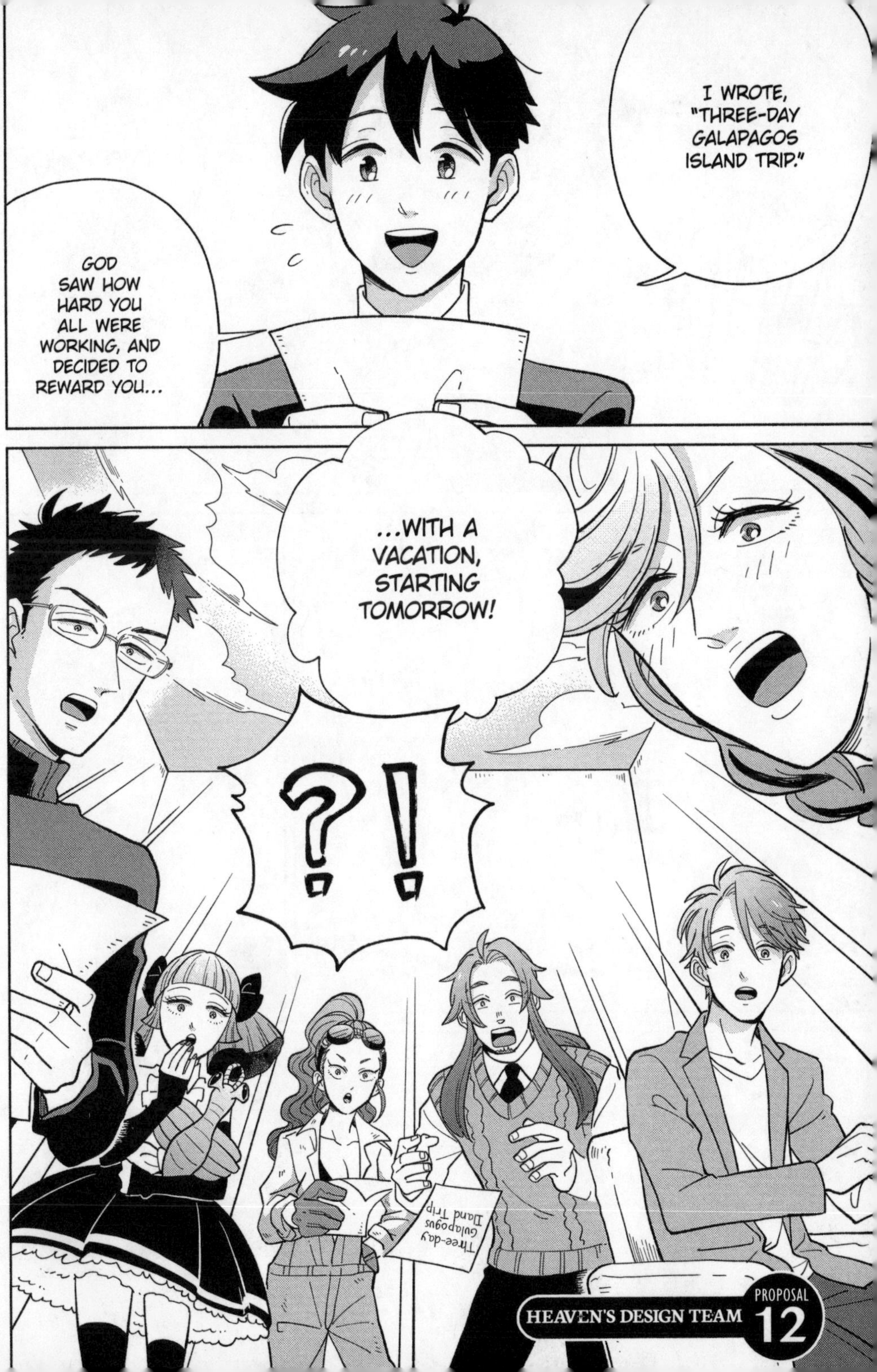
I WROTE, "THREE-DAY GALAPAGOS ISLAND TRIP."
GOD SAW HOW HARD YOU ALL WERE WORKING, AND DECIDED TO REWARD YOU...
...WITH A VACATION, STARTING TOMORROW!
?!
HEAVEN'S DESIGN TEAM
PROPOSAL 12

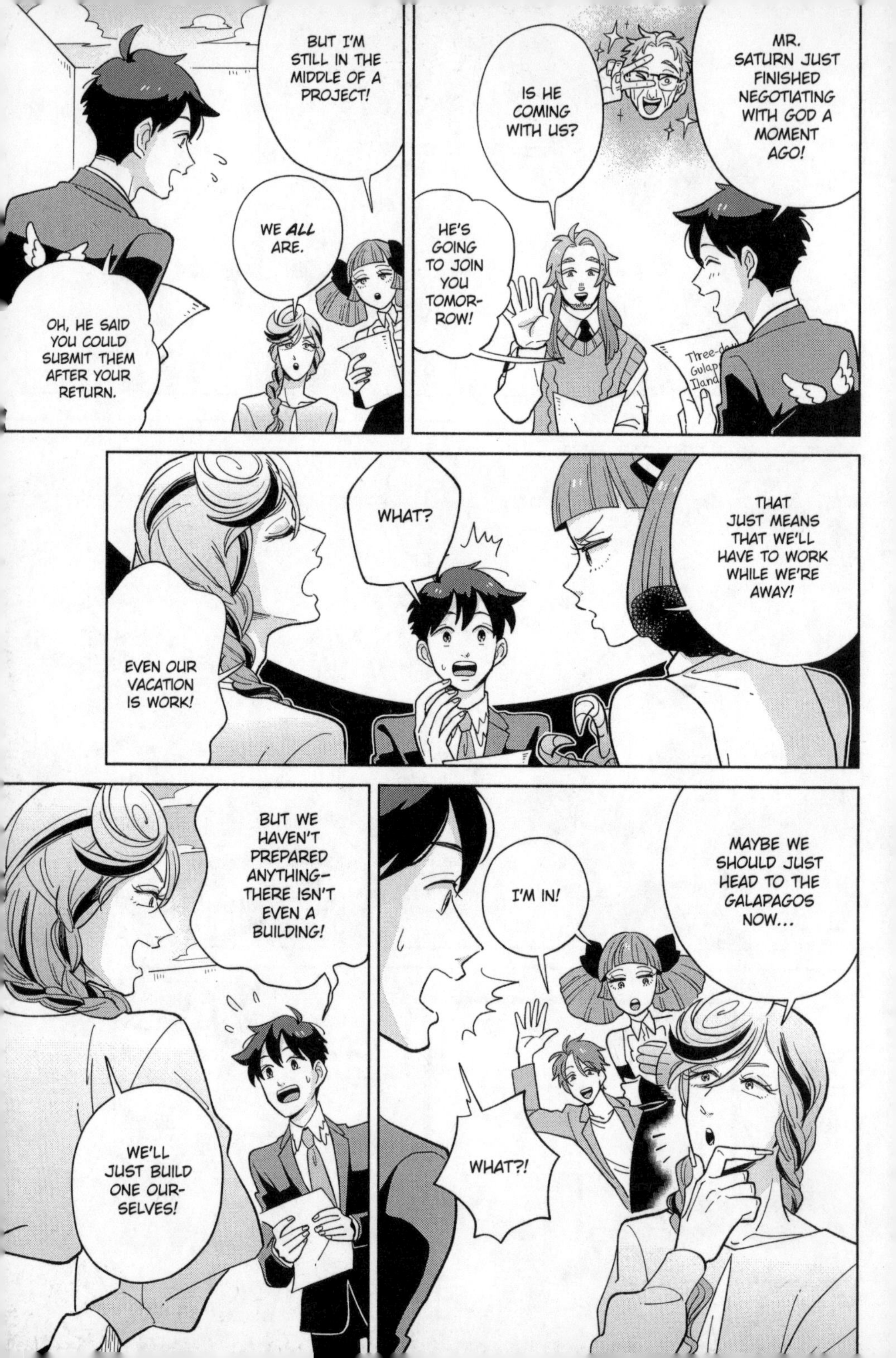
MR. SATURN JUST FINISHED NEGOTIATING WITH GOD A MOMENT AGO!
IS HE COMING WITH US?
HE'S GOING TO JOIN YOU TOMORROW!
BUT I'M STILL IN THE MIDDLE OF A PROJECT!
WE **ALL** ARE.
OH, HE SAID YOU COULD SUBMIT THEM AFTER YOUR RETURN.
THAT JUST MEANS THAT WE'LL HAVE TO WORK WHILE WE'RE AWAY!
WHAT?
EVEN OUR VACATION IS WORK!
MAYBE WE SHOULD JUST HEAD TO THE GALAPAGOS NOW...
I'M IN!
WHAT?!
BUT WE HAVEN'T PREPARED ANYTHING—THERE ISN'T EVEN A BUILDING!
WE'LL JUST BUILD ONE OURSELVES!

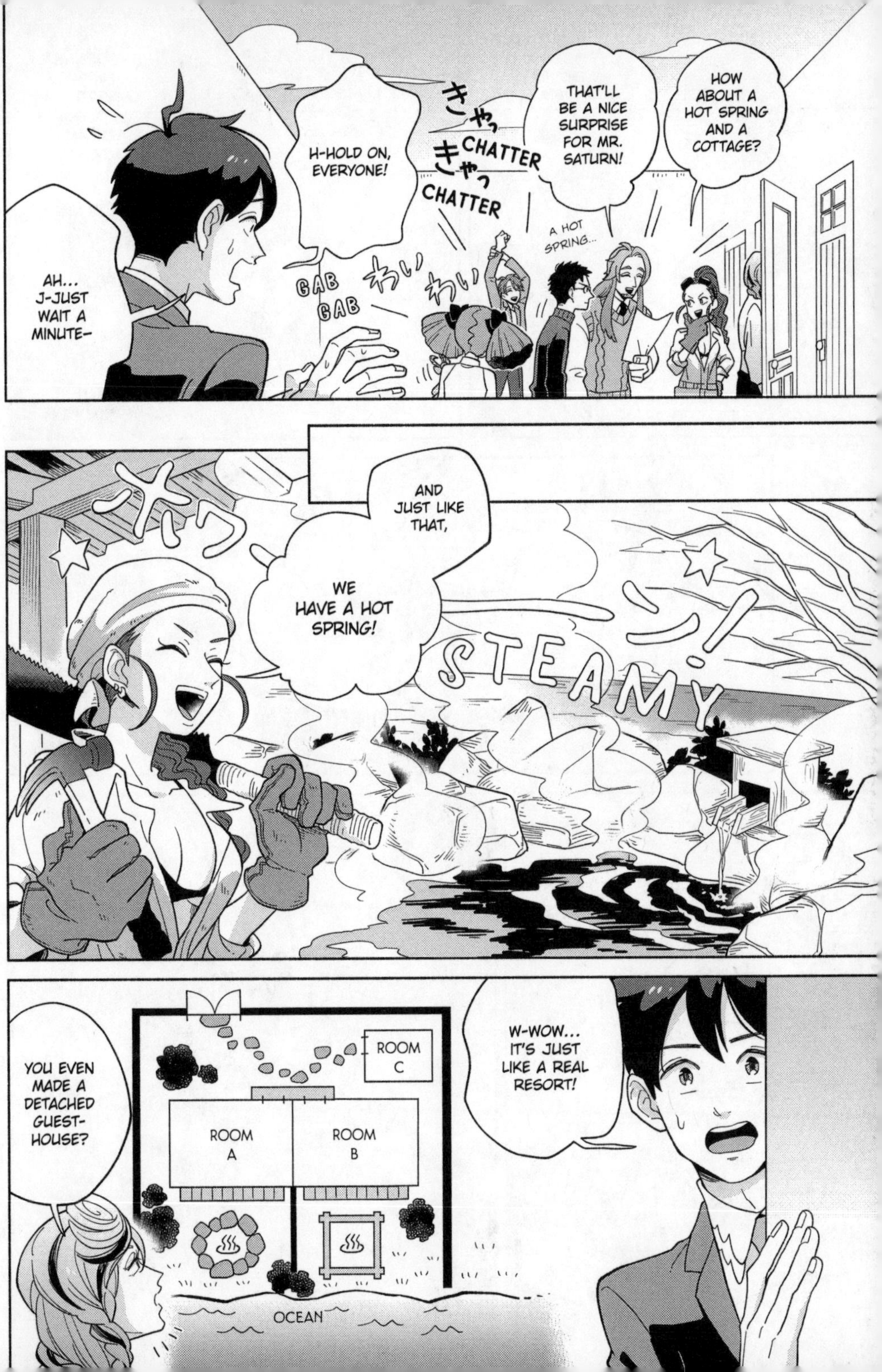
HOW ABOUT A HOT SPRING AND A COTTAGE?
THAT'LL BE A NICE SURPRISE FOR MR. SATURN!
A HOT SPRING...
きゃっ CHATTER
きゃっ CHATTER
H-HOLD ON, EVERYONE!
わい GAB
わい GAB
AH... J-JUST WAIT A MINUTE-
AND JUST LIKE THAT,
WE HAVE A HOT SPRING!
ホワーン!
STEAMY!
W-WOW... IT'S JUST LIKE A REAL RESORT!
ROOM C
ROOM B
ROOM A
OCEAN
YOU EVEN MADE A DETACHED GUEST-HOUSE?

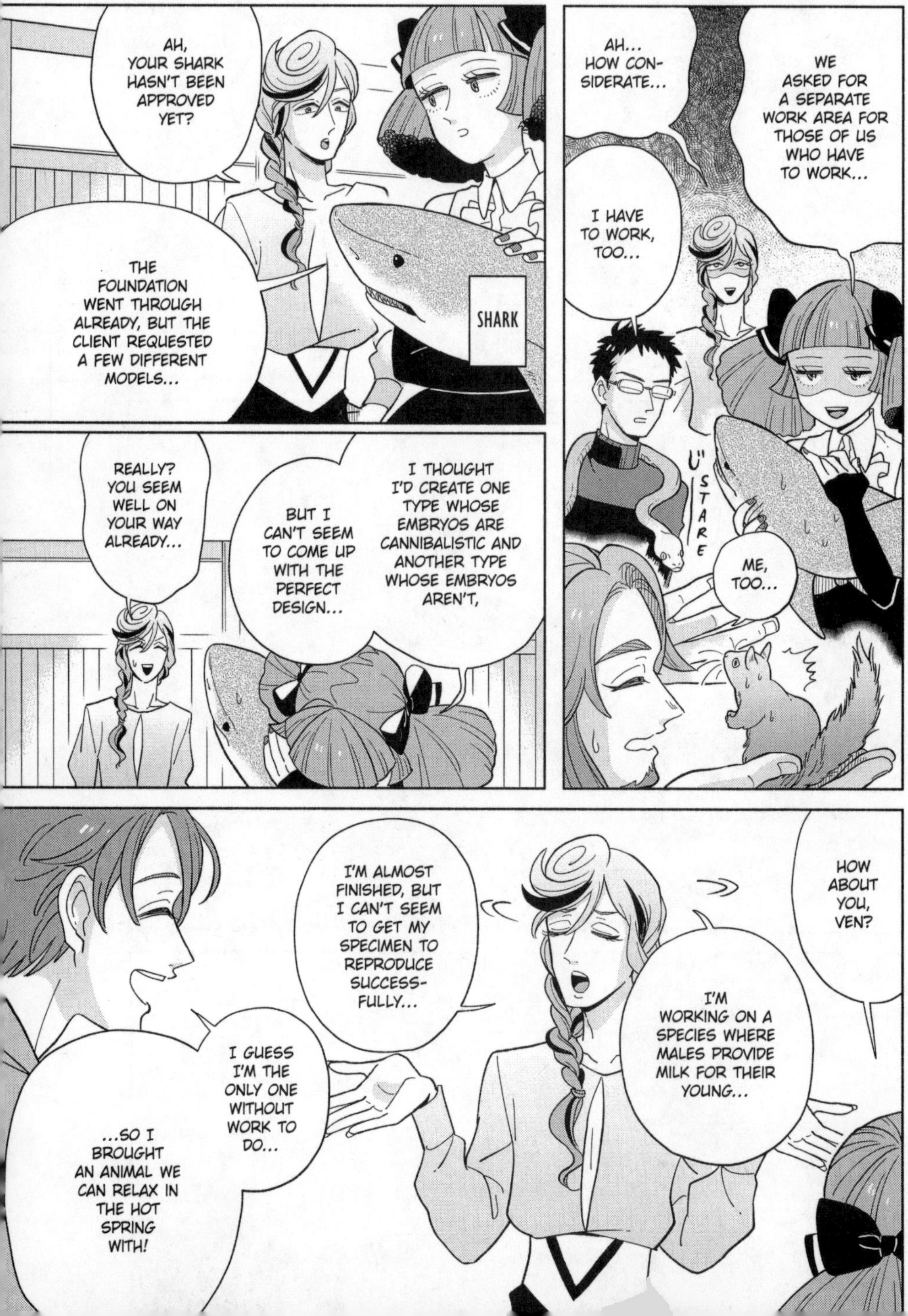
WE ASKED FOR A SEPARATE WORK AREA FOR THOSE OF US WHO HAVE TO WORK...
AH... HOW CON- SIDERATE...
I HAVE TO WORK, TOO...
STARE
ME, TOO...
AH, YOUR SHARK HASN'T BEEN APPROVED YET?
SHARK
THE FOUNDATION WENT THROUGH ALREADY, BUT THE CLIENT REQUESTED A FEW DIFFERENT MODELS...
I THOUGHT I'D CREATE ONE TYPE WHOSE EMBRYOS ARE CANNIBALISTIC AND ANOTHER TYPE WHOSE EMBRYOS AREN'T,
BUT I CAN'T SEEM TO COME UP WITH THE PERFECT DESIGN...
REALLY? YOU SEEM WELL ON YOUR WAY ALREADY...
HOW ABOUT YOU, VEN?
I'M WORKING ON A SPECIES WHERE MALES PROVIDE MILK FOR THEIR YOUNG...
I'M ALMOST FINISHED, BUT I CAN'T SEEM TO GET MY SPECIMEN TO REPRODUCE SUCCESS- FULLY...
I GUESS I'M THE ONLY ONE WITHOUT WORK TO DO...
...SO I BROUGHT AN ANIMAL WE CAN RELAX IN THE HOT SPRING WITH!

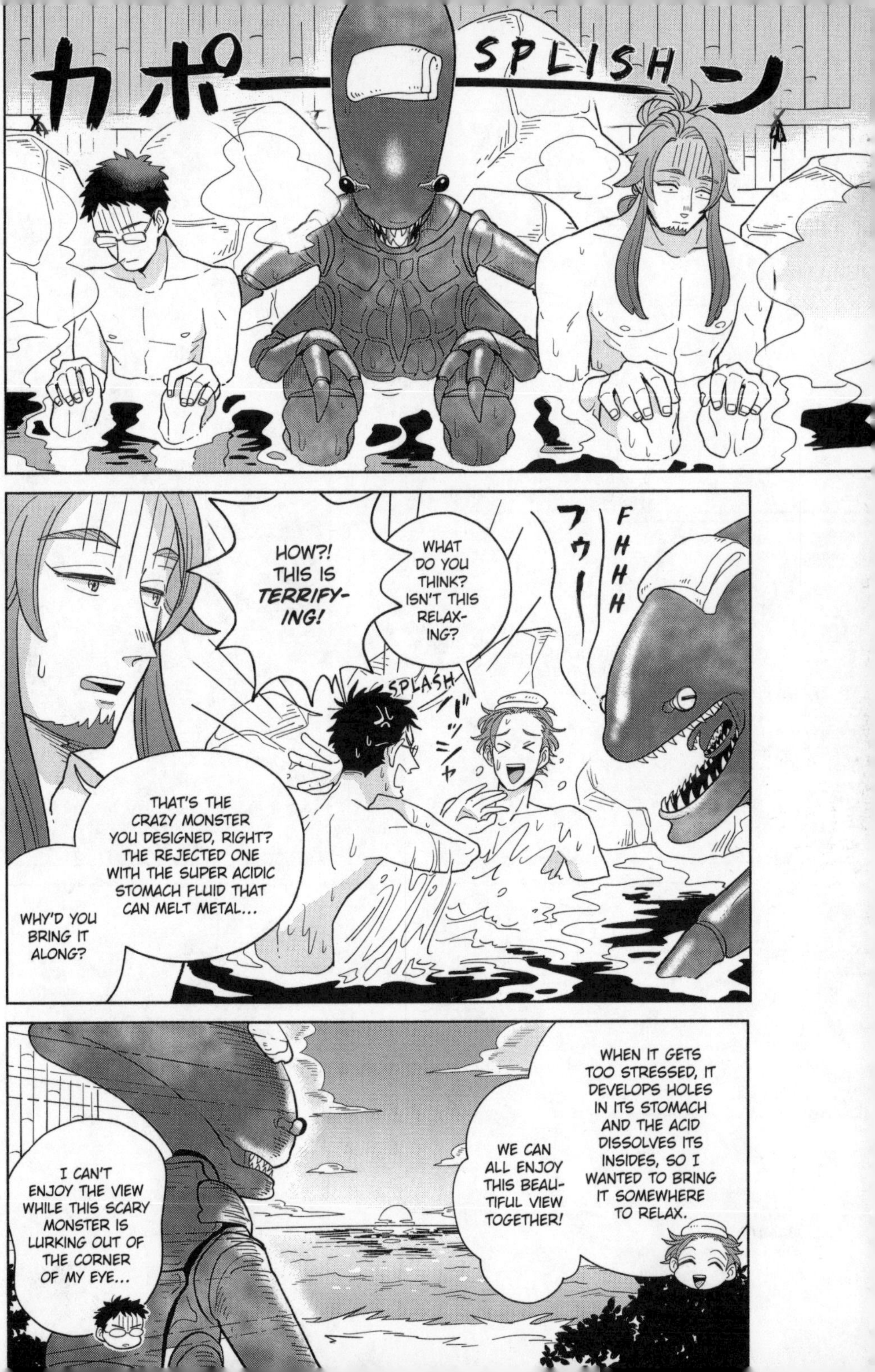
カポーン
SPLISH
フウー
FHHH
WHAT DO YOU THINK? ISN'T THIS RELAXING?
HOW?! THIS IS *TERRIFYING!*
SPLASH
THAT'S THE CRAZY MONSTER YOU DESIGNED, RIGHT? THE REJECTED ONE WITH THE SUPER ACIDIC STOMACH FLUID THAT CAN MELT METAL...
WHY'D YOU BRING IT ALONG?
WHEN IT GETS TOO STRESSED, IT DEVELOPS HOLES IN ITS STOMACH AND THE ACID DISSOLVES ITS INSIDES, SO I WANTED TO BRING IT SOMEWHERE TO RELAX.
WE CAN ALL ENJOY THIS BEAUTIFUL VIEW TOGETHER!
I CAN'T ENJOY THE VIEW WHILE THIS SCARY MONSTER IS LURKING OUT OF THE CORNER OF MY EYE...

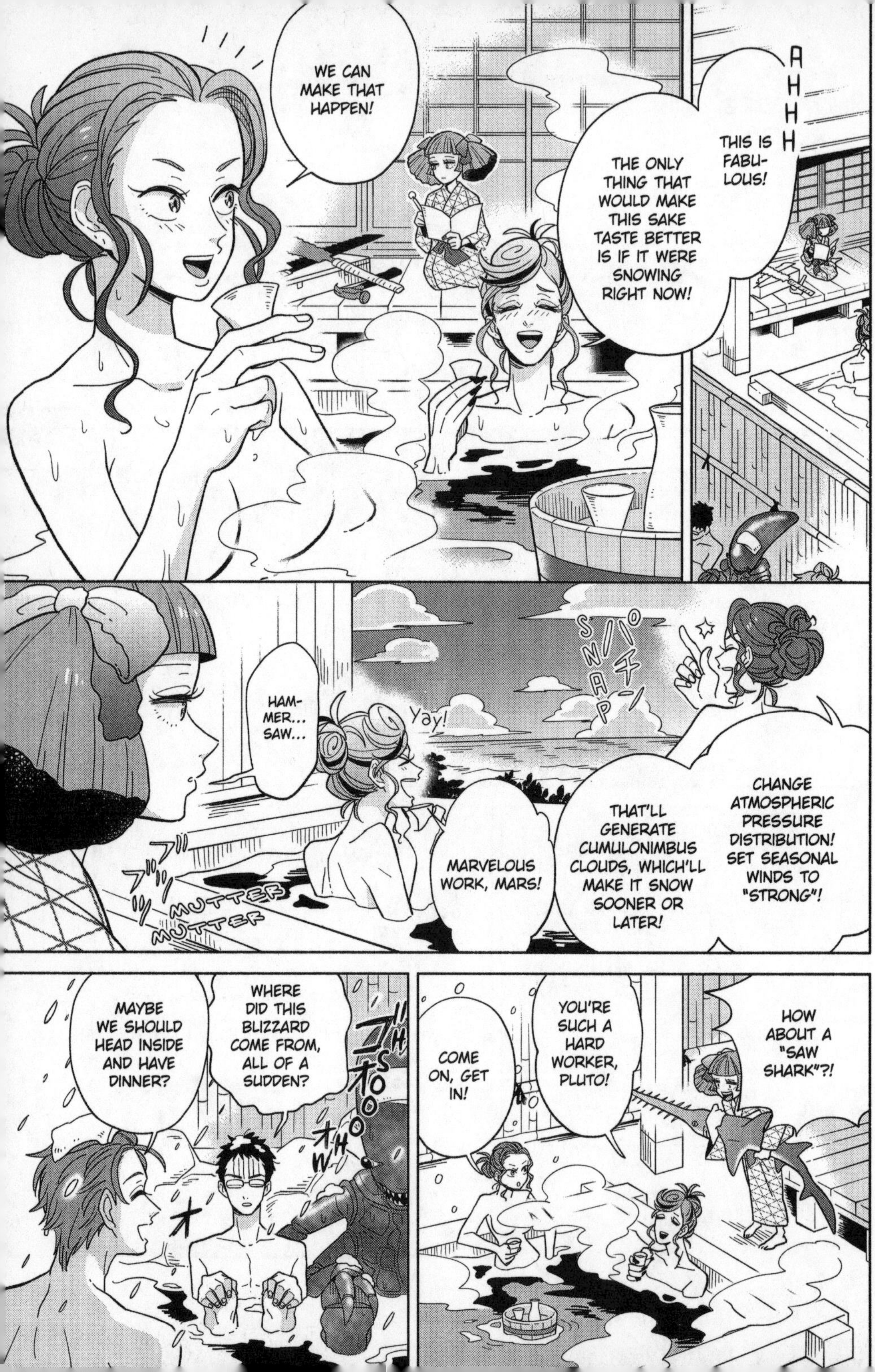
AHHHH
THIS IS FABU-LOUS!
THE ONLY THING THAT WOULD MAKE THIS SAKE TASTE BETTER IS IF IT WERE SNOWING RIGHT NOW!
WE CAN MAKE THAT HAPPEN!
SNAP
CHANGE ATMOSPHERIC PRESSURE DISTRIBUTION! SET SEASONAL WINDS TO "STRONG"!
THAT'LL GENERATE CUMULONIMBUS CLOUDS, WHICH'LL MAKE IT SNOW SOONER OR LATER!
MARVELOUS WORK, MARS!
Yay!
HAM-MER... SAW...
MUTTER MUTTER
HOW ABOUT A "SAW SHARK"?!
YOU'RE SUCH A HARD WORKER, PLUTO!
COME ON, GET IN!
WHOOSH
WHERE DID THIS BLIZZARD COME FROM, ALL OF A SUDDEN?
MAYBE WE SHOULD HEAD INSIDE AND HAVE DINNER?

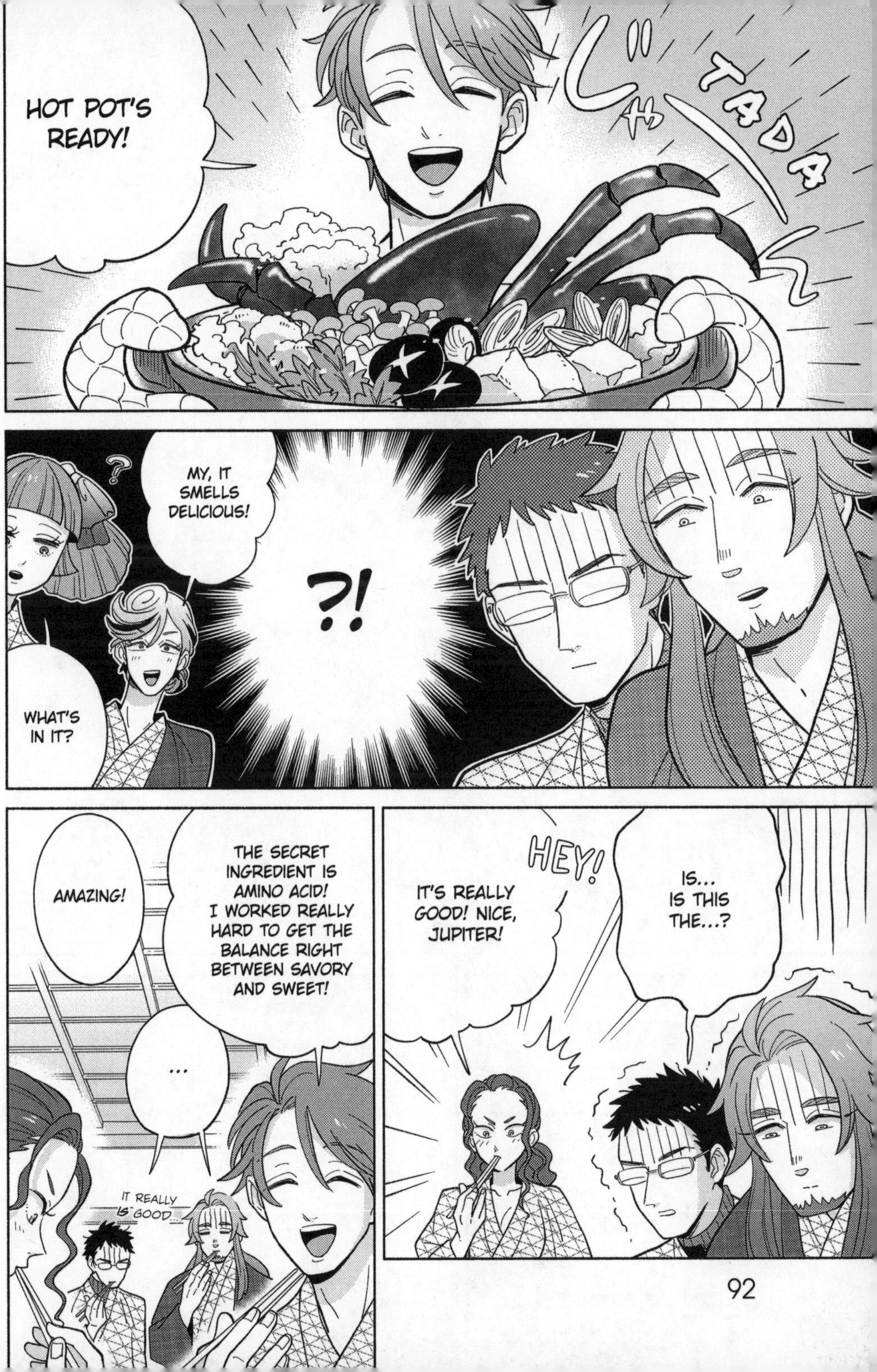
HOT POT'S READY!
TADA
?!
?
MY, IT SMELLS DELICIOUS!
WHAT'S IN IT?
IS... IS THIS THE...?
HEY!
IT'S REALLY GOOD! NICE, JUPITER!
THE SECRET INGREDIENT IS AMINO ACID! I WORKED REALLY HARD TO GET THE BALANCE RIGHT BETWEEN SAVORY AND SWEET!
AMAZING!
...
IT REALLY IS GOOD...

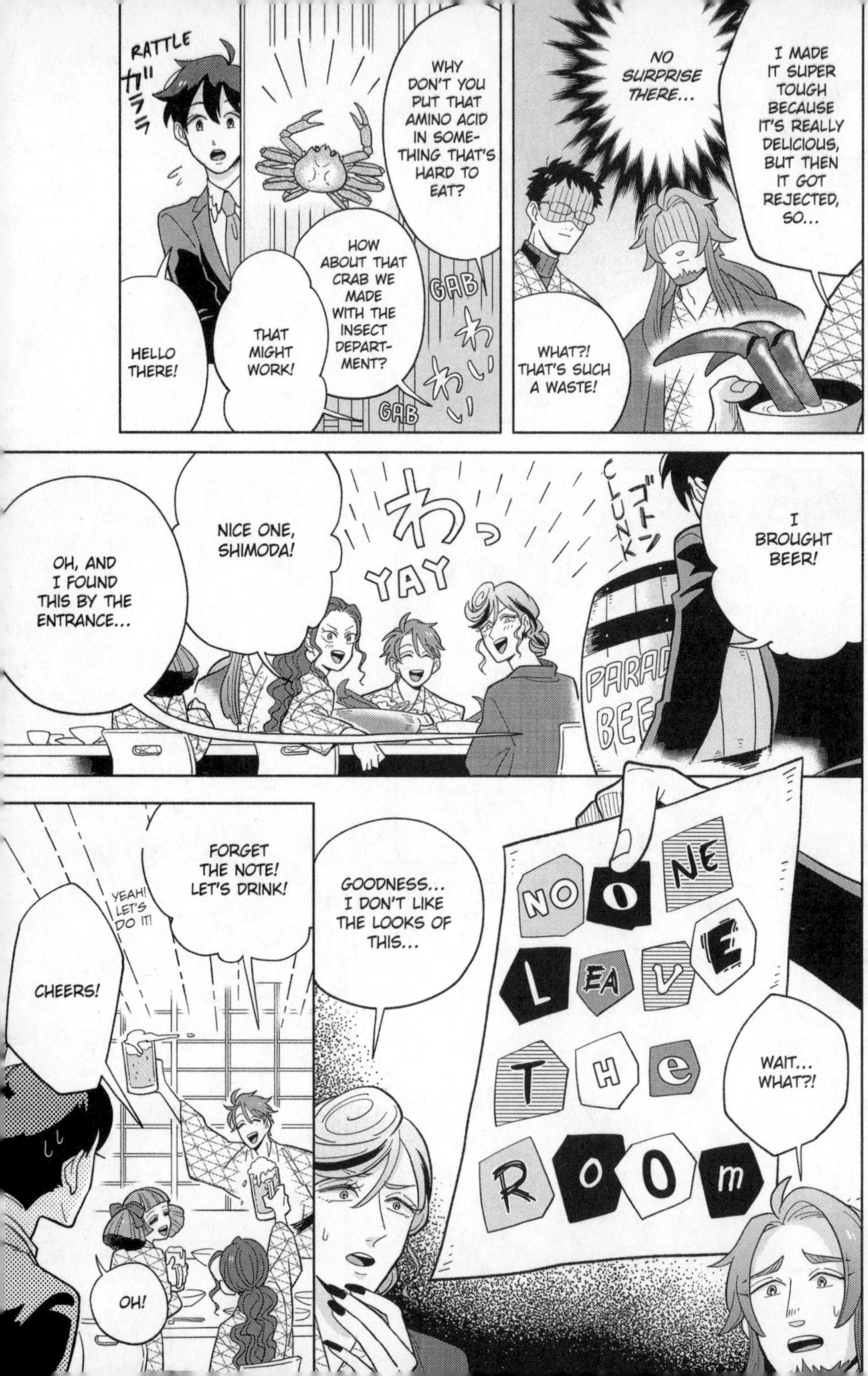
I MADE IT SUPER TOUGH BECAUSE IT'S REALLY DELICIOUS, BUT THEN IT GOT REJECTED, SO...
NO SURPRISE THERE...
WHAT?! THAT'S SUCH A WASTE!
WHY DON'T YOU PUT THAT AMINO ACID IN SOME-THING THAT'S HARD TO EAT?
RATTLE
ガララ
HOW ABOUT THAT CRAB WE MADE WITH THE INSECT DEPART-MENT?
GAB
わいわい
GAB
THAT MIGHT WORK!
HELLO THERE!
I BROUGHT BEER!
CLUNK
ゴトン
わっ
YAY
NICE ONE, SHIMODA!
OH, AND I FOUND THIS BY THE ENTRANCE...
NO ONE LEAVE THE ROOM
WAIT... WHAT?!
GOODNESS... I DON'T LIKE THE LOOKS OF THIS...
FORGET THE NOTE! LET'S DRINK!
YEAH! LET'S DO IT!
CHEERS!
OH!

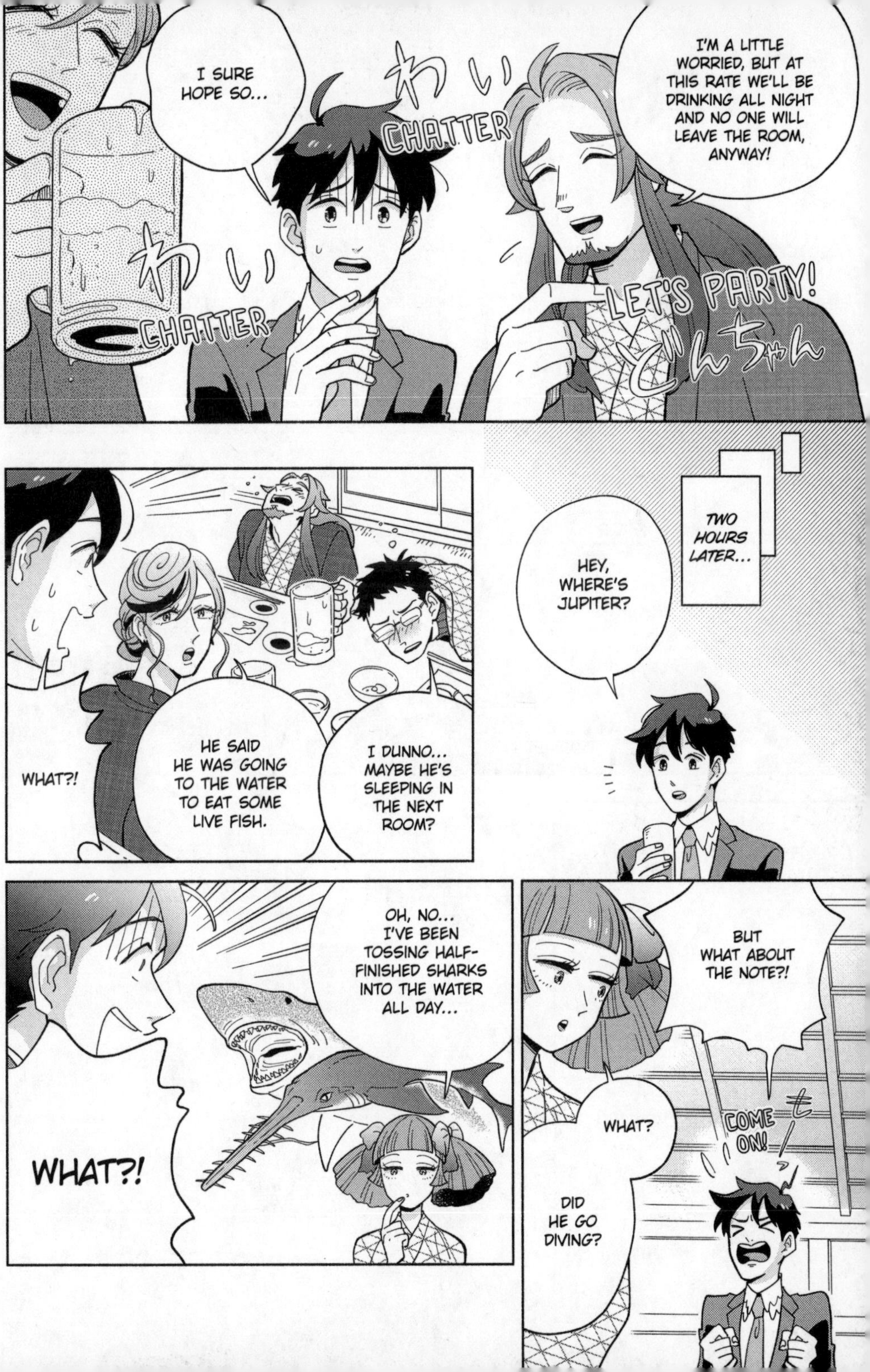
I'M A LITTLE WORRIED, BUT AT THIS RATE WE'LL BE DRINKING ALL NIGHT AND NO ONE WILL LEAVE THE ROOM, ANYWAY!
わい
CHATTER
I SURE HOPE SO...
LET'S PARTY!
どんちゃん
わい
CHATTER
TWO HOURS LATER...
HEY, WHERE'S JUPITER?
I DUNNO... MAYBE HE'S SLEEPING IN THE NEXT ROOM?
HE SAID HE WAS GOING TO THE WATER TO EAT SOME LIVE FISH.
WHAT?!
BUT WHAT ABOUT THE NOTE?!
WHAT?
COME ON!
もー
DID HE GO DIVING?
OH, NO... I'VE BEEN TOSSING HALF-FINISHED SHARKS INTO THE WATER ALL DAY...
WHAT?!

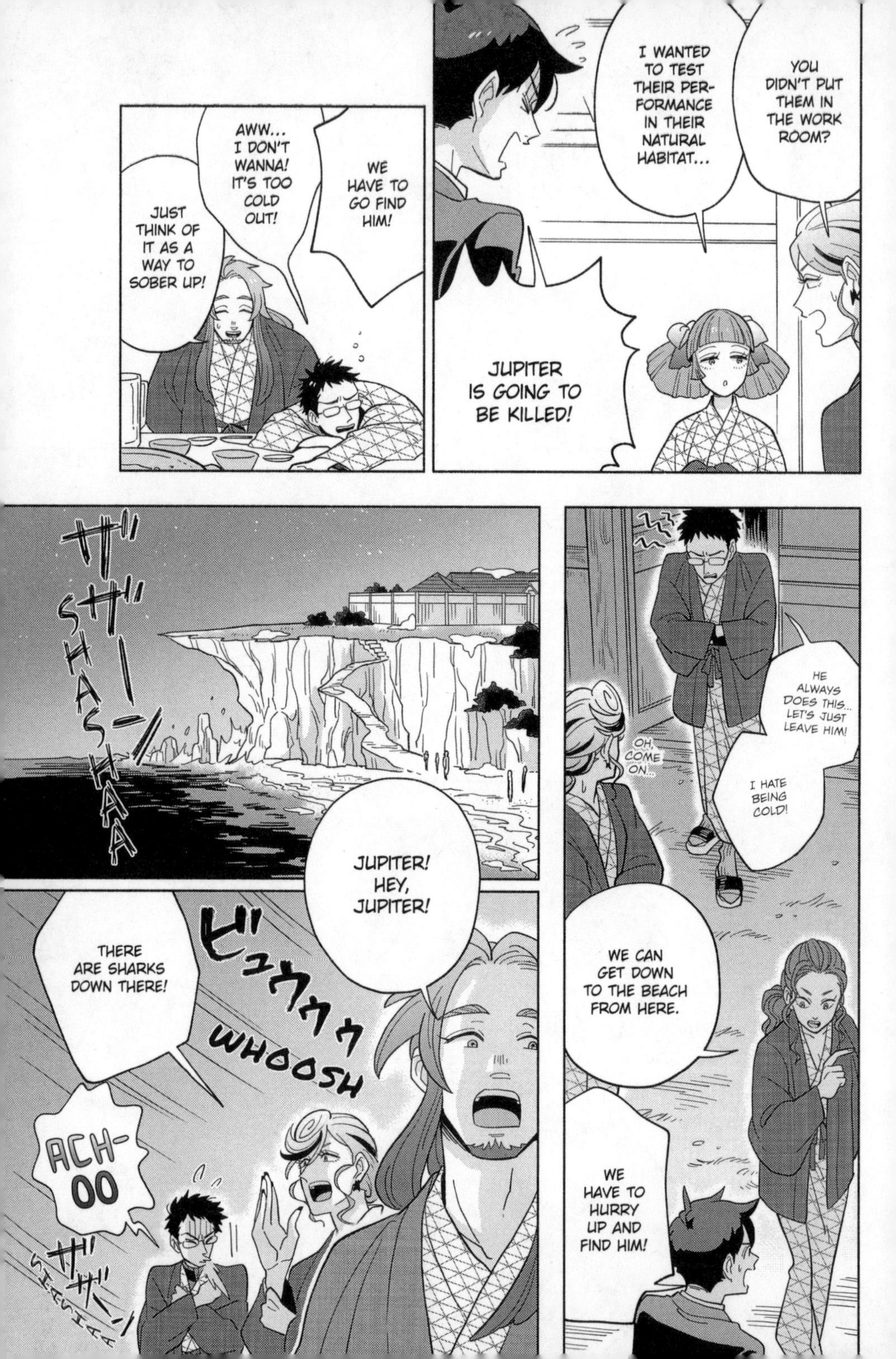
YOU DIDN'T PUT THEM IN THE WORK ROOM?
I WANTED TO TEST THEIR PER-FORMANCE IN THEIR NATURAL HABITAT...
JUPITER IS GOING TO BE KILLED!
WE HAVE TO GO FIND HIM!
AWW... I DON'T WANNA! IT'S TOO COLD OUT!
JUST THINK OF IT AS A WAY TO SOBER UP!
HE ALWAYS DOES THIS... LET'S JUST LEAVE HIM!
I HATE BEING COLD!
OH, COME ON...
WE CAN GET DOWN TO THE BEACH FROM HERE.
WE HAVE TO HURRY UP AND FIND HIM!
ザザー
SHASHAA
JUPITER! HEY, JUPITER!
ビュウゥゥ
WHOOSH
THERE ARE SHARKS DOWN THERE!
ACH-OO
ザザー

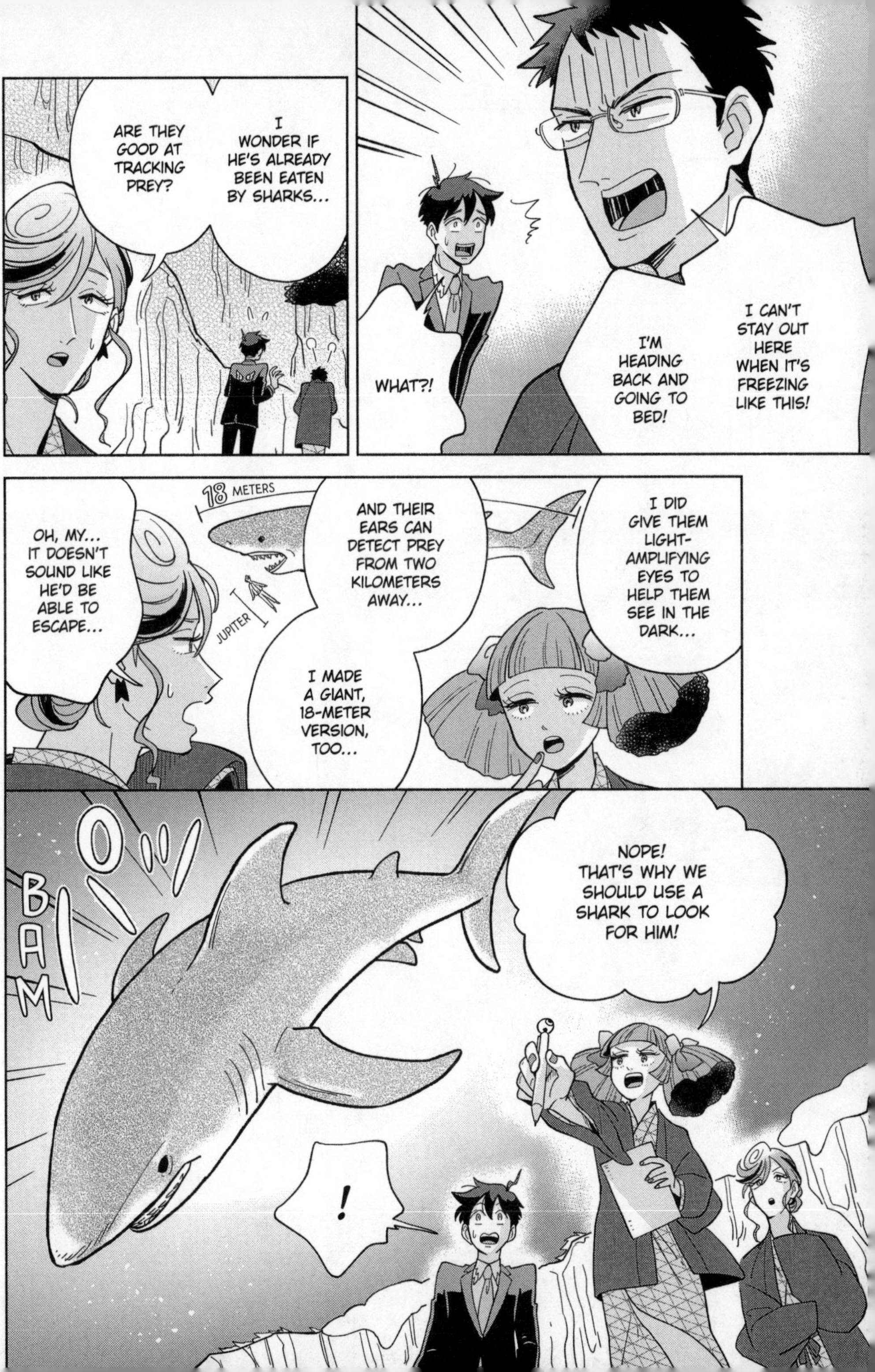
I CAN'T STAY OUT HERE WHEN IT'S FREEZING LIKE THIS!
I'M HEADING BACK AND GOING TO BED!
WHAT?!
I WONDER IF HE'S ALREADY BEEN EATEN BY SHARKS...
ARE THEY GOOD AT TRACKING PREY?
I DID GIVE THEM LIGHT-AMPLIFYING EYES TO HELP THEM SEE IN THE DARK...
AND THEIR EARS CAN DETECT PREY FROM TWO KILOMETERS AWAY...
I MADE A GIANT, 18-METER VERSION, TOO...
18 METERS
JUPITER
OH, MY... IT DOESN'T SOUND LIKE HE'D BE ABLE TO ESCAPE...
NOPE! THAT'S WHY WE SHOULD USE A SHARK TO LOOK FOR HIM!
BAM
!

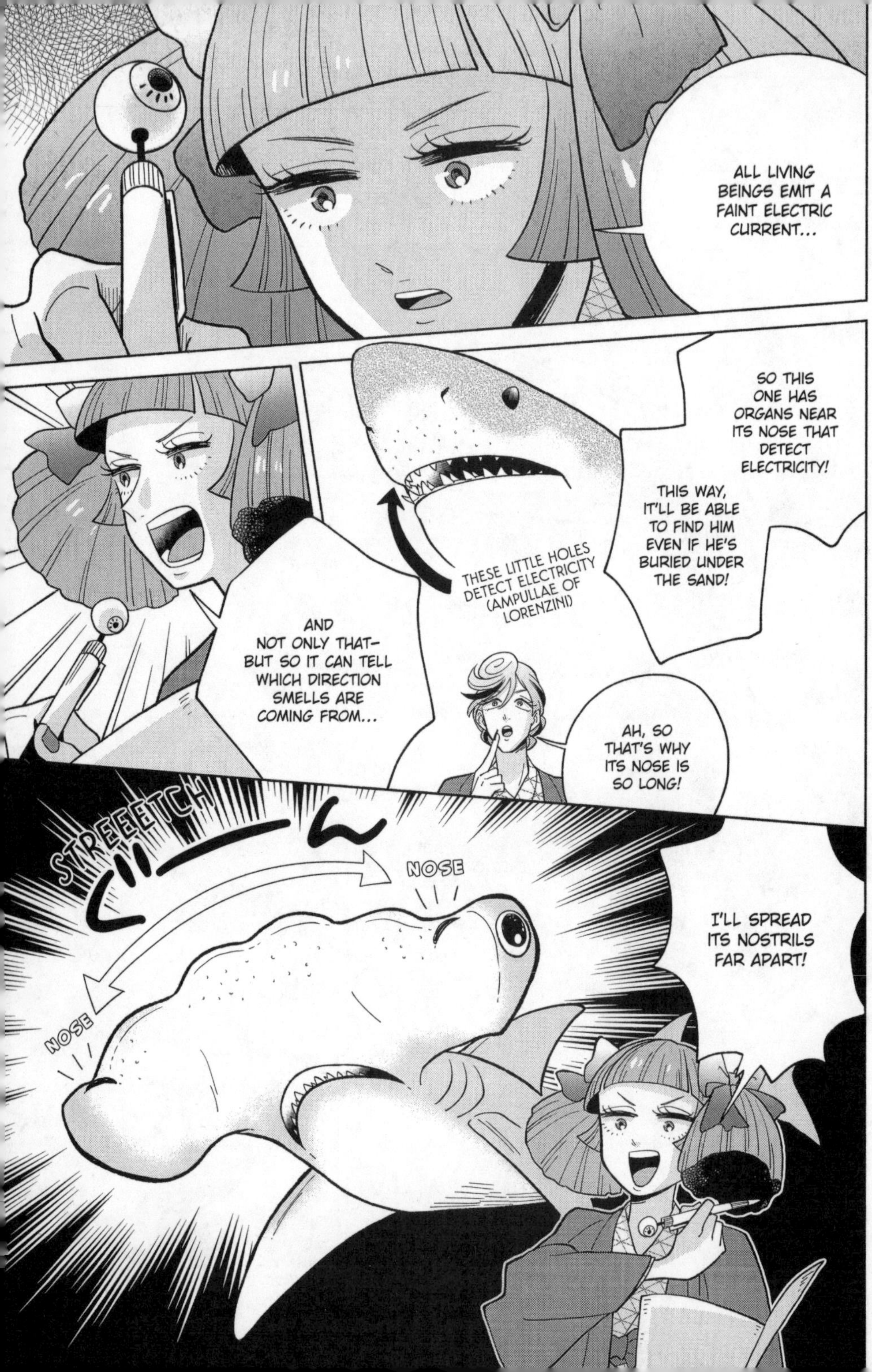
ALL LIVING BEINGS EMIT A FAINT ELECTRIC CURRENT...
SO THIS ONE HAS ORGANS NEAR ITS NOSE THAT DETECT ELECTRICITY!
THIS WAY, IT'LL BE ABLE TO FIND HIM EVEN IF HE'S BURIED UNDER THE SAND!
THESE LITTLE HOLES DETECT ELECTRICITY (AMPULLAE OF LORENZINI)
AND NOT ONLY THAT- BUT SO IT CAN TELL WHICH DIRECTION SMELLS ARE COMING FROM...
AH, SO THAT'S WHY ITS NOSE IS SO LONG!
I'LL SPREAD ITS NOSTRILS FAR APART!
NOSE
STREEETCH
NOSE

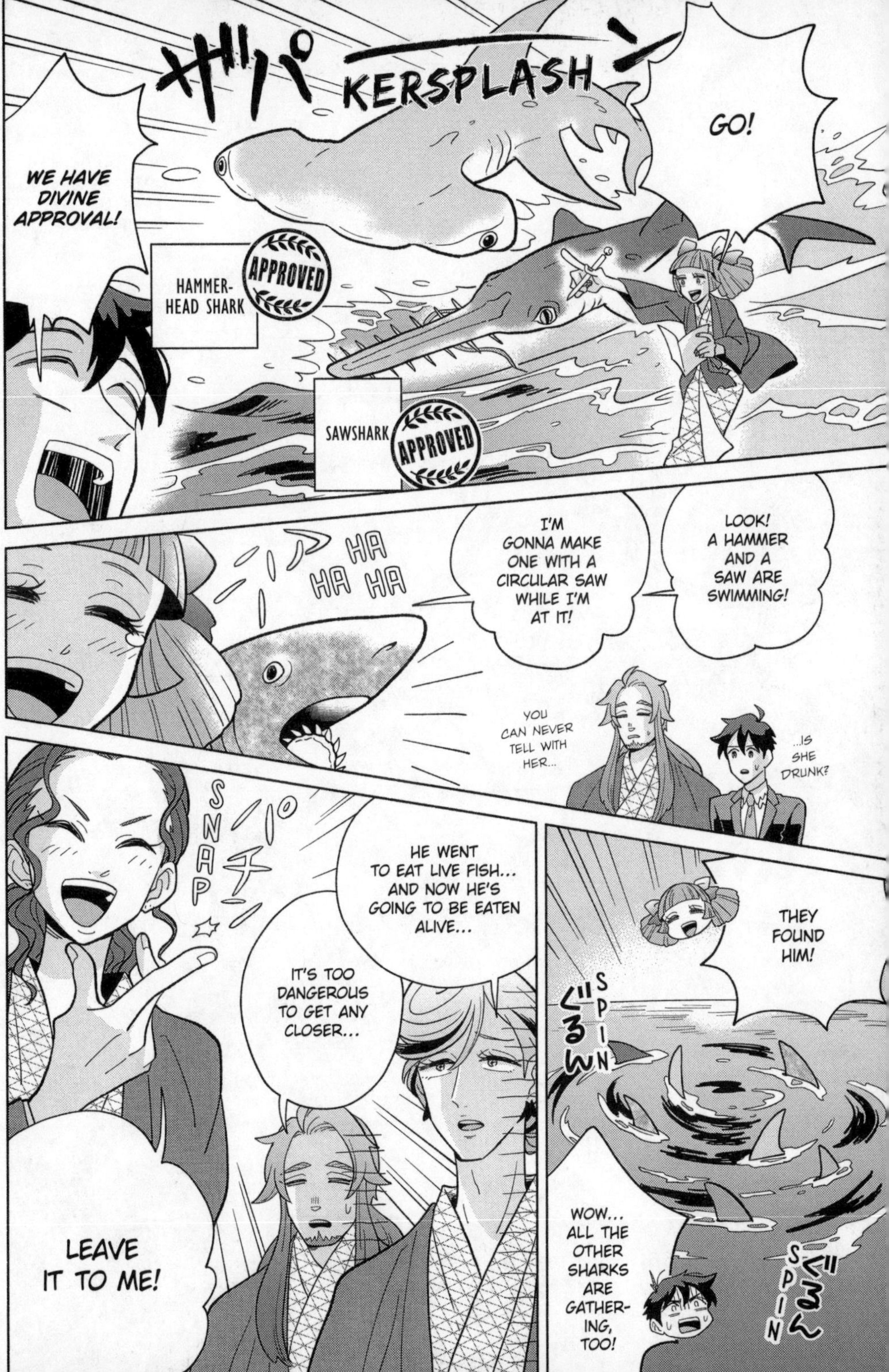
GO!
ザパーン
KERSPLASH
WE HAVE DIVINE APPROVAL!
HAMMER-HEAD SHARK
APPROVED
SAWSHARK
APPROVED
LOOK! A HAMMER AND A SAW ARE SWIMMING!
I'M GONNA MAKE ONE WITH A CIRCULAR SAW WHILE I'M AT IT!
HA HA HA
...IS SHE DRUNK?
YOU CAN NEVER TELL WITH HER...
THEY FOUND HIM!
ぐるん
SPIN
WOW... ALL THE OTHER SHARKS ARE GATHERING, TOO!
ぐるん
SPIN
HE WENT TO EAT LIVE FISH... AND NOW HE'S GOING TO BE EATEN ALIVE...
IT'S TOO DANGEROUS TO GET ANY CLOSER...
パチ
SNAP
LEAVE IT TO ME!

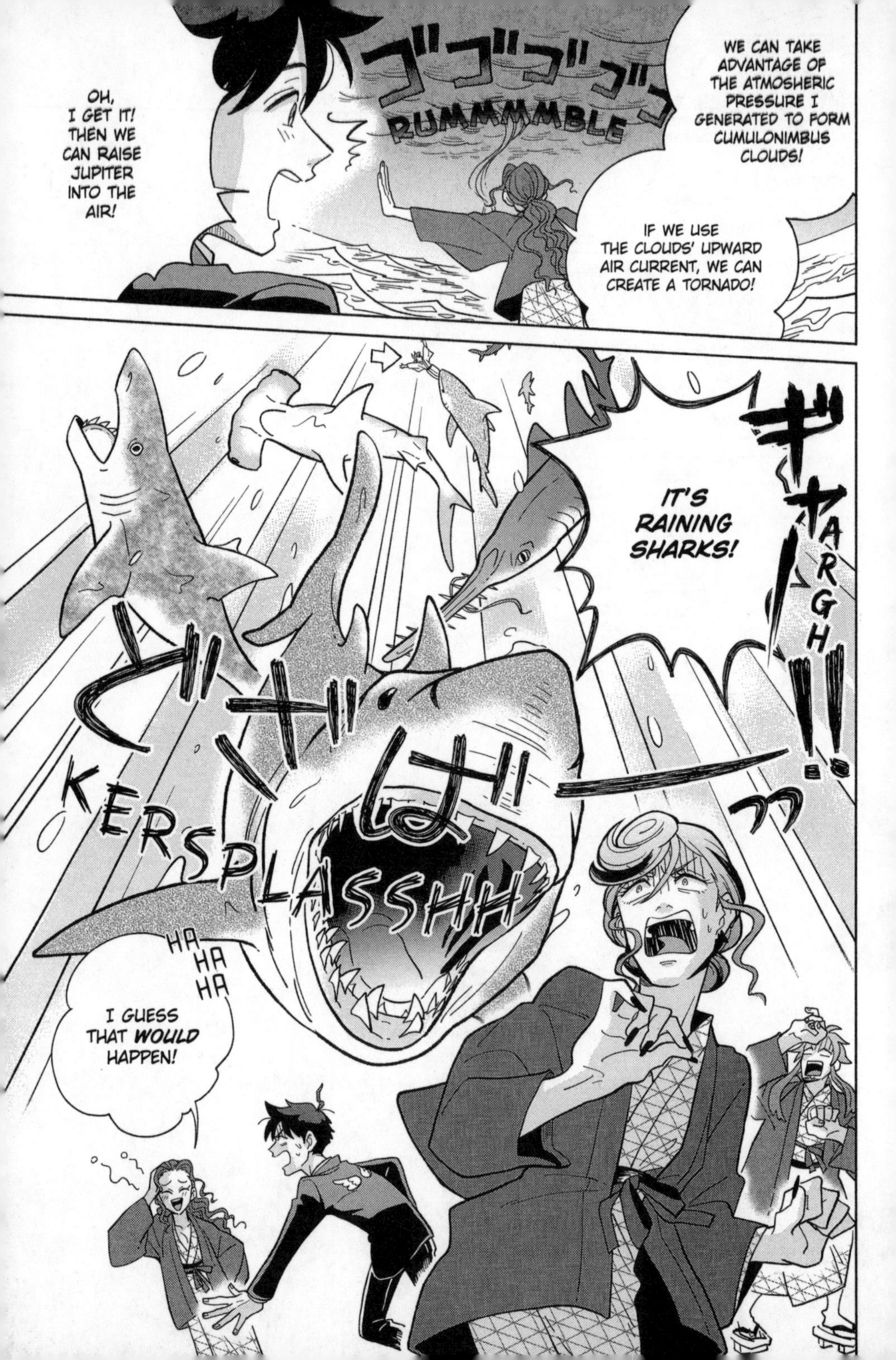
WE CAN TAKE ADVANTAGE OF THE ATMOSHERIC PRESSURE I GENERATED TO FORM CUMULONIMBUS CLOUDS!
IF WE USE THE CLOUDS' UPWARD AIR CURRENT, WE CAN CREATE A TORNADO!
RUMMMMMBLE
OH, I GET IT! THEN WE CAN RAISE JUPITER INTO THE AIR!
ARGH!!
IT'S RAINING SHARKS!
KERSPLASSHH
HA HA HA
I GUESS THAT WOULD HAPPEN!

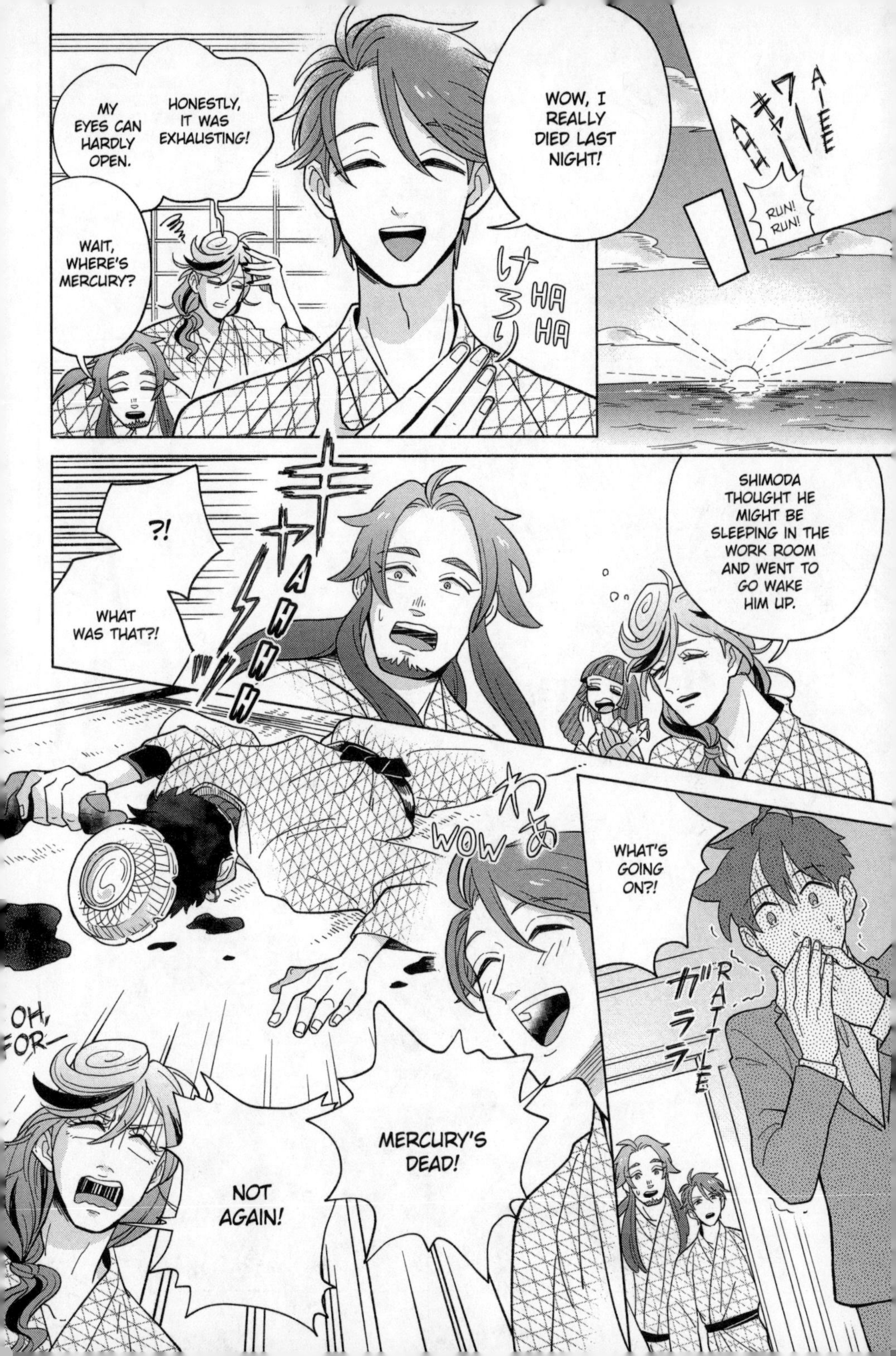
キャー
AIEE
AHH
RUN! RUN!
WOW, I REALLY DIED LAST NIGHT!
けろり
HA HA
HONESTLY, IT WAS EXHAUSTING!
MY EYES CAN HARDLY OPEN.
WAIT, WHERE'S MERCURY?
SHIMODA THOUGHT HE MIGHT BE SLEEPING IN THE WORK ROOM AND WENT TO GO WAKE HIM UP.
キャ
AHHHHH
?!
WHAT WAS THAT?!
WHAT'S GOING ON?!
ガラ
RATTLE
わあ
WOW
MERCURY'S DEAD!
NOT AGAIN!
OH, FOR—

# THE ENCYCLOPEDIA OF REAL ANIMALS 12

## ANIMAL 33 | HELICOPRION

ILLUSTRATION
2005
1902
1993
1953
2015
1911
Different visualizations of helicoprions over the years.

Illustration: Hebi-Zou

THE REAL THING
A fossilized portion of a helicoprion's lower jaw on display at the Paleozoological Museum of China in Beijing.

Photo: Alamy/Alfo

Helicoprions were shark-like eugeneodontids that lived approximately 270 million years ago. After fossilized remains of their teeth, arranged in a spiral pattern and called tooth-whorls, were discovered, a debate began as to the placement of the whorls on the individuals' bodies. Over 100 years of speculation, scientists conceptualized a wide variety of different helicoprion forms. It was believed that the tooth-whorls were composed only of the animals' teeth until 2013, when a CT scan was performed on a helicoprion fossil which revealed that a portion of jawbone was still attached. This discovery finally placed the tooth-whorl on the lower jaw. The giant 18-meter (59-foot) shark that appeared as a prototype in this chapter is a megalodon, a species of shark that went extinct approximately 1.5 million years ago. 18 meters (59 feet) is around the same size as a train car—imagine how scary a shark that size would be!

| | |
|---|---|
| **[Name]** | *Helicoprion* |
| **[Classification]** | Class: Chondrichthyes<br>Order: Eugeneodontida<br>Family: Agassizodontidae<br>Genus: *Helicoprion* |
| **[Temporal range]** | 200~300 million years ago |

## ANIMAL 34 HAMMERHEAD SHARK

THE REAL THING

NOSE
NOSE

A scalloped hammerhead swimming off the coast of Colombia.

Photo: F1 online/Aflo

**[Name]** Hammerhead shark
**[Classification]** Class: Chondrichthyes
Order: Carcharhiniformes
Family: Sphyrnidae
**[Habitat]** Warmer waters worldwide
**[Length]** 4-6 m (13-20 ft)

In Japanese, hammerhead sharks are known as *shumoku* sharks for their resemblance to the wooden bell hammers (*shumoku*) used to strike gongs. They have many sensory pores called ampullae of Lorenzini on their extra-wide heads which allow them to sense the electricity given off by other living creatures. The positioning of their eyes on either side of their head enhances their field of vision. This, combined with their directional sense of smell, makes them formidable hunters. Their wide heads also serve as a steering system.

## ANIMAL 35 JAPANESE SAWSHARK

The long, saw-like part of Japanese sawsharks are known as rostrums and are used to attack during hunting and to dig in the sand. Sawsharks' rostrums have many ampullae of Lorenzini that help them find prey on the sea floor effectively. The species is ovoviviparous and gives live birth to pups. Sharks bear their young in a variety of ways, including those that lay eggs (like the Japanese bullhead shark) and those whose embyros feed on its siblings inside the womb (like the sand tiger shark).

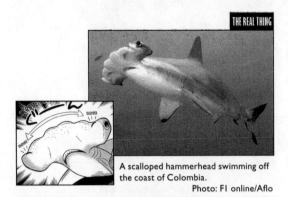

THE REAL THING

A young sawshark.

Photo: Uryu/Aflo

**[Name]** *Pristiophorus japonicus*
**[Classification]** Class: Chondrichthyes
Order: Pristiophoriformes
Family: Pristiophoridae
Genus: *Pristiophorus*
**[Habitat]** Northern Pacific Ocean around Japan and northern China
**[Length]** Approximately 1.7 m (5.6 ft)

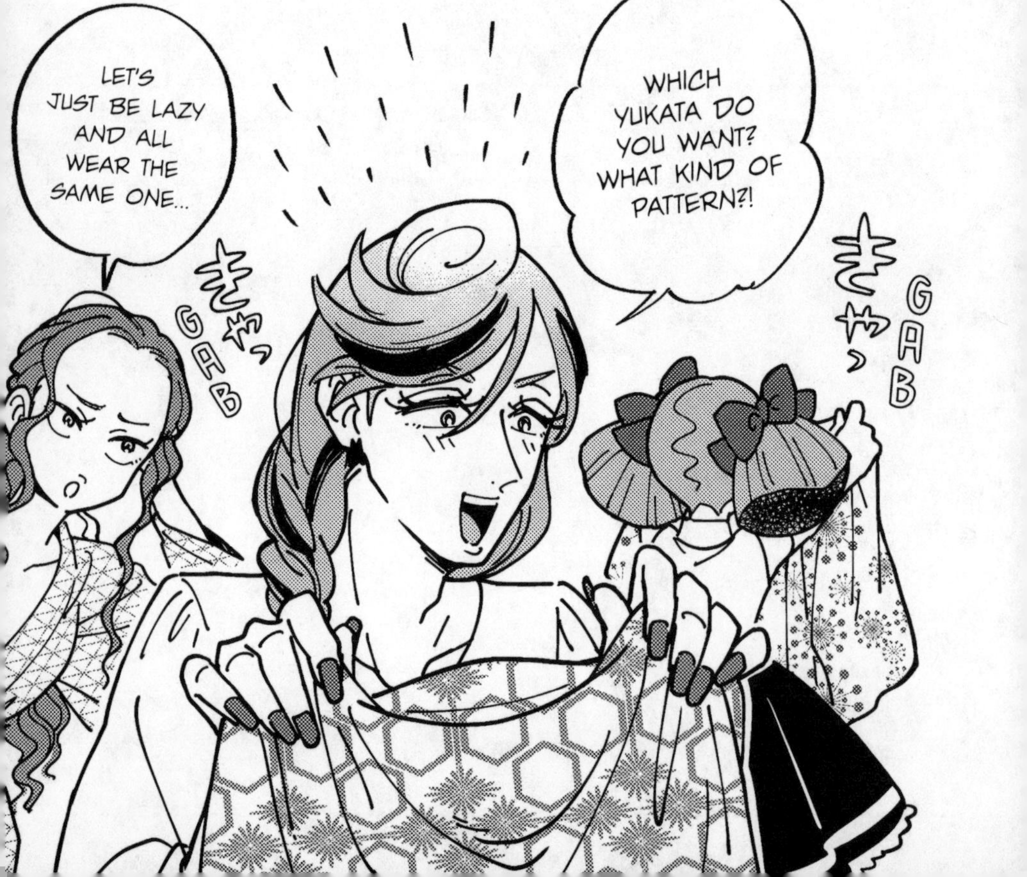
WHICH YUKATA DO YOU WANT? WHAT KIND OF PATTERN?!
GAB
LET'S JUST BE LAZY AND ALL WEAR THE SAME ONE...
GAB

# HEAVEN'S
# DESIGN TEAM

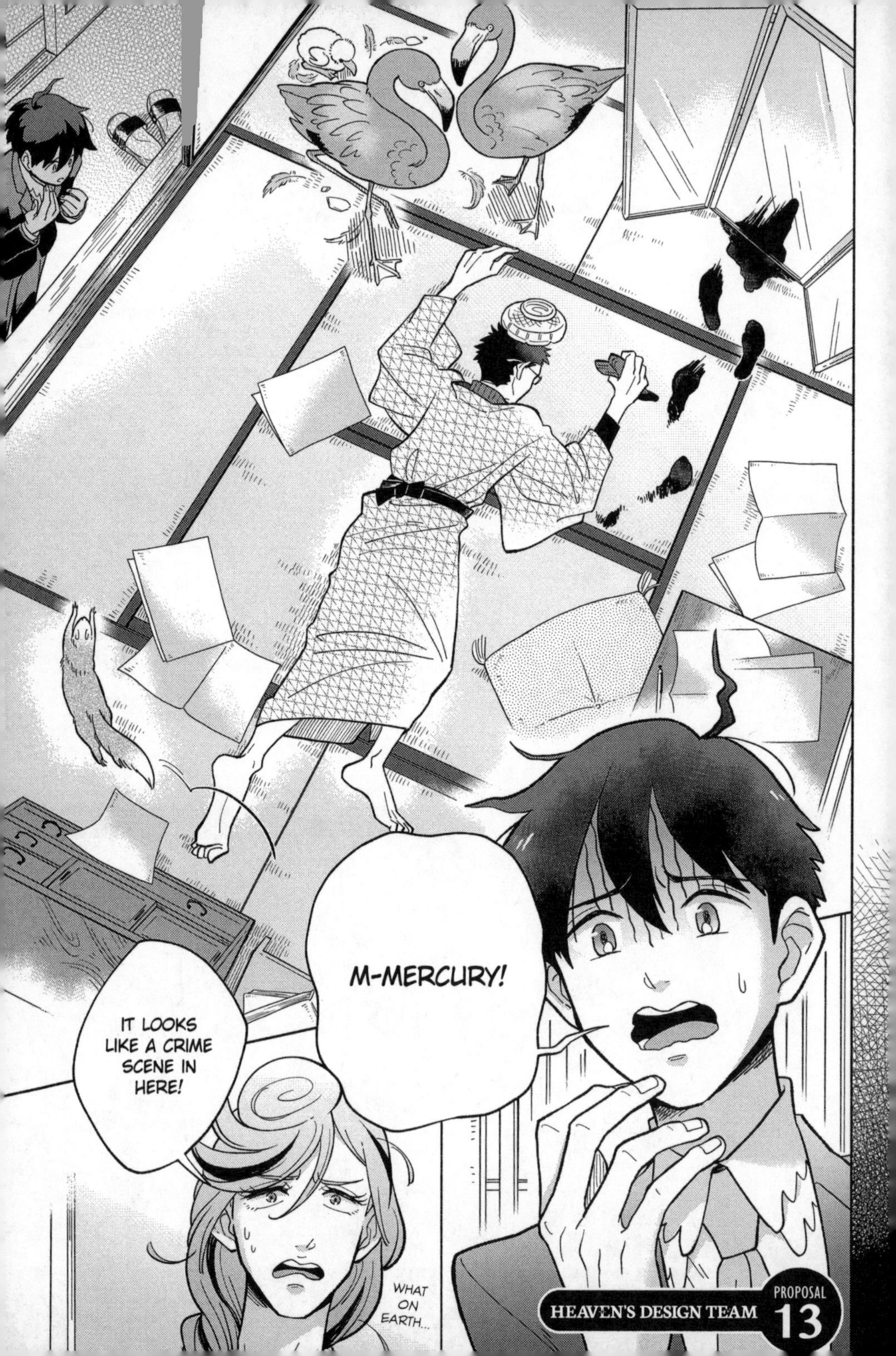
M-MERCURY!
IT LOOKS LIKE A CRIME SCENE IN HERE!
WHAT ON EARTH...
HEAVEN'S DESIGN TEAM
PROPOSAL 13

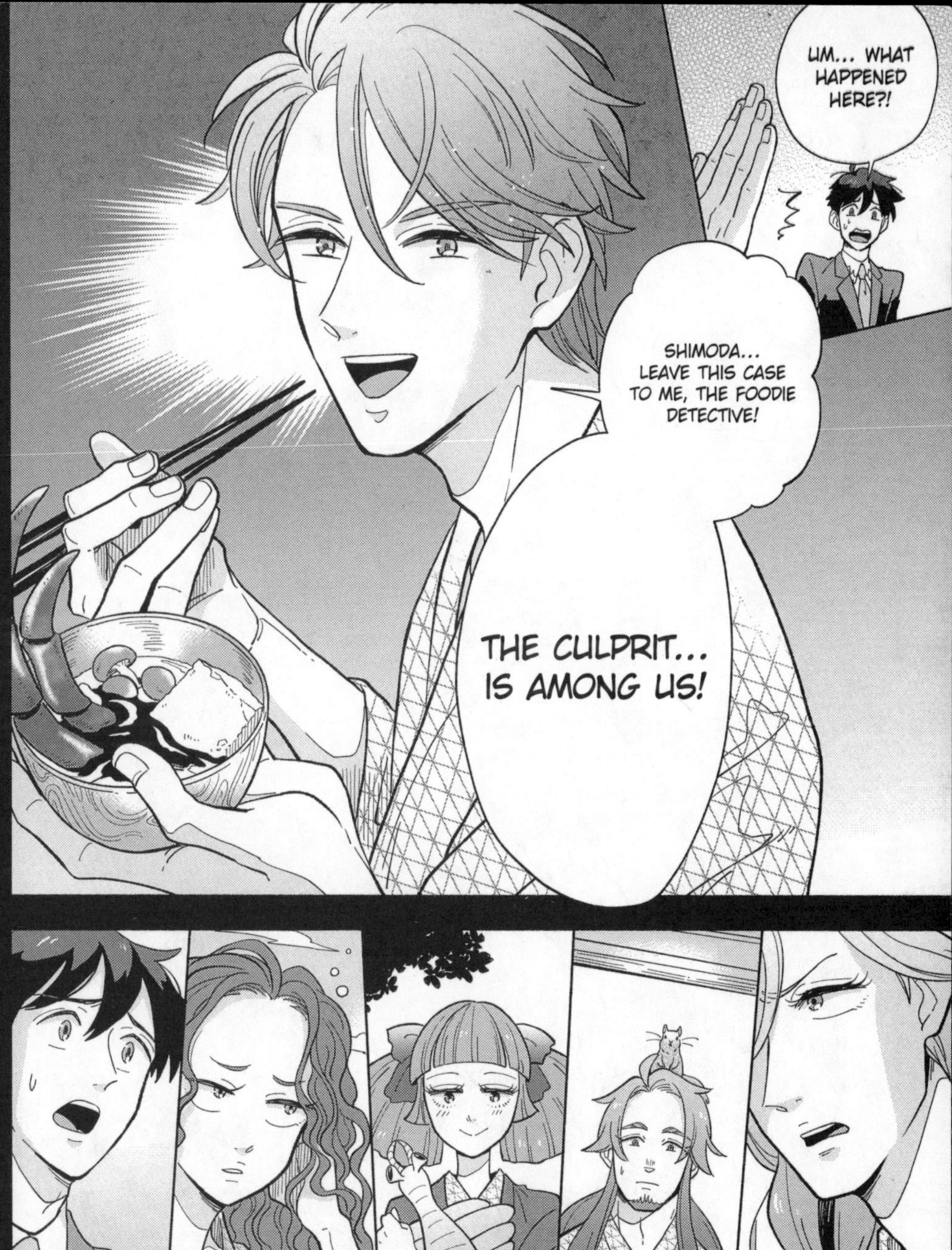
UM... WHAT HAPPENED HERE?!
SHIMODA... LEAVE THIS CASE TO ME, THE FOODIE DETECTIVE!
THE CULPRIT... IS AMONG US!

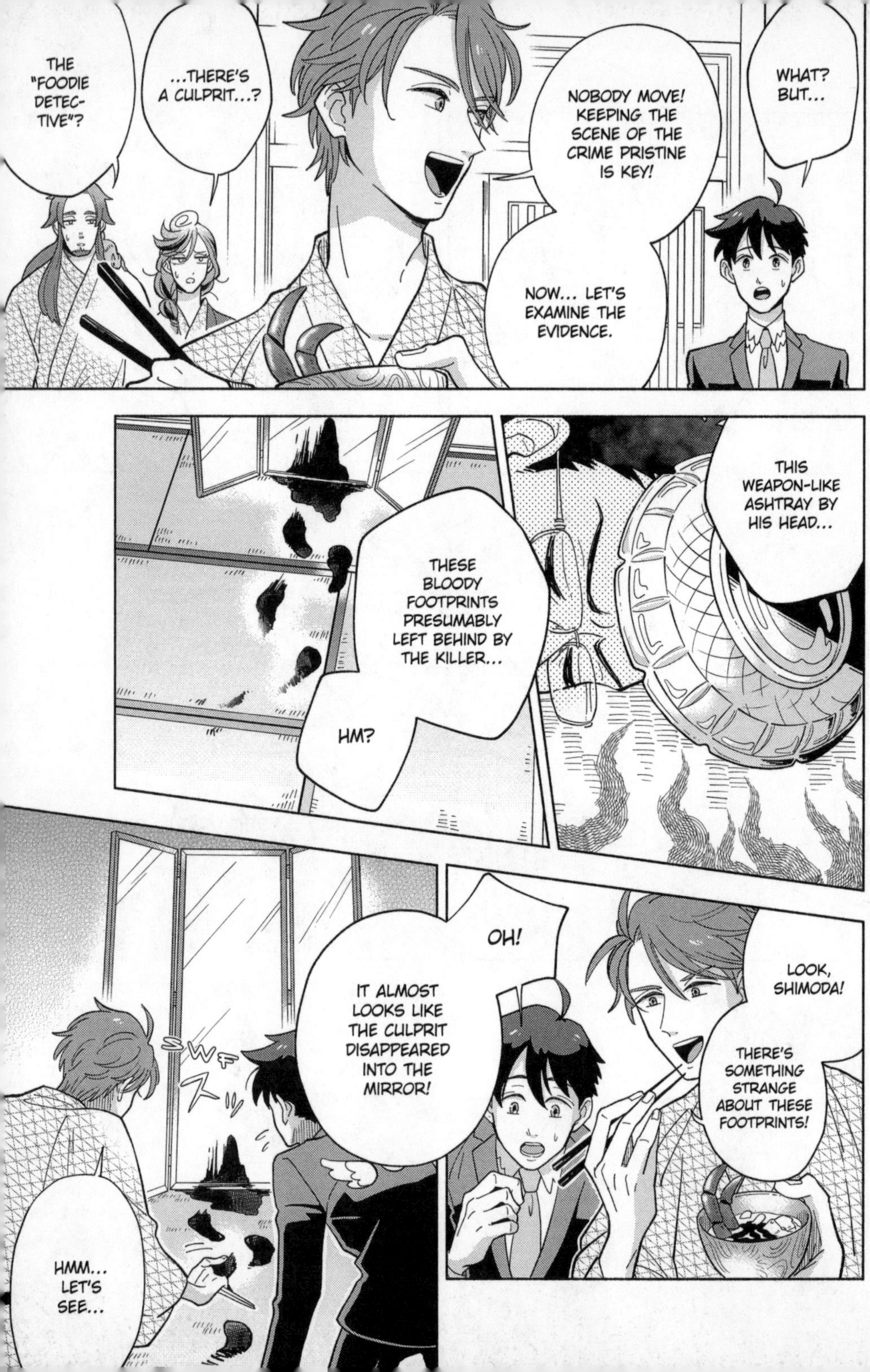
WHAT? BUT...
NOBODY MOVE! KEEPING THE SCENE OF THE CRIME PRISTINE IS KEY!
NOW... LET'S EXAMINE THE EVIDENCE.
...THERE'S A CULPRIT...?
THE "FOODIE DETECTIVE"?
THIS WEAPON-LIKE ASHTRAY BY HIS HEAD...
THESE BLOODY FOOTPRINTS PRESUMABLY LEFT BEHIND BY THE KILLER...
HM?
LOOK, SHIMODA!
THERE'S SOMETHING STRANGE ABOUT THESE FOOTPRINTS!
OH!
IT ALMOST LOOKS LIKE THE CULPRIT DISAPPEARED INTO THE MIRROR!
SWF
HMM... LET'S SEE...

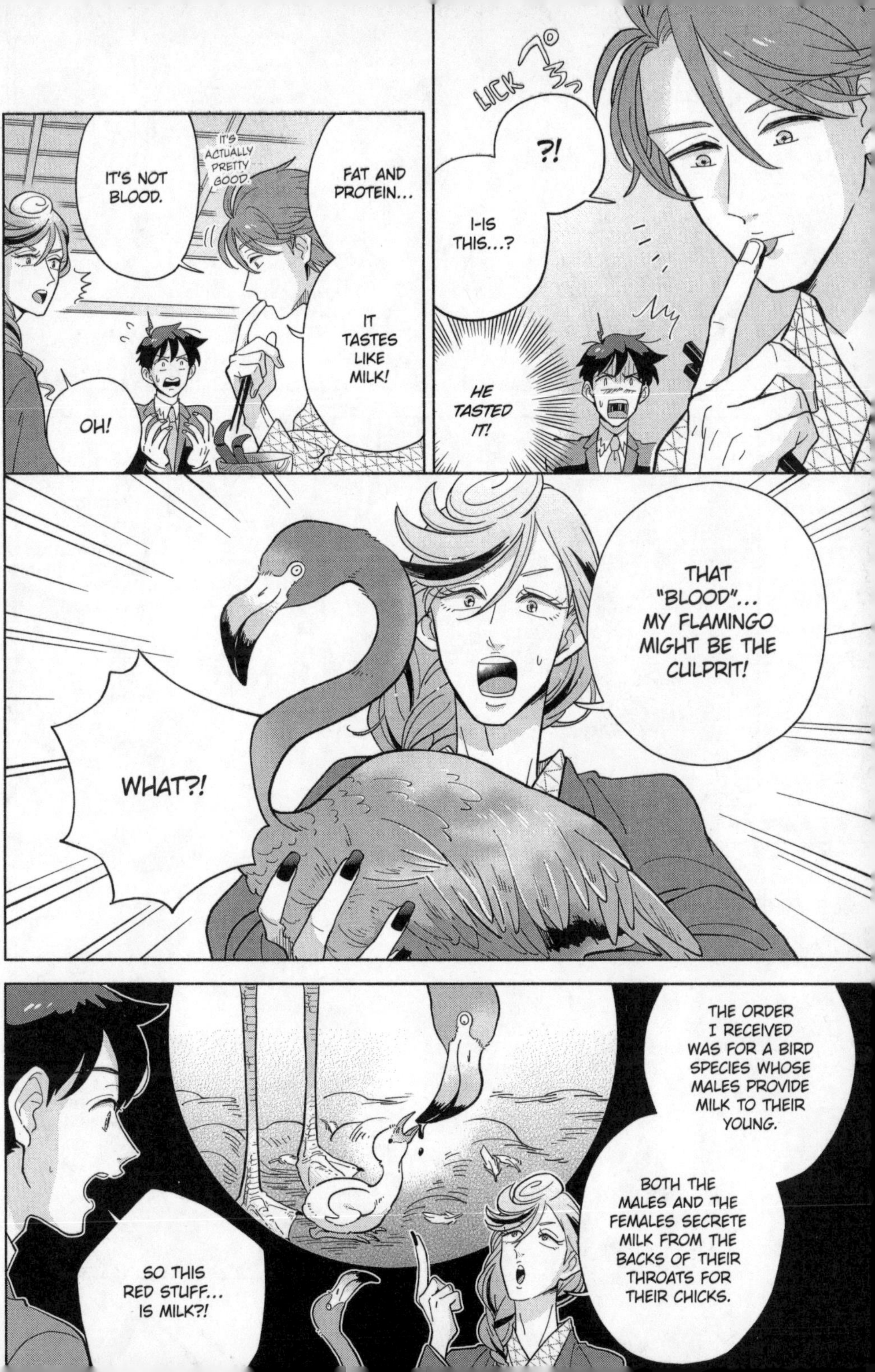
LICK
?!
I-IS THIS...?
HE TASTED IT!
FAT AND PROTEIN...
IT'S ACTUALLY PRETTY GOOD.
IT'S NOT BLOOD.
IT TASTES LIKE MILK!
OH!
THAT "BLOOD"... MY FLAMINGO MIGHT BE THE CULPRIT!
WHAT?!
THE ORDER I RECEIVED WAS FOR A BIRD SPECIES WHOSE MALES PROVIDE MILK TO THEIR YOUNG.
BOTH THE MALES AND THE FEMALES SECRETE MILK FROM THE BACKS OF THEIR THROATS FOR THEIR CHICKS.
SO THIS RED STUFF... IS MILK?!

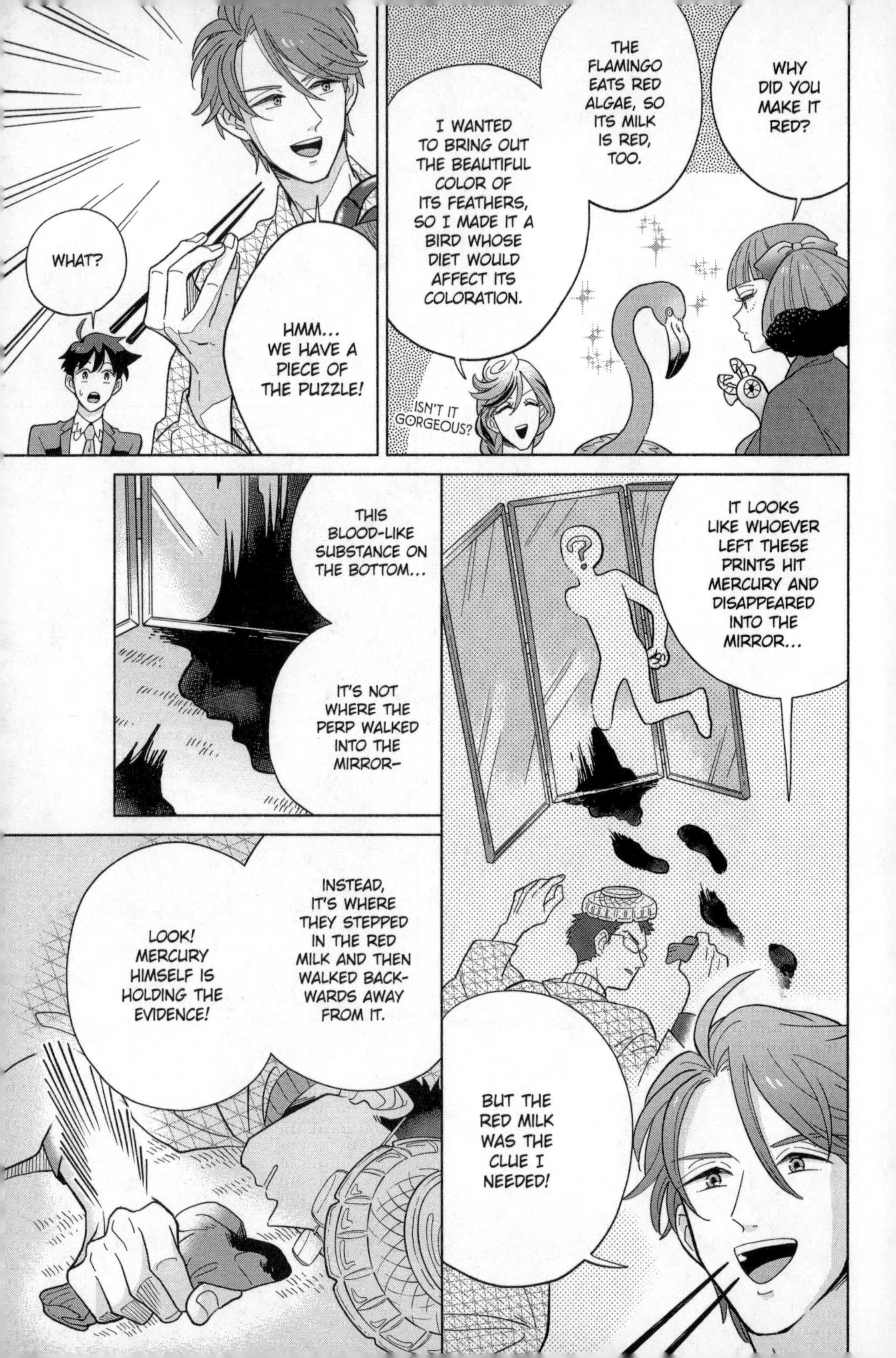
WHY DID YOU MAKE IT RED?
THE FLAMINGO EATS RED ALGAE, SO ITS MILK IS RED, TOO.
I WANTED TO BRING OUT THE BEAUTIFUL COLOR OF ITS FEATHERS, SO I MADE IT A BIRD WHOSE DIET WOULD AFFECT ITS COLORATION.
ISN'T IT GORGEOUS?
HMM... WE HAVE A PIECE OF THE PUZZLE!
WHAT?
IT LOOKS LIKE WHOEVER LEFT THESE PRINTS HIT MERCURY AND DISAPPEARED INTO THE MIRROR...
BUT THE RED MILK WAS THE CLUE I NEEDED!
THIS BLOOD-LIKE SUBSTANCE ON THE BOTTOM...
IT'S NOT WHERE THE PERP WALKED INTO THE MIRROR-
INSTEAD, IT'S WHERE THEY STEPPED IN THE RED MILK AND THEN WALKED BACK-WARDS AWAY FROM IT.
LOOK! MERCURY HIMSELF IS HOLDING THE EVIDENCE!

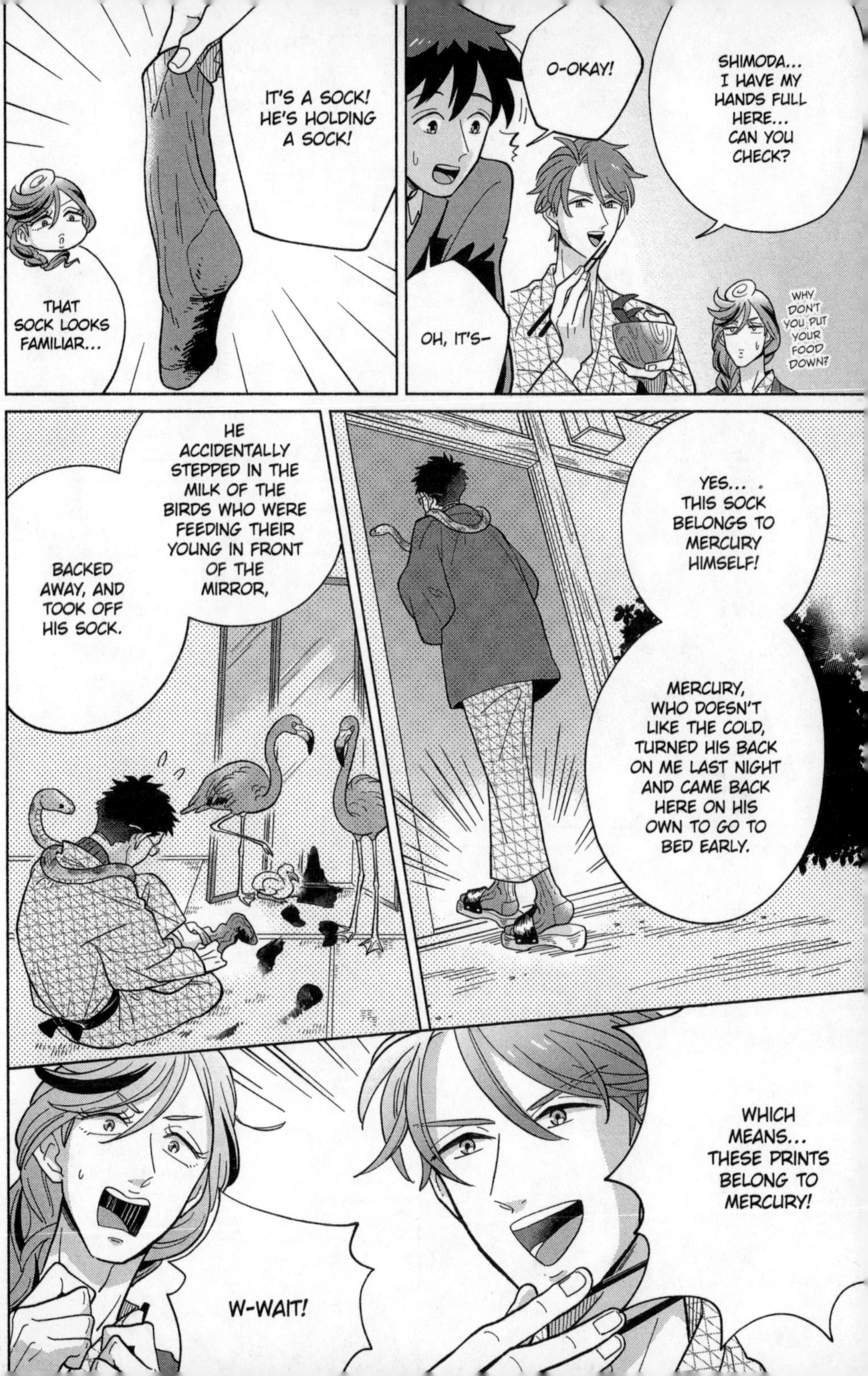
SHIMODA... I HAVE MY HANDS FULL HERE... CAN YOU CHECK?
O-OKAY!
WHY DON'T YOU PUT YOUR FOOD DOWN?
OH, IT'S-
IT'S A SOCK! HE'S HOLDING A SOCK!
THAT SOCK LOOKS FAMILIAR...
YES... THIS SOCK BELONGS TO MERCURY HIMSELF!
MERCURY, WHO DOESN'T LIKE THE COLD, TURNED HIS BACK ON ME LAST NIGHT AND CAME BACK HERE ON HIS OWN TO GO TO BED EARLY.
HE ACCIDENTALLY STEPPED IN THE MILK OF THE BIRDS WHO WERE FEEDING THEIR YOUNG IN FRONT OF THE MIRROR,
BACKED AWAY, AND TOOK OFF HIS SOCK.
WHICH MEANS... THESE PRINTS BELONG TO MERCURY!
W-WAIT!

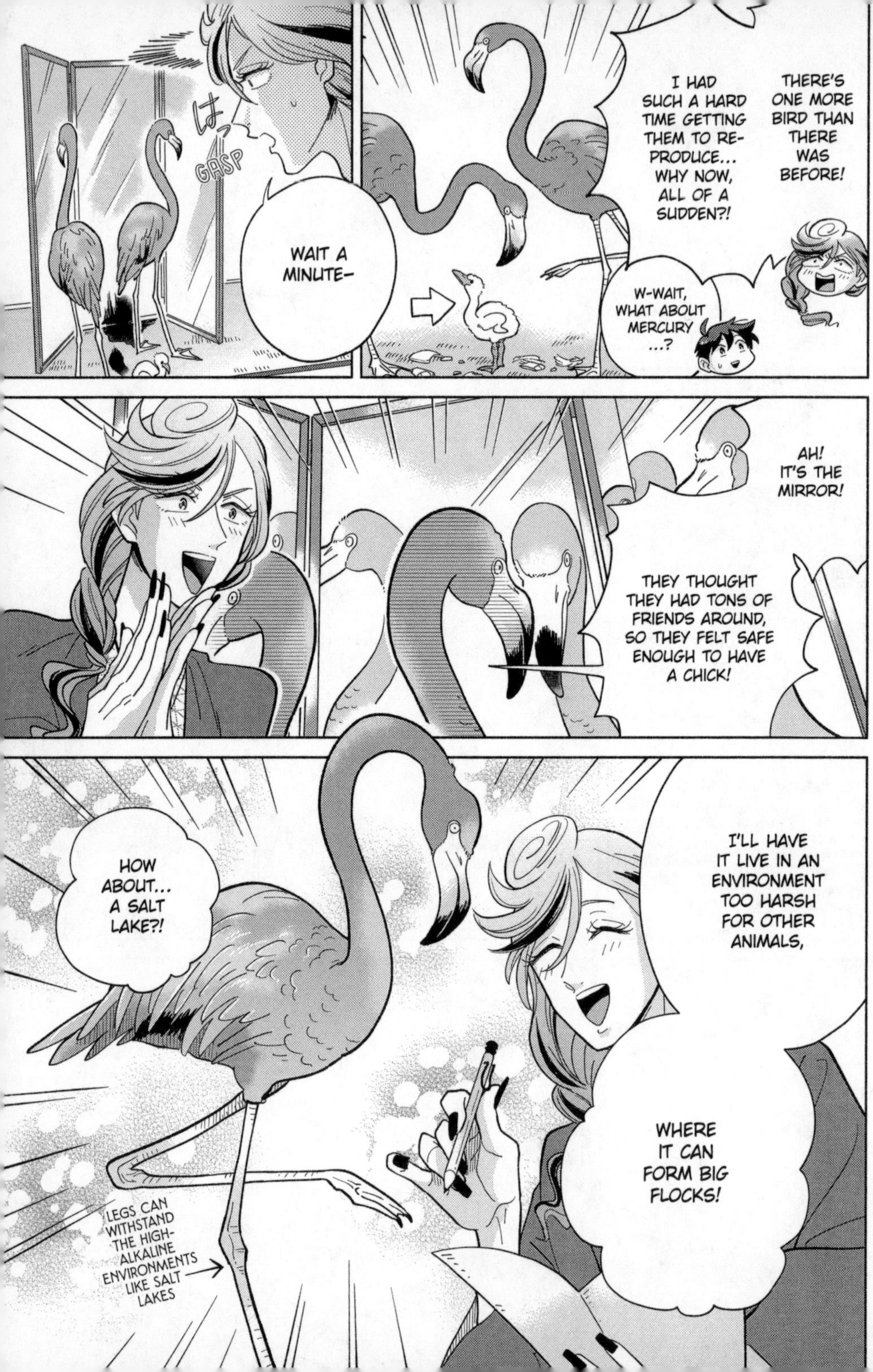
THERE'S ONE MORE BIRD THAN THERE WAS BEFORE!
I HAD SUCH A HARD TIME GETTING THEM TO RE-PRODUCE… WHY NOW, ALL OF A SUDDEN?!
W-WAIT, WHAT ABOUT MERCURY …?
はっ
GASP
WAIT A MINUTE–
AH! IT'S THE MIRROR!
THEY THOUGHT THEY HAD TONS OF FRIENDS AROUND, SO THEY FELT SAFE ENOUGH TO HAVE A CHICK!
I'LL HAVE IT LIVE IN AN ENVIRONMENT TOO HARSH FOR OTHER ANIMALS,
WHERE IT CAN FORM BIG FLOCKS!
HOW ABOUT… A SALT LAKE?!
LEGS CAN WITHSTAND THE HIGH-ALKALINE ENVIRONMENTS LIKE SALT LAKES

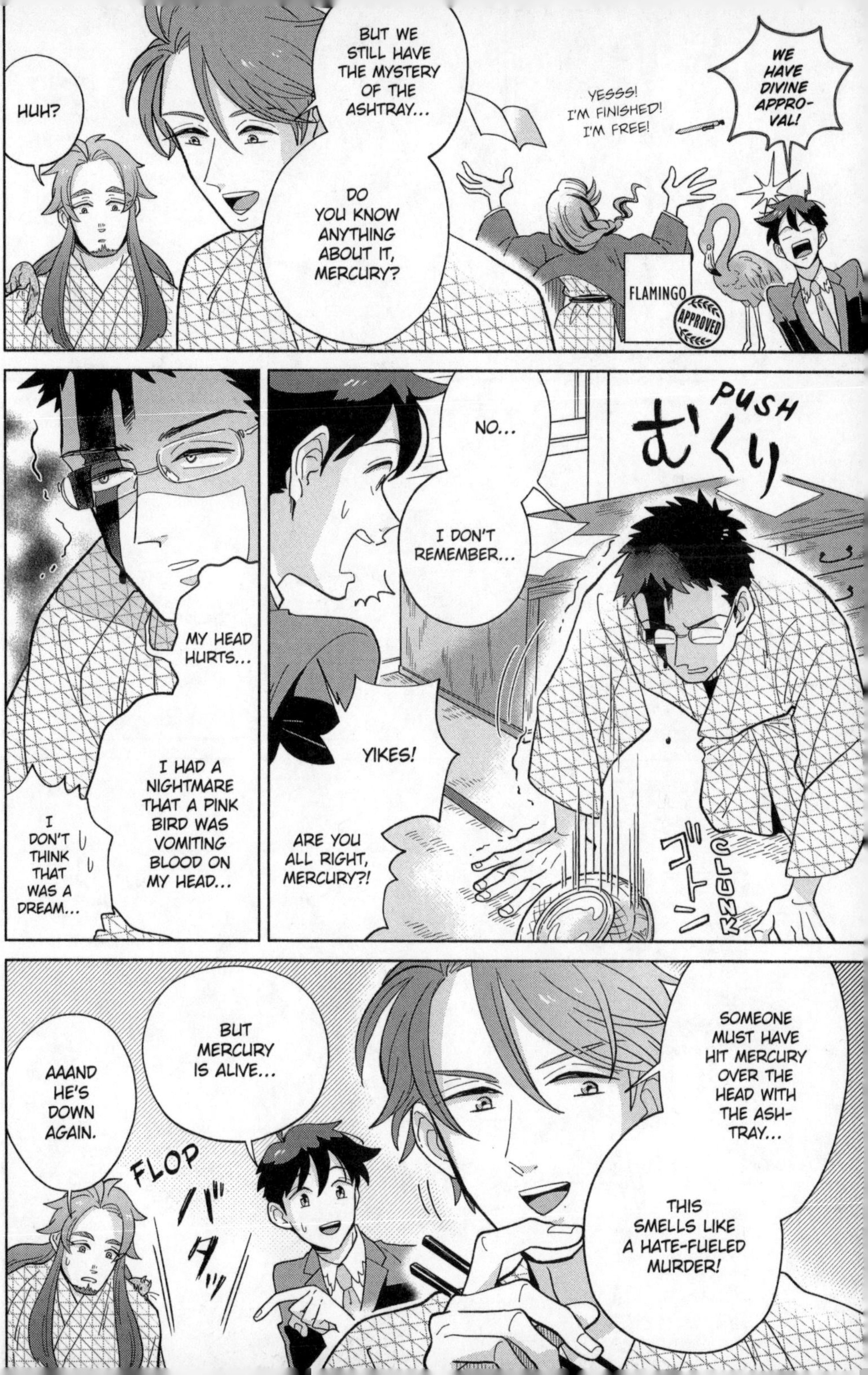
WE HAVE DIVINE APPRO-VAL!
YESSS! I'M FINISHED! I'M FREE!
FLAMINGO
APPROVED
BUT WE STILL HAVE THE MYSTERY OF THE ASHTRAY...
DO YOU KNOW ANYTHING ABOUT IT, MERCURY?
HUH?
PUSH
むくり
CLUNK
NO...
I DON'T REMEMBER...
YIKES!
ARE YOU ALL RIGHT, MERCURY?!
MY HEAD HURTS...
I HAD A NIGHTMARE THAT A PINK BIRD WAS VOMITING BLOOD ON MY HEAD...
I DON'T THINK THAT WAS A DREAM...
SOMEONE MUST HAVE HIT MERCURY OVER THE HEAD WITH THE ASH-TRAY...
THIS SMELLS LIKE A HATE-FUELED MURDER!
BUT MERCURY IS ALIVE...
FLOP
AAAND HE'S DOWN AGAIN.

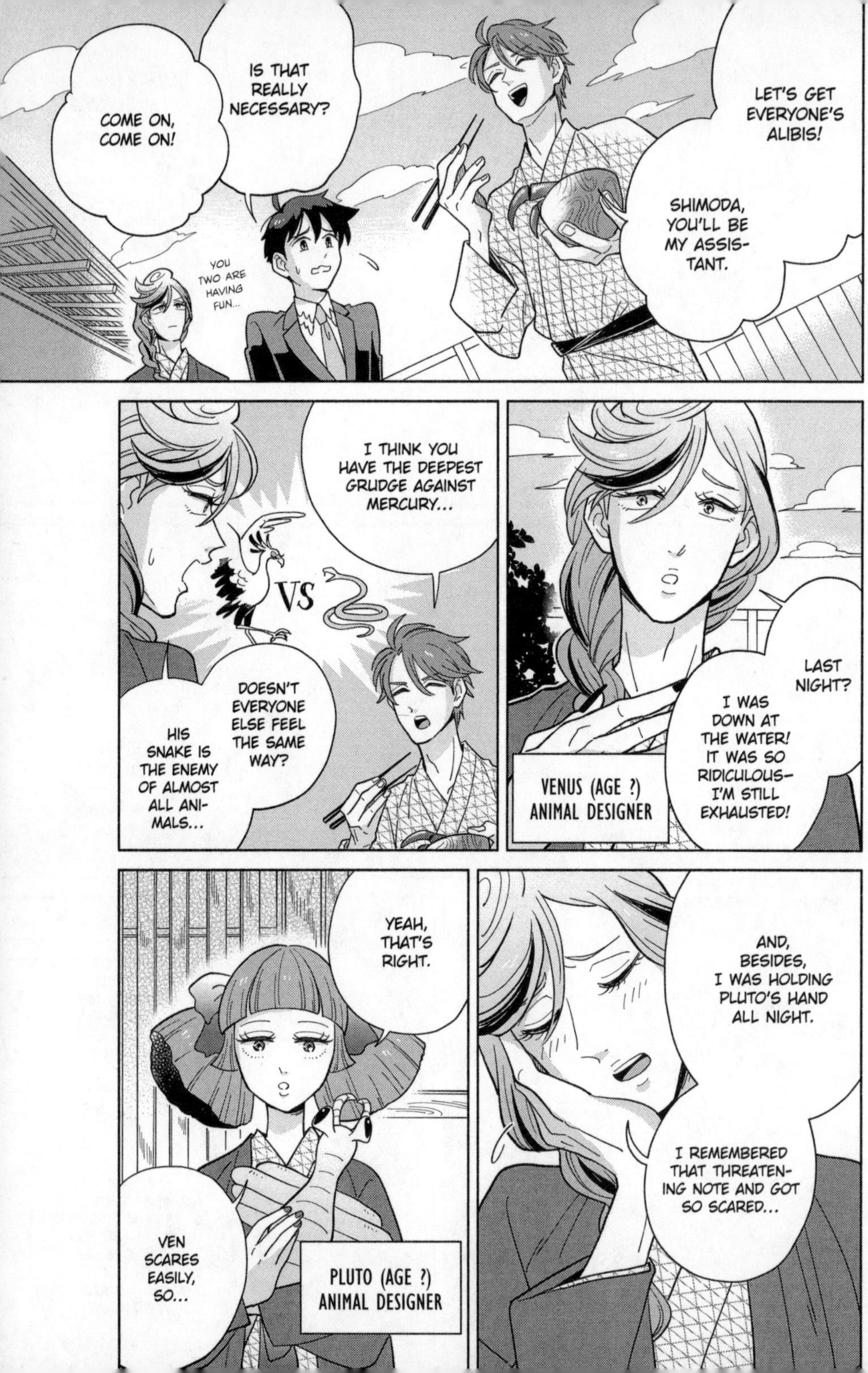
LET'S GET EVERYONE'S ALIBIS!
SHIMODA, YOU'LL BE MY ASSIS-TANT.
IS THAT REALLY NECESSARY?
COME ON, COME ON!
YOU TWO ARE HAVING FUN...
LAST NIGHT?
I WAS DOWN AT THE WATER! IT WAS SO RIDICULOUS— I'M STILL EXHAUSTED!
VENUS (AGE ?) ANIMAL DESIGNER
I THINK YOU HAVE THE DEEPEST GRUDGE AGAINST MERCURY...
VS
DOESN'T EVERYONE ELSE FEEL THE SAME WAY?
HIS SNAKE IS THE ENEMY OF ALMOST ALL ANI-MALS...
AND, BESIDES, I WAS HOLDING PLUTO'S HAND ALL NIGHT.
I REMEMBERED THAT THREATEN-ING NOTE AND GOT SO SCARED...
YEAH, THAT'S RIGHT.
VEN SCARES EASILY, SO...
PLUTO (AGE ?) ANIMAL DESIGNER

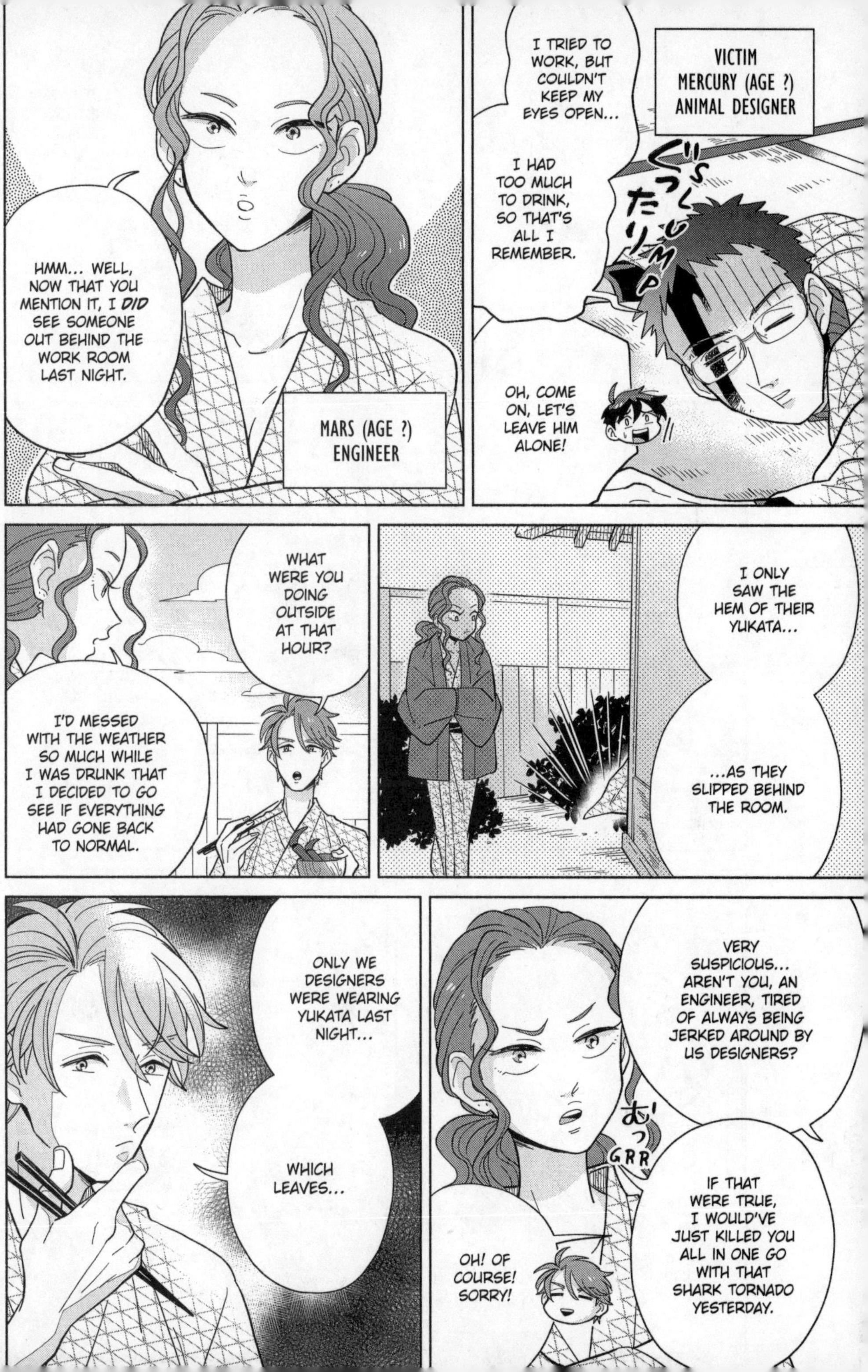
VICTIM
MERCURY (AGE ?)
ANIMAL DESIGNER
I TRIED TO WORK, BUT COULDN'T KEEP MY EYES OPEN...
I HAD TOO MUCH TO DRINK, SO THAT'S ALL I REMEMBER.
ぐったり
SLUMP
OH, COME ON, LET'S LEAVE HIM ALONE!
HMM... WELL, NOW THAT YOU MENTION IT, I *DID* SEE SOMEONE OUT BEHIND THE WORK ROOM LAST NIGHT.
MARS (AGE ?)
ENGINEER
I ONLY SAW THE HEM OF THEIR YUKATA...
...AS THEY SLIPPED BEHIND THE ROOM.
WHAT WERE YOU DOING OUTSIDE AT THAT HOUR?
I'D MESSED WITH THE WEATHER SO MUCH WHILE I WAS DRUNK THAT I DECIDED TO GO SEE IF EVERYTHING HAD GONE BACK TO NORMAL.
VERY SUSPICIOUS... AREN'T YOU, AN ENGINEER, TIRED OF ALWAYS BEING JERKED AROUND BY US DESIGNERS?
むっ
GRR
IF THAT WERE TRUE, I WOULD'VE JUST KILLED YOU ALL IN ONE GO WITH THAT SHARK TORNADO YESTERDAY.
OH! OF COURSE! SORRY!
ONLY WE DESIGNERS WERE WEARING YUKATA LAST NIGHT...
WHICH LEAVES...

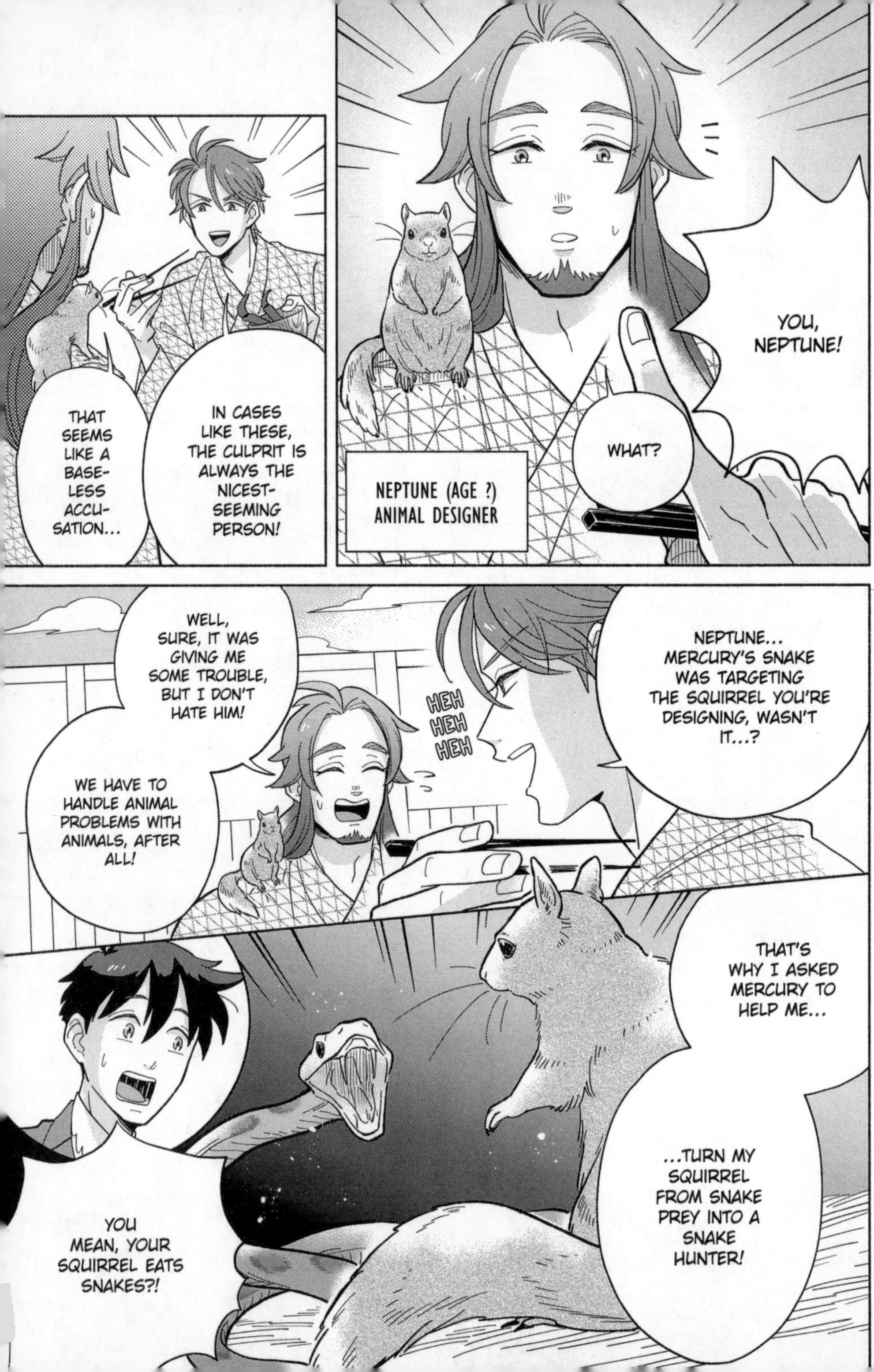
YOU, NEPTUNE!
WHAT?
NEPTUNE (AGE ?) ANIMAL DESIGNER
IN CASES LIKE THESE, THE CULPRIT IS ALWAYS THE NICEST-SEEMING PERSON!
THAT SEEMS LIKE A BASELESS ACCUSATION...
NEPTUNE... MERCURY'S SNAKE WAS TARGETING THE SQUIRREL YOU'RE DESIGNING, WASN'T IT...?
HEH HEH HEH
WELL, SURE, IT WAS GIVING ME SOME TROUBLE, BUT I DON'T HATE HIM!
WE HAVE TO HANDLE ANIMAL PROBLEMS WITH ANIMALS, AFTER ALL!
THAT'S WHY I ASKED MERCURY TO HELP ME...
...TURN MY SQUIRREL FROM SNAKE PREY INTO A SNAKE HUNTER!
YOU MEAN, YOUR SQUIRREL EATS SNAKES?!

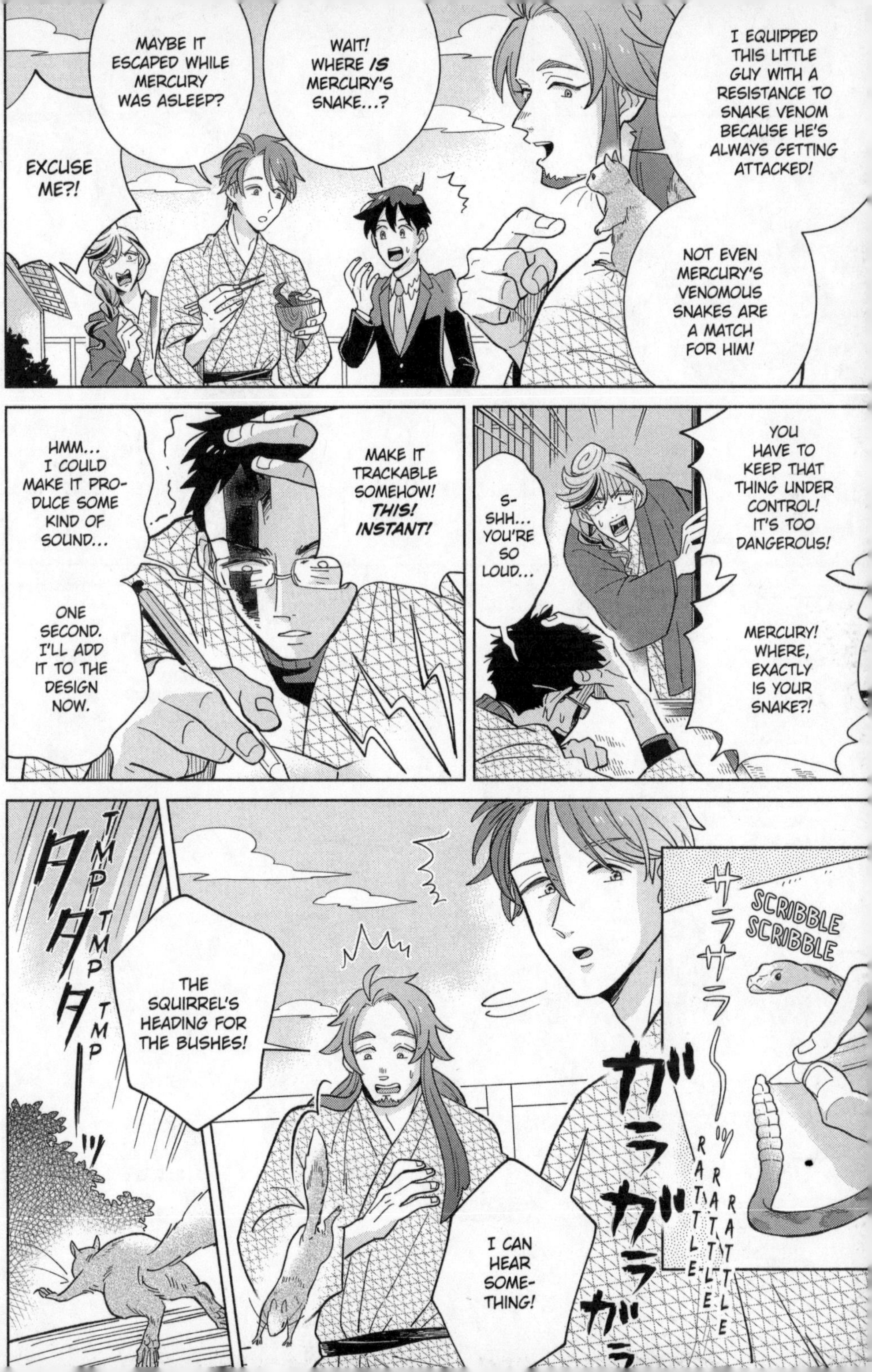

I EQUIPPED THIS LITTLE GUY WITH A RESISTANCE TO SNAKE VENOM BECAUSE HE'S ALWAYS GETTING ATTACKED!
NOT EVEN MERCURY'S VENOMOUS SNAKES ARE A MATCH FOR HIM!
WAIT! WHERE *IS* MERCURY'S SNAKE...?
MAYBE IT ESCAPED WHILE MERCURY WAS ASLEEP?
EXCUSE ME?!
YOU HAVE TO KEEP THAT THING UNDER CONTROL! IT'S TOO DANGEROUS!
MERCURY! WHERE, EXACTLY IS YOUR SNAKE?!
S-SHH... YOU'RE SO LOUD...
MAKE IT TRACKABLE SOMEHOW! *THIS! INSTANT!*
HMM... I COULD MAKE IT PRO-DUCE SOME KIND OF SOUND...
ONE SECOND. I'LL ADD IT TO THE DESIGN NOW.
SCRIBBLE SCRIBBLE
サラサラ〜ッ
RATTLE RATTLE RATTLE
ガラガラ
I CAN HEAR SOME-THING!
THE SQUIRREL'S HEADING FOR THE BUSHES!
TMP TMP TMP
タタターッ

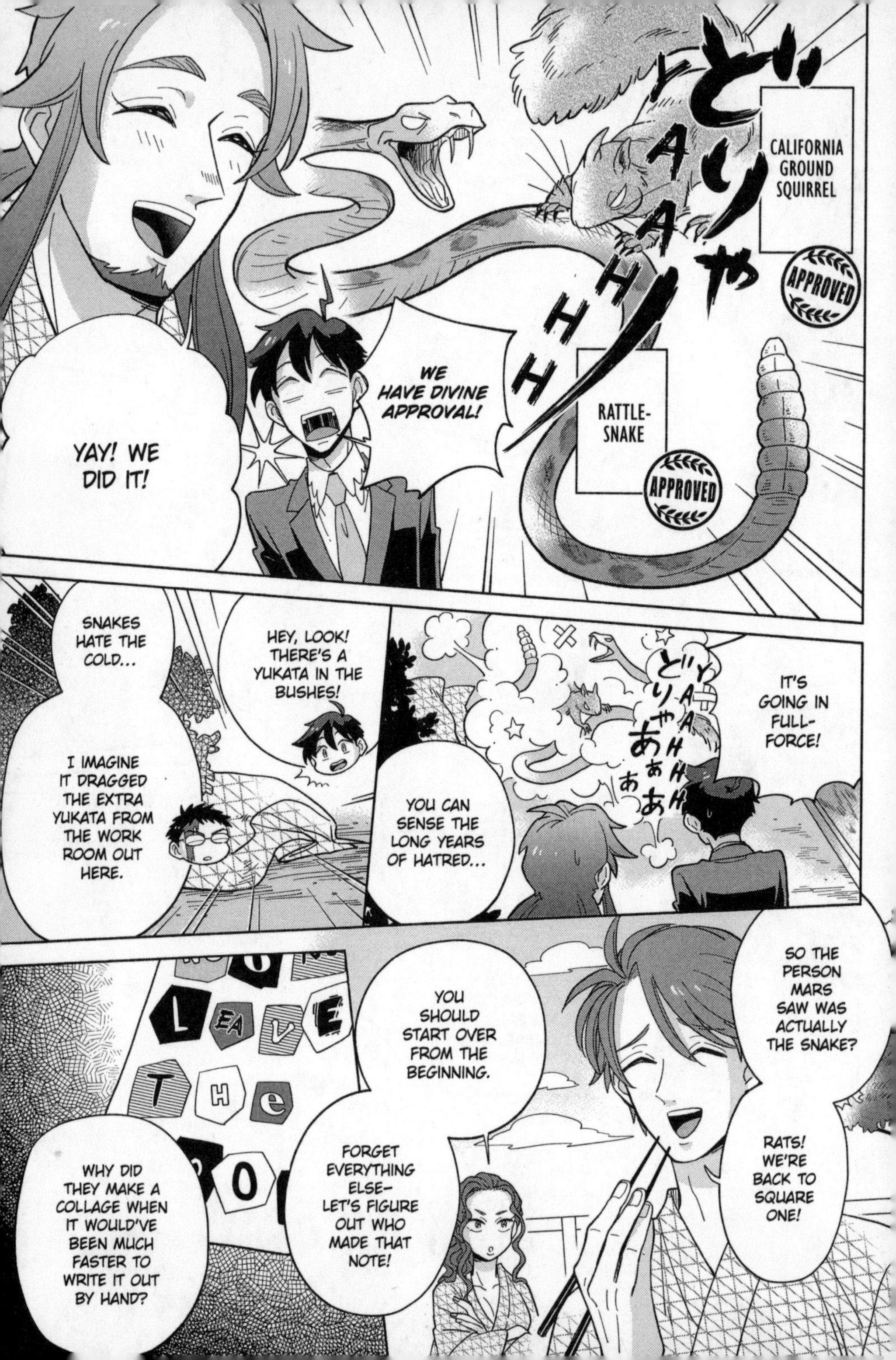
どりゃ
AAAHHHHH
CALIFORNIA GROUND SQUIRREL
APPROVED
RATTLE-SNAKE
APPROVED
WE HAVE DIVINE APPROVAL!
YAY! WE DID IT!
IT'S GOING IN FULL-FORCE!
どりゃあぁあ
YAAHHHH
YOU CAN SENSE THE LONG YEARS OF HATRED...
HEY, LOOK! THERE'S A YUKATA IN THE BUSHES!
SNAKES HATE THE COLD...
I IMAGINE IT DRAGGED THE EXTRA YUKATA FROM THE WORK ROOM OUT HERE.
SO THE PERSON MARS SAW WAS ACTUALLY THE SNAKE?
RATS! WE'RE BACK TO SQUARE ONE!
YOU SHOULD START OVER FROM THE BEGINNING.
FORGET EVERYTHING ELSE— LET'S FIGURE OUT WHO MADE THAT NOTE!
LEAVE THe
WHY DID THEY MAKE A COLLAGE WHEN IT WOULD'VE BEEN MUCH FASTER TO WRITE IT OUT BY HAND?

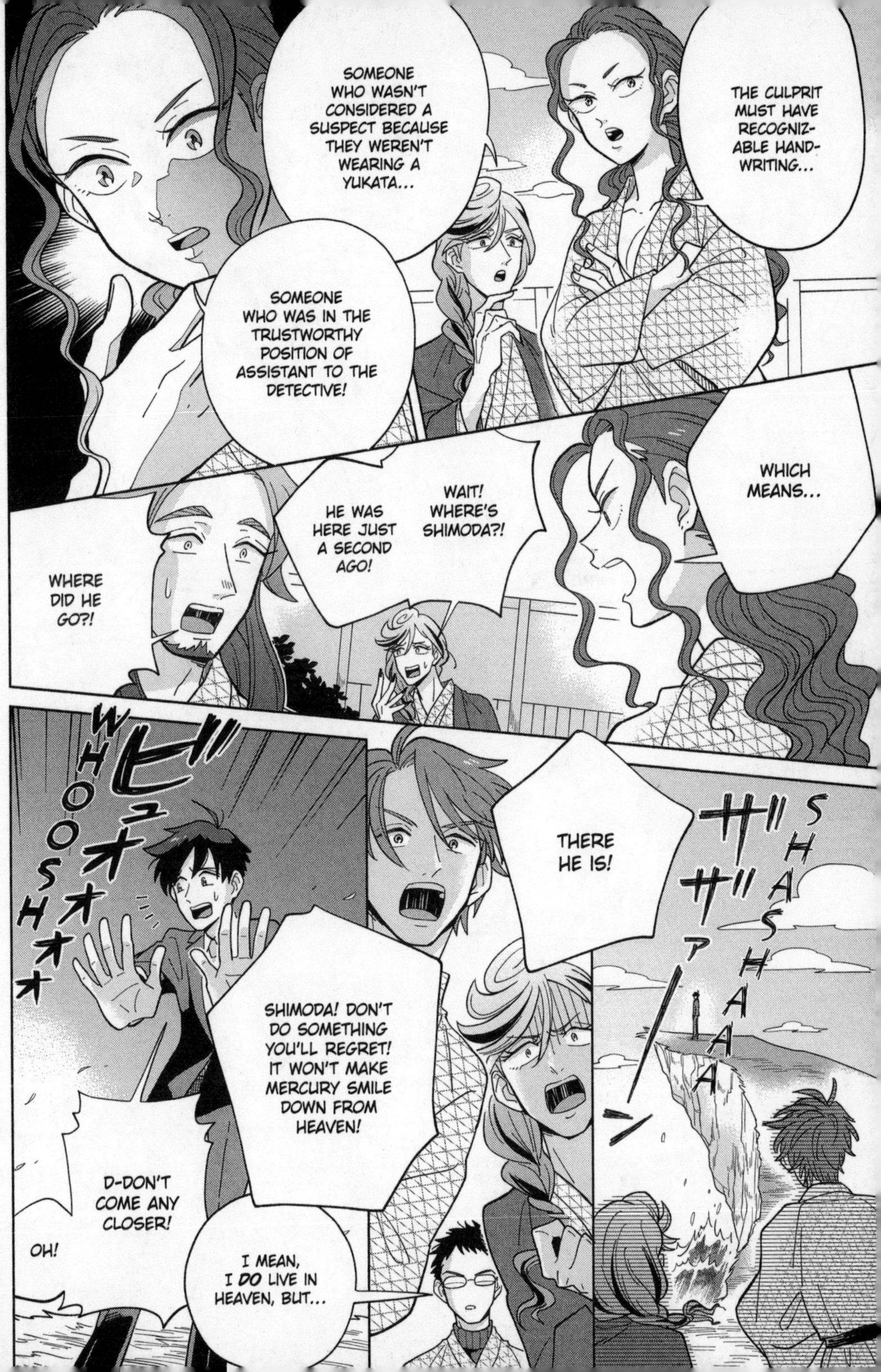
THE CULPRIT MUST HAVE RECOGNIZABLE HANDWRITING...
SOMEONE WHO WASN'T CONSIDERED A SUSPECT BECAUSE THEY WEREN'T WEARING A YUKATA...
SOMEONE WHO WAS IN THE TRUSTWORTHY POSITION OF ASSISTANT TO THE DETECTIVE!
WHICH MEANS...
WAIT! WHERE'S SHIMODA?!
HE WAS HERE JUST A SECOND AGO!
WHERE DID HE GO?!
SHASHAAAA
THERE HE IS!
SHIMODA! DON'T DO SOMETHING YOU'LL REGRET! IT WON'T MAKE MERCURY SMILE DOWN FROM HEAVEN!
WHOOOOSH
D-DON'T COME ANY CLOSER!
OH!
I MEAN, I *DO* LIVE IN HEAVEN, BUT...

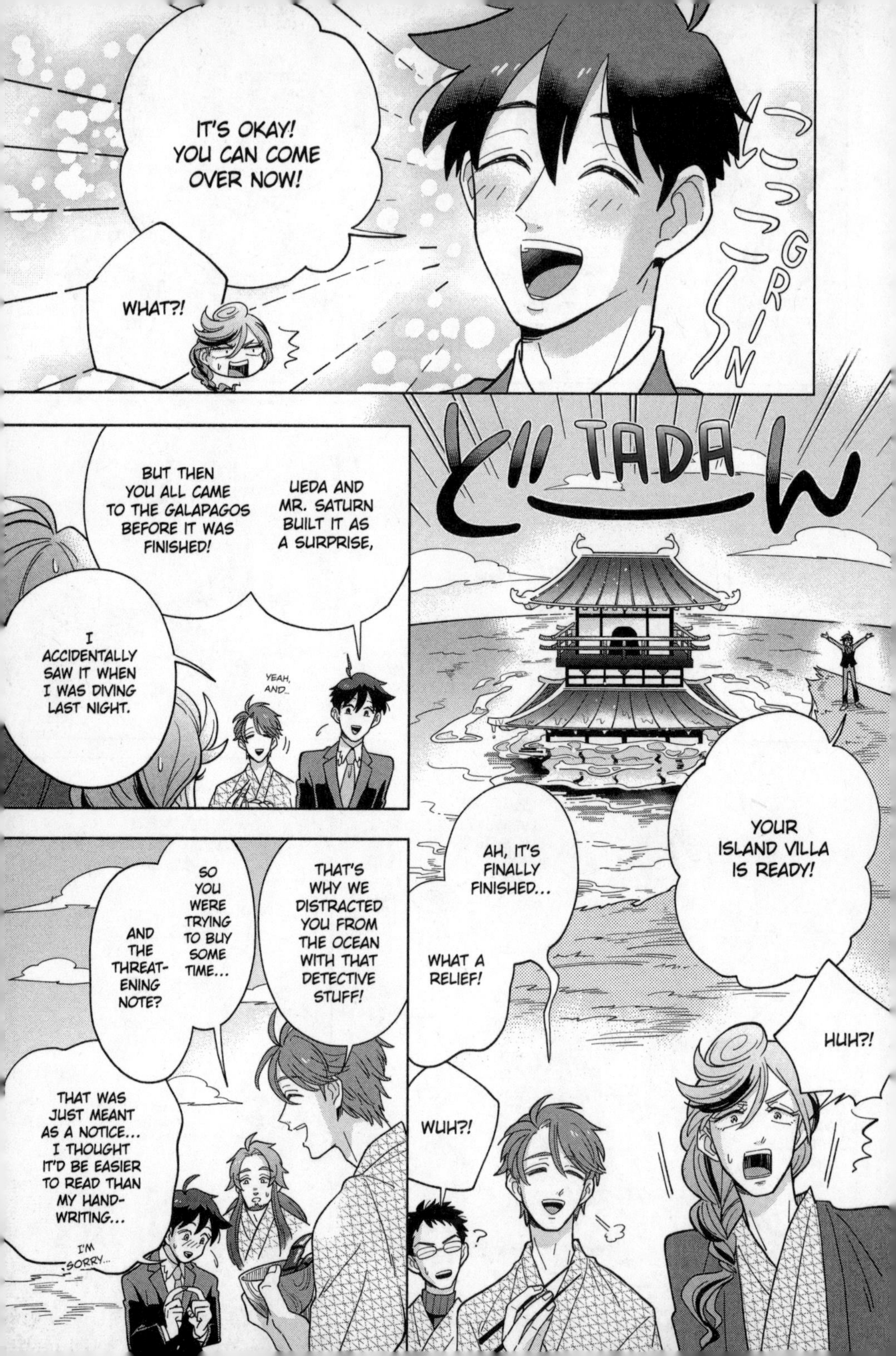
GRIN
IT'S OKAY! YOU CAN COME OVER NOW!
WHAT?!
TADA
YOUR ISLAND VILLA IS READY!
AH, IT'S FINALLY FINISHED...
WHAT A RELIEF!
UEDA AND MR. SATURN BUILT IT AS A SURPRISE,
BUT THEN YOU ALL CAME TO THE GALAPAGOS BEFORE IT WAS FINISHED!
YEAH, AND...
I ACCIDENTALLY SAW IT WHEN I WAS DIVING LAST NIGHT.
HUH?!
WUH?!
THAT'S WHY WE DISTRACTED YOU FROM THE OCEAN WITH THAT DETECTIVE STUFF!
SO YOU WERE TRYING TO BUY SOME TIME...
AND THE THREAT-ENING NOTE?
THAT WAS JUST MEANT AS A NOTICE... I THOUGHT IT'D BE EASIER TO READ THAN MY HAND-WRITING...
I'M SORRY...

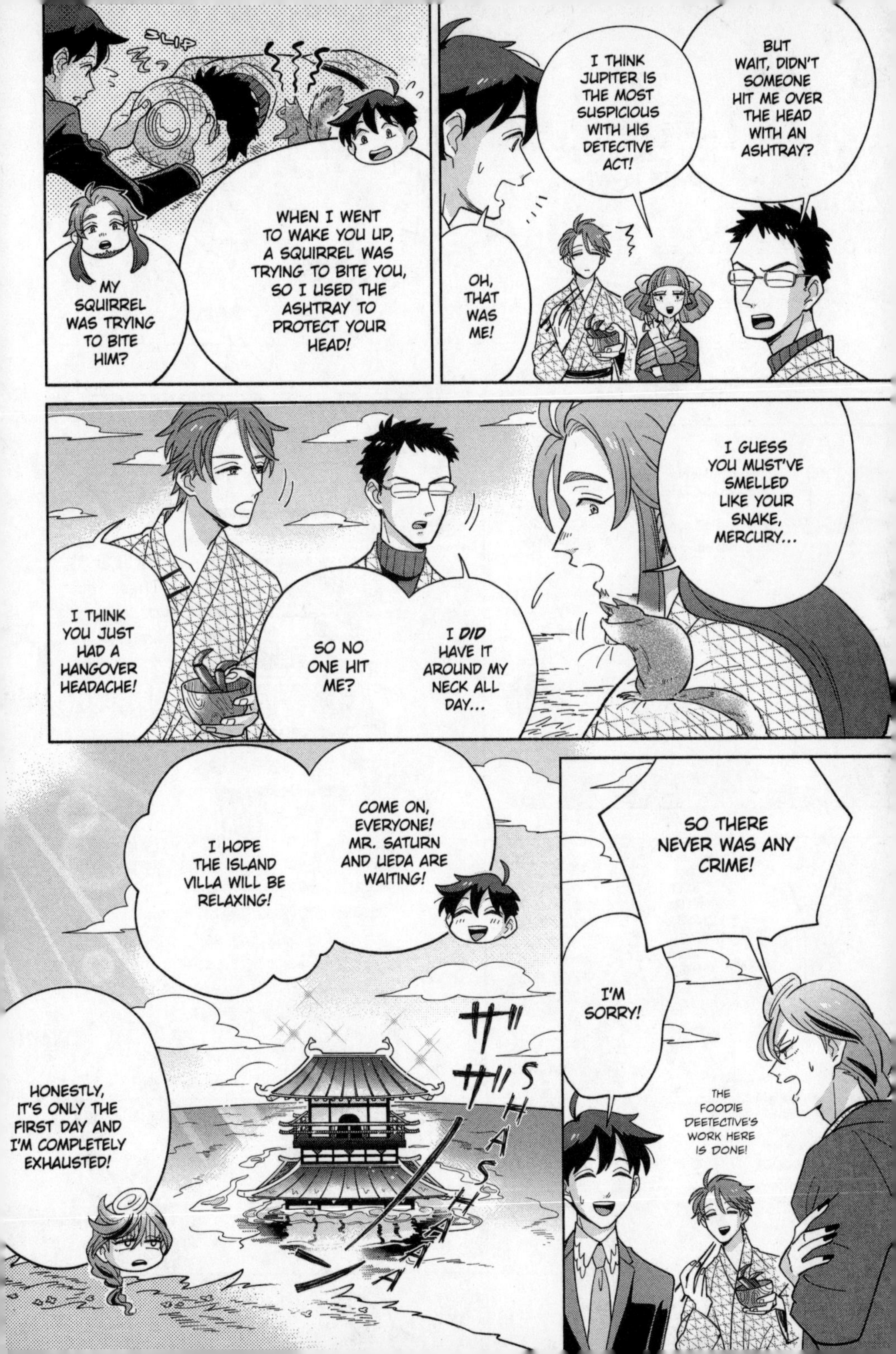
BUT WAIT, DIDN'T SOMEONE HIT ME OVER THE HEAD WITH AN ASHTRAY?
I THINK JUPITER IS THE MOST SUSPICIOUS WITH HIS DETECTIVE ACT!
OH, THAT WAS ME!
SLIP
WHEN I WENT TO WAKE YOU UP, A SQUIRREL WAS TRYING TO BITE YOU, SO I USED THE ASHTRAY TO PROTECT YOUR HEAD!
MY SQUIRREL WAS TRYING TO BITE HIM?
I GUESS YOU MUST'VE SMELLED LIKE YOUR SNAKE, MERCURY...
I DID HAVE IT AROUND MY NECK ALL DAY...
SO NO ONE HIT ME?
I THINK YOU JUST HAD A HANGOVER HEADACHE!
SO THERE NEVER WAS ANY CRIME!
I'M SORRY!
THE FOODIE DEETECTIVE'S WORK HERE IS DONE!
COME ON, EVERYONE! MR. SATURN AND UEDA ARE WAITING!
I HOPE THE ISLAND VILLA WILL BE RELAXING!
SHASHAAA
HONESTLY, IT'S ONLY THE FIRST DAY AND I'M COMPLETELY EXHAUSTED!

# THE ENCYCLOPEDIA OF REAL ANIMALS 13

## ANIMAL 36 | CALIFORNIA GROUND SQUIRREL

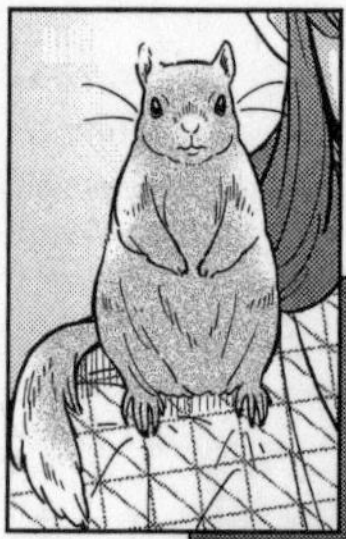

THE REAL THING

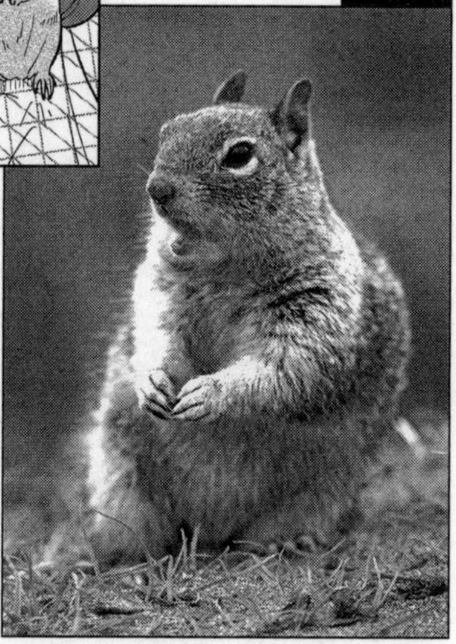

Squirrels rub the scent of rattlesnakes onto their bodies by chewing on snakeskins.
Photo: Arco Images/Aflo

Snakes are the archenemy of squirrels, but California ground squirrels stand their ground against rattlesnakes as if they were the predators (in reality, ground squirrels are herbivores and don't actually eat snakes). These squirrels attack rattlesnakes in order to get their scent on their bodies, and will sometimes bite discarded snakeskins or chew on the areas where a snake recently was in order to achieve the same effect. By disguising their scent, the squirrels can avoid being hunted.

Ground squirrels also use their tails to determine an approaching snake's condition and behavior. They purposely heat and swish around their tails, which activates the snake's infrared radiation detector and provokes it into producing a rattling sound. This allows the squirrels to determine the size and location of the snake.

| | |
|---|---|
| **[Name]** | *Otospermophilus beecheyi* |
| **[Classification]** | Class: Mammalia<br>Order: Rodentia<br>Family: Sciuridae |
| **[Length]** | Approximately 30-50 cm (12-20 in) |

## ANIMAL 37 RATTLESNAKE

THE REAL THING

A western diamondback rattlesnake in Arizona. The rattle can be seen at the bottom right.

Photo: Ardea/Aflo

Rattlesnakes are venomous snakes that can reach up to 240 centimeters (8 ft) in length. They have a rattle made of scales at the ends of their tails that they shake when threatened in order to produce a rattling sound. They are ovoviviparous and give birth to live young after theirs eggs hatch internally. They have some resistance to the venom of others of their own species, but because being bitten is still harmful, they tend to avoid each other. California squirrels use this behavior to their advantage.

| | |
|---|---|
| **[Name]** | Rattlesnake |
| **[Classification]** | Class: Reptilia<br>Order: Squamata<br>Family: Viperidae<br>Subfamily: Crotalinae |
| **[Habitat]** | The Americas |
| **[Length]** | 60-240 cm (2-8 ft) |

## ANIMAL 38 FLAMINGO

Flamingos live in salt lakes in colonies of tens of thousands. They use their beaks to scoop and eat the red algae growing at the bottom of lakes, which gives their feathers a pink hue. Flamingos feed their young a kind of bright red milk that is produced in the throats of both the females and males of the species.

LEGS CAN WITHSTAND THE HIGH-ALKALINE ENVIRONMENTS LIKE SALT LAKES

An American flamingo and its chick. The chicks' fur is white, not pink.

Photo: Juniors Bildarchiv/Aflo

THE REAL THING

| | |
|---|---|
| **[Name]** | Flamingo |
| **[Classification]** | Class: Aves<br>Order: Phoenicopteriformes<br>Family: Phoenicopteridae |
| **[Habitat]** | Southern Europe, Africa, Central and South America |
| **[Height]** | 90-140 cm (3-4.6 ft) |

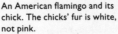

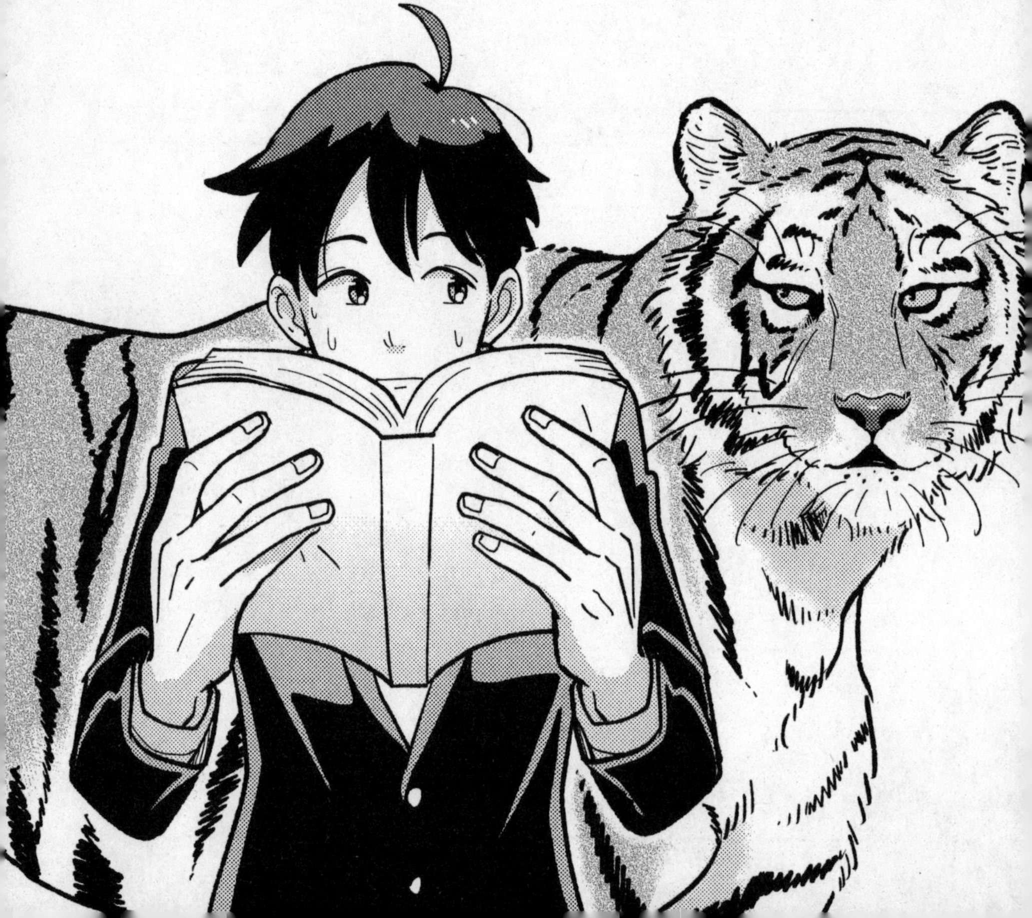

# HEAVEN'S
# DESIGN TEAM

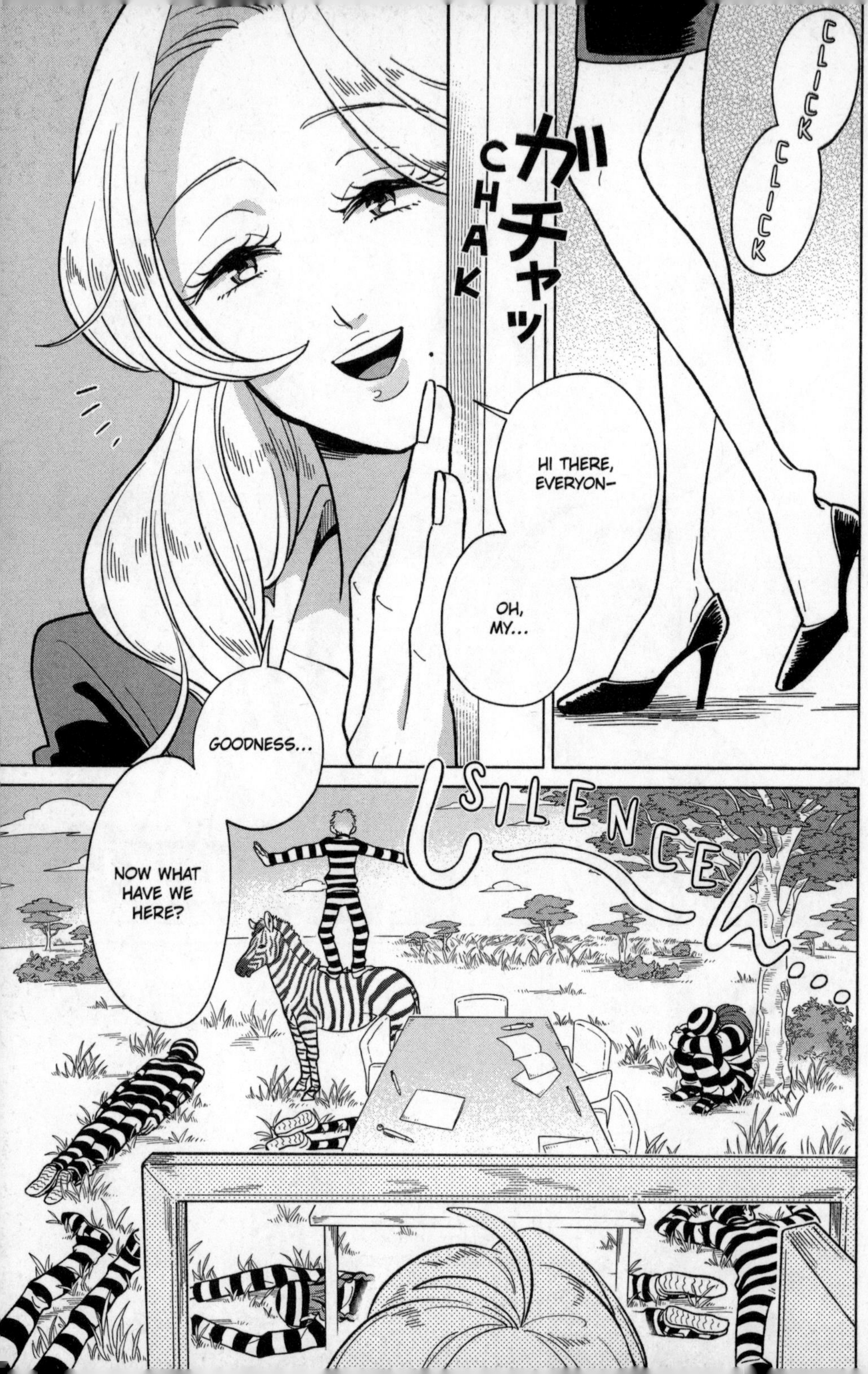
CLICK CLICK
ガチャッ
CHAK
HI THERE, EVERYON–
OH, MY...
GOODNESS...
NOW WHAT HAVE WE HERE?
SILENCE...

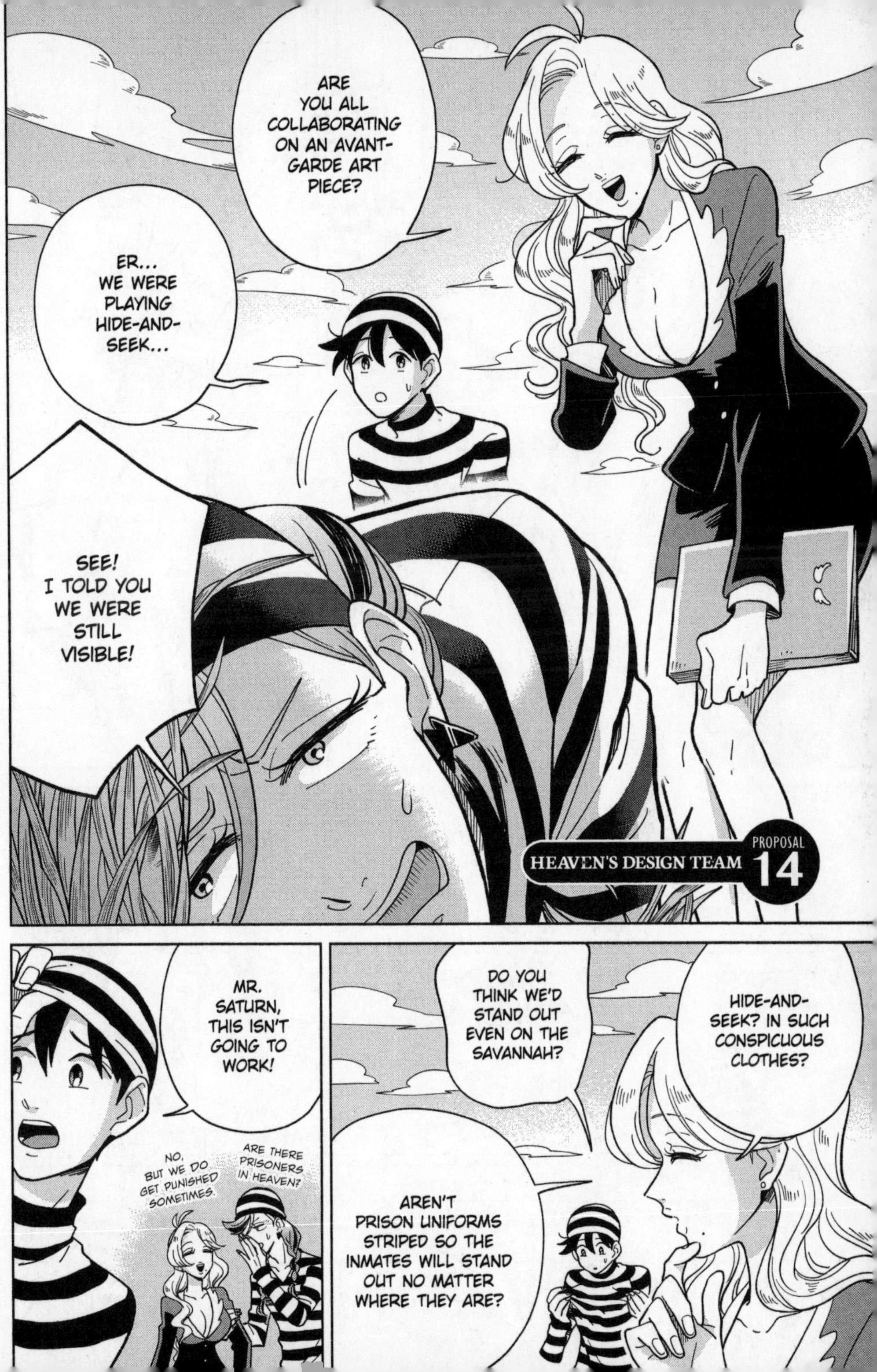
ARE YOU ALL COLLABORATING ON AN AVANT-GARDE ART PIECE?
ER... WE WERE PLAYING HIDE-AND-SEEK...
SEE! I TOLD YOU WE WERE STILL VISIBLE!
HEAVEN'S DESIGN TEAM
PROPOSAL 14
HIDE-AND-SEEK? IN SUCH CONSPICUOUS CLOTHES?
DO YOU THINK WE'D STAND OUT EVEN ON THE SAVANNAH?
AREN'T PRISON UNIFORMS STRIPED SO THE INMATES WILL STAND OUT NO MATTER WHERE THEY ARE?
MR. SATURN, THIS ISN'T GOING TO WORK!
ARE THERE PRISONERS IN HEAVEN?
NO, BUT WE DO GET PUNISHED SOMETIMES.

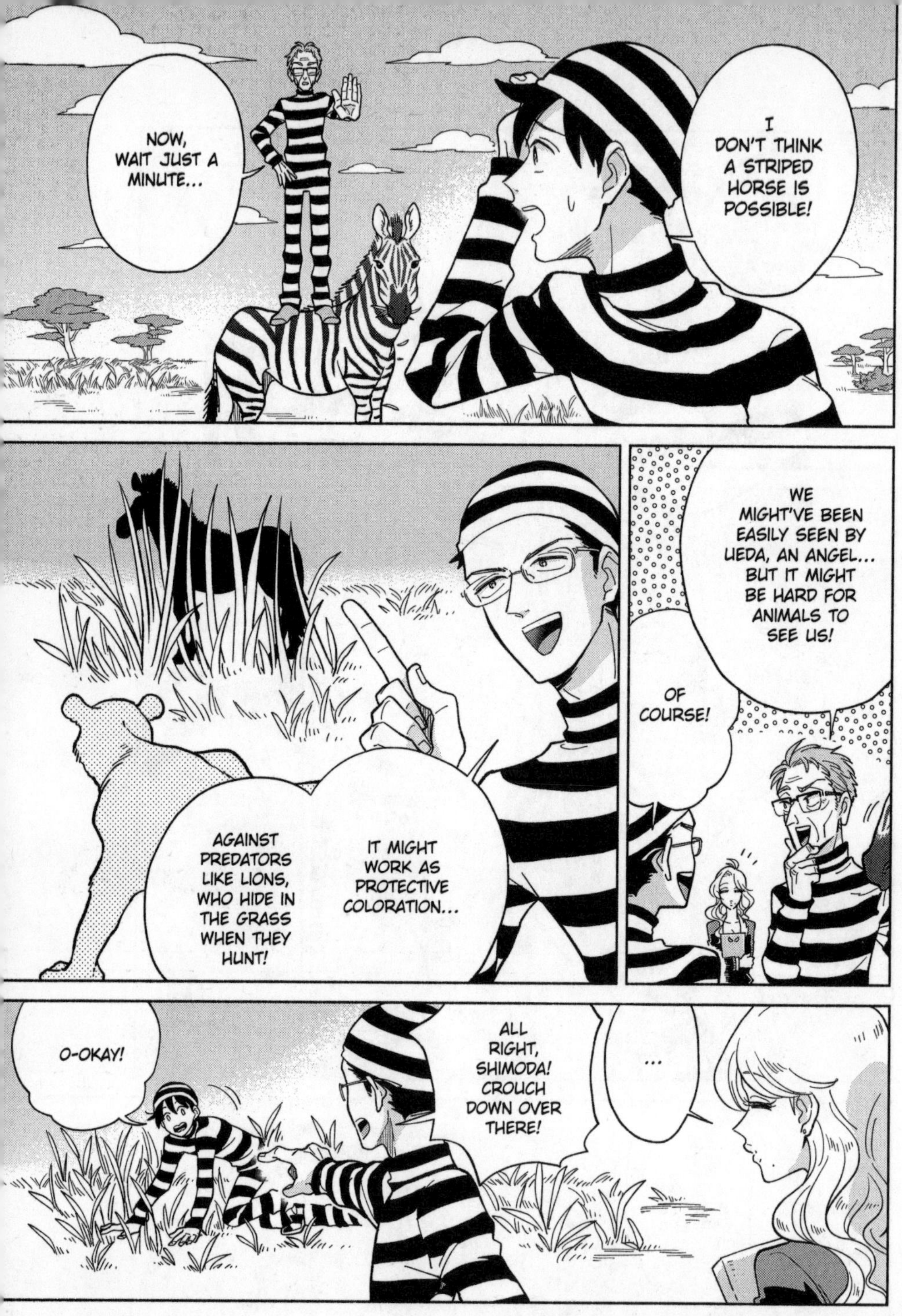
I DON'T THINK A STRIPED HORSE IS POSSIBLE!
NOW, WAIT JUST A MINUTE...
WE MIGHT'VE BEEN EASILY SEEN BY UEDA, AN ANGEL... BUT IT MIGHT BE HARD FOR ANIMALS TO SEE US!
OF COURSE!
IT MIGHT WORK AS PROTECTIVE COLORATION...
AGAINST PREDATORS LIKE LIONS, WHO HIDE IN THE GRASS WHEN THEY HUNT!
...
ALL RIGHT, SHIMODA! CROUCH DOWN OVER THERE!
O-OKAY!

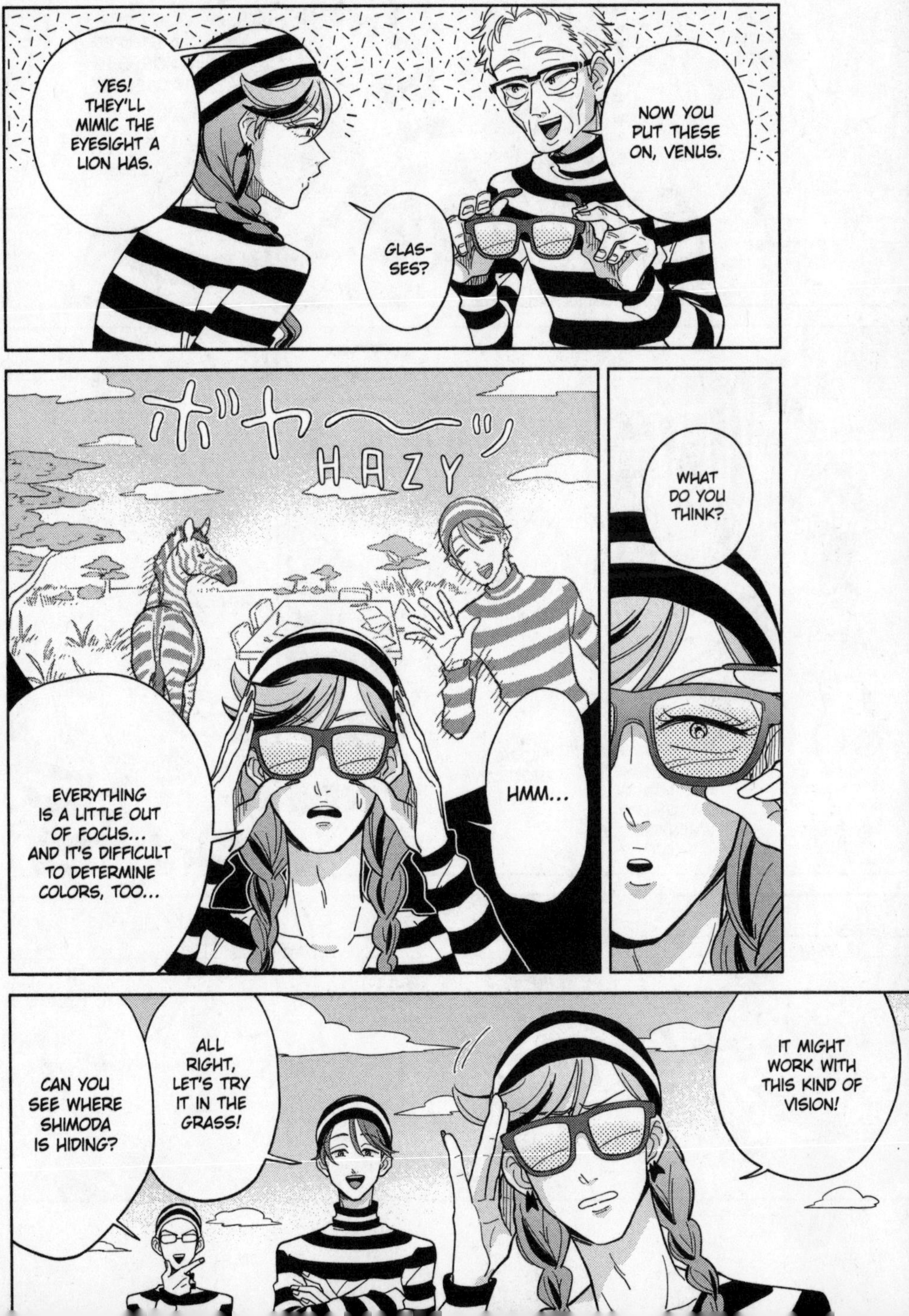
NOW YOU PUT THESE ON, VENUS.
GLAS-SES?
YES! THEY'LL MIMIC THE EYESIGHT A LION HAS.
WHAT DO YOU THINK?
ボヤ〜〜ッ
HAZY
HMM...
EVERYTHING IS A LITTLE OUT OF FOCUS... AND IT'S DIFFICULT TO DETERMINE COLORS, TOO...
IT MIGHT WORK WITH THIS KIND OF VISION!
ALL RIGHT, LET'S TRY IT IN THE GRASS!
CAN YOU SEE WHERE SHIMODA IS HIDING?

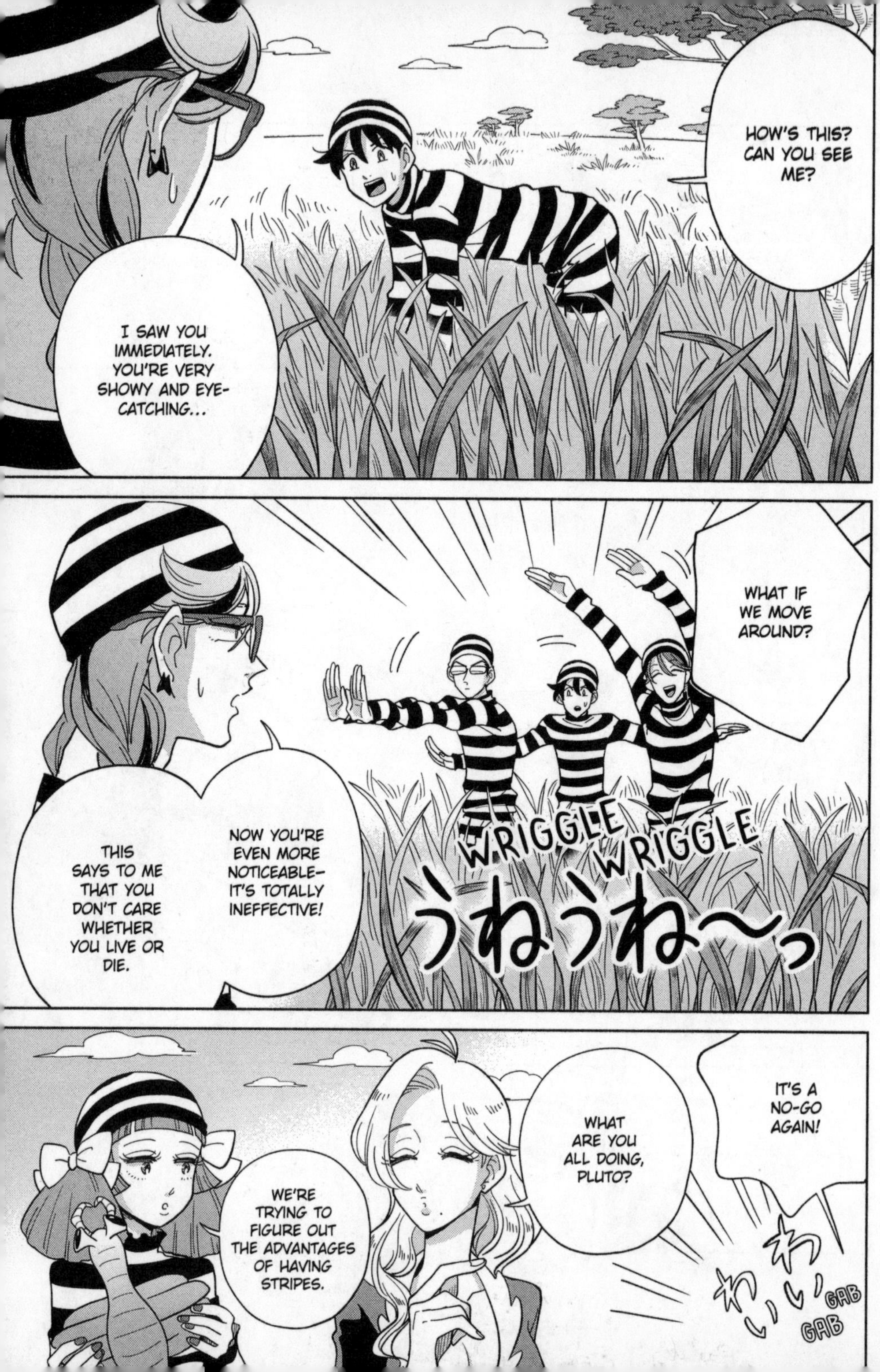
HOW'S THIS? CAN YOU SEE ME?
I SAW YOU IMMEDIATELY. YOU'RE VERY SHOWY AND EYE-CATCHING...
WHAT IF WE MOVE AROUND?
WRIGGLE WRIGGLE
うねうね～っ
NOW YOU'RE EVEN MORE NOTICEABLE-IT'S TOTALLY INEFFECTIVE!
THIS SAYS TO ME THAT YOU DON'T CARE WHETHER YOU LIVE OR DIE.
IT'S A NO-GO AGAIN!
わいわい
GAB GAB
WHAT ARE YOU ALL DOING, PLUTO?
WE'RE TRYING TO FIGURE OUT THE ADVANTAGES OF HAVING STRIPES.

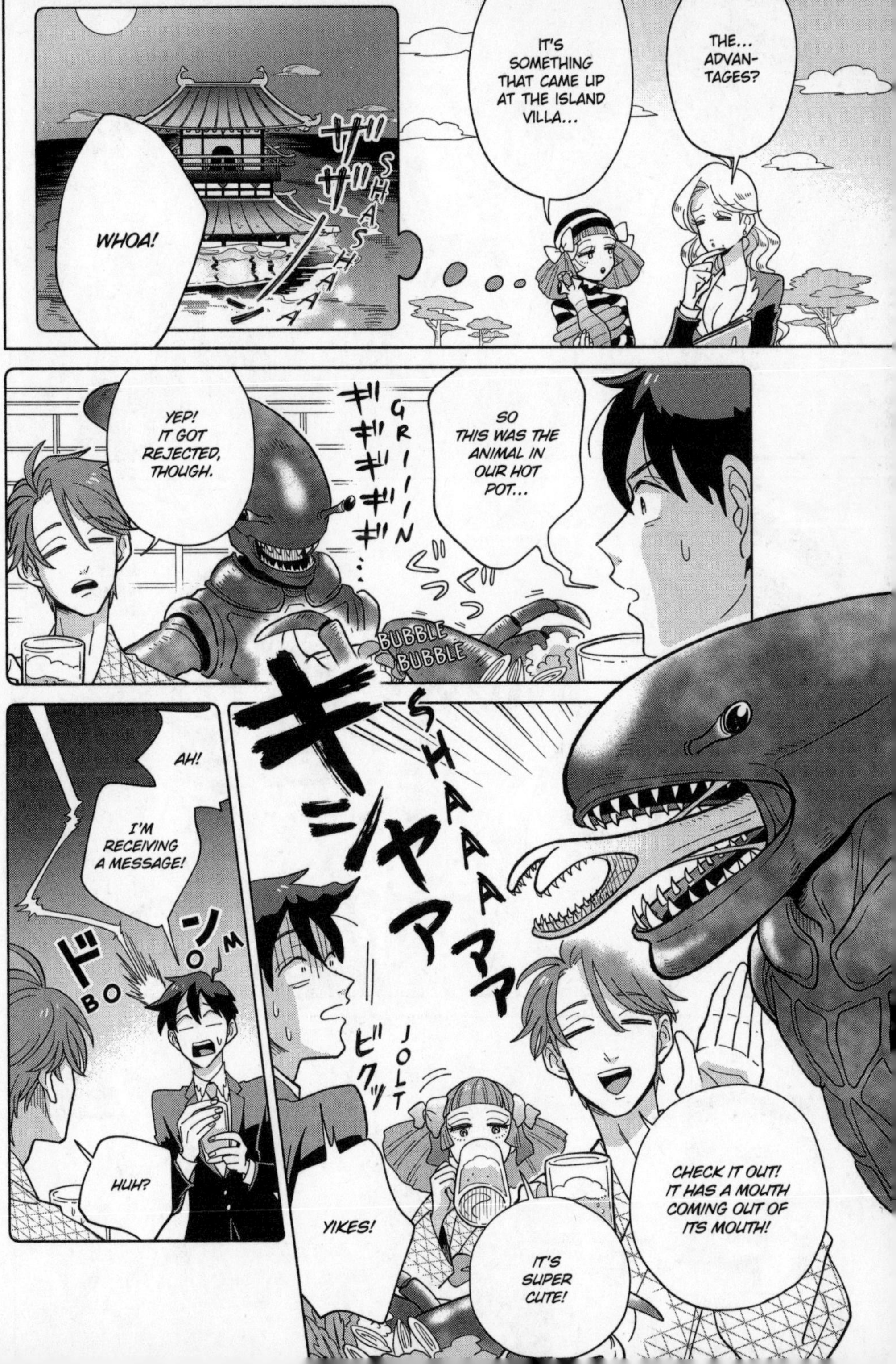
THE... ADVANTAGES?
IT'S SOMETHING THAT CAME UP AT THE ISLAND VILLA...
SHASHAAA
WHOA!
SO THIS WAS THE ANIMAL IN OUR HOT POT...
GRIIIN
YEP! IT GOT REJECTED, THOUGH.
BUBBLE BUBBLE
SHAAAA
CHECK IT OUT! IT HAS A MOUTH COMING OUT OF ITS MOUTH!
JOLT
IT'S SUPER CUTE!
YIKES!
AH!
I'M RECEIVING A MESSAGE!
BOOM
HUH?

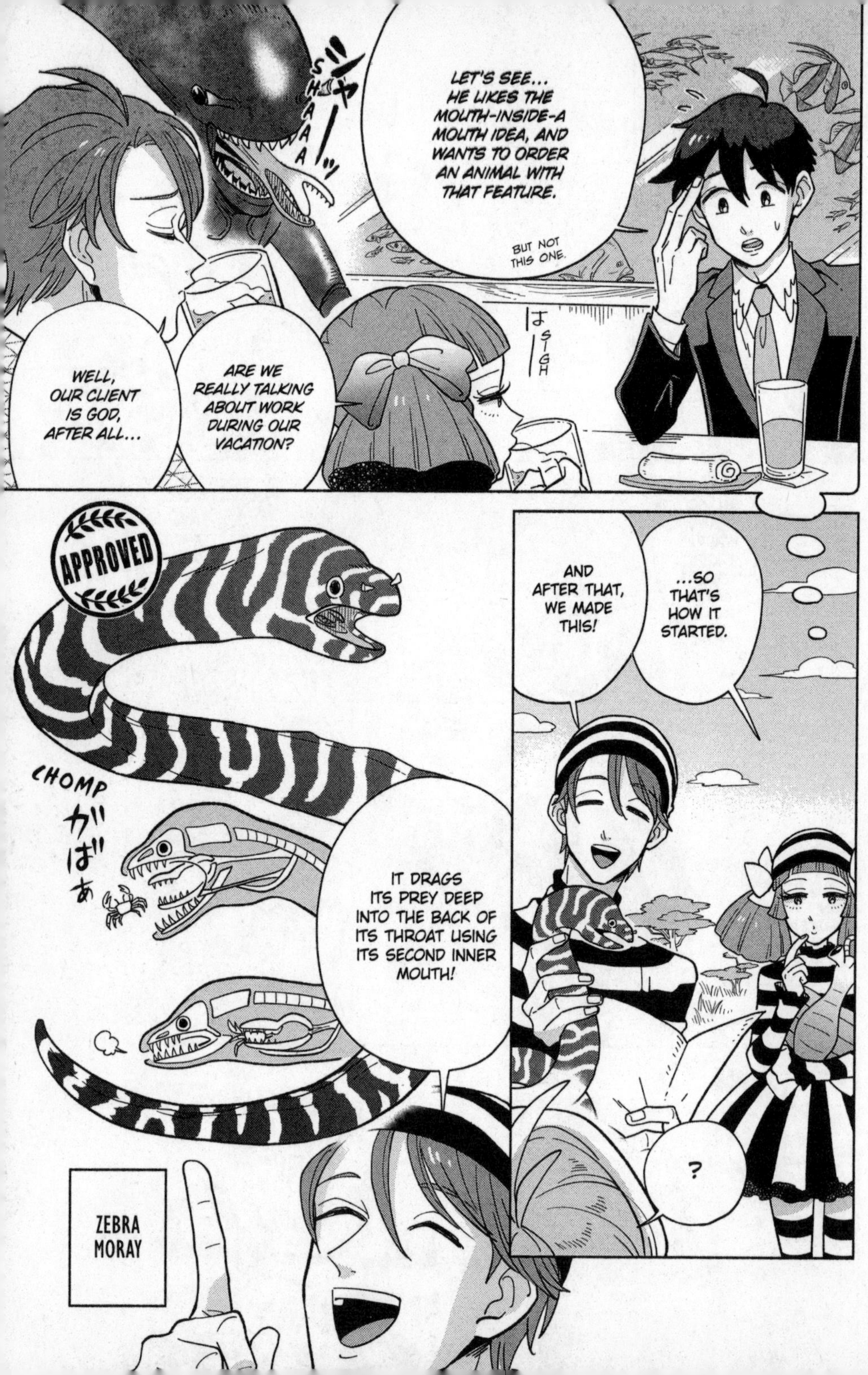

LET'S SEE... HE LIKES THE MOUTH-INSIDE-A MOUTH IDEA, AND WANTS TO ORDER AN ANIMAL WITH THAT FEATURE.
BUT NOT THIS ONE.
ジャーッ SHAAAA
は SIGH
ARE WE REALLY TALKING ABOUT WORK DURING OUR VACATION?
WELL, OUR CLIENT IS GOD, AFTER ALL...
...SO THAT'S HOW IT STARTED.
AND AFTER THAT, WE MADE THIS!
?
APPROVED
CHOMP がばぁ
IT DRAGS ITS PREY DEEP INTO THE BACK OF ITS THROAT USING ITS SECOND INNER MOUTH!
ZEBRA MORAY

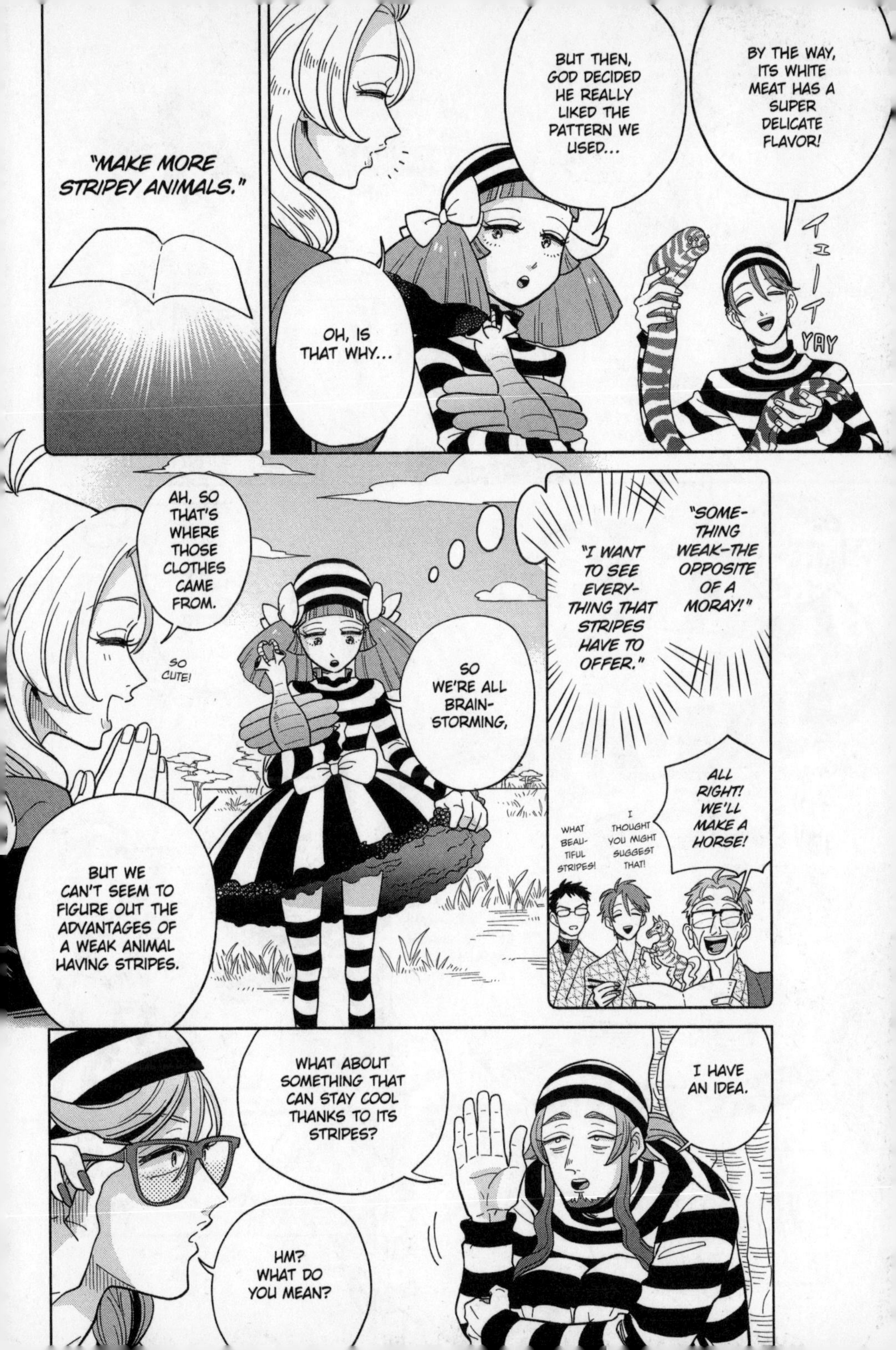

BY THE WAY, ITS WHITE MEAT HAS A SUPER DELICATE FLAVOR!
イェーイ
YAY
BUT THEN, GOD DECIDED HE REALLY LIKED THE PATTERN WE USED...
OH, IS THAT WHY...
"MAKE MORE STRIPEY ANIMALS."
"SOMETHING WEAK—THE OPPOSITE OF A MORAY!"
"I WANT TO SEE EVERYTHING THAT STRIPES HAVE TO OFFER."
ALL RIGHT! WE'LL MAKE A HORSE!
I THOUGHT YOU MIGHT SUGGEST THAT!
WHAT BEAUTIFUL STRIPES!
SO WE'RE ALL BRAINSTORMING,
AH, SO THAT'S WHERE THOSE CLOTHES CAME FROM.
SO CUTE!
BUT WE CAN'T SEEM TO FIGURE OUT THE ADVANTAGES OF A WEAK ANIMAL HAVING STRIPES.
I HAVE AN IDEA.
WHAT ABOUT SOMETHING THAT CAN STAY COOL THANKS TO ITS STRIPES?
HM? WHAT DO YOU MEAN?

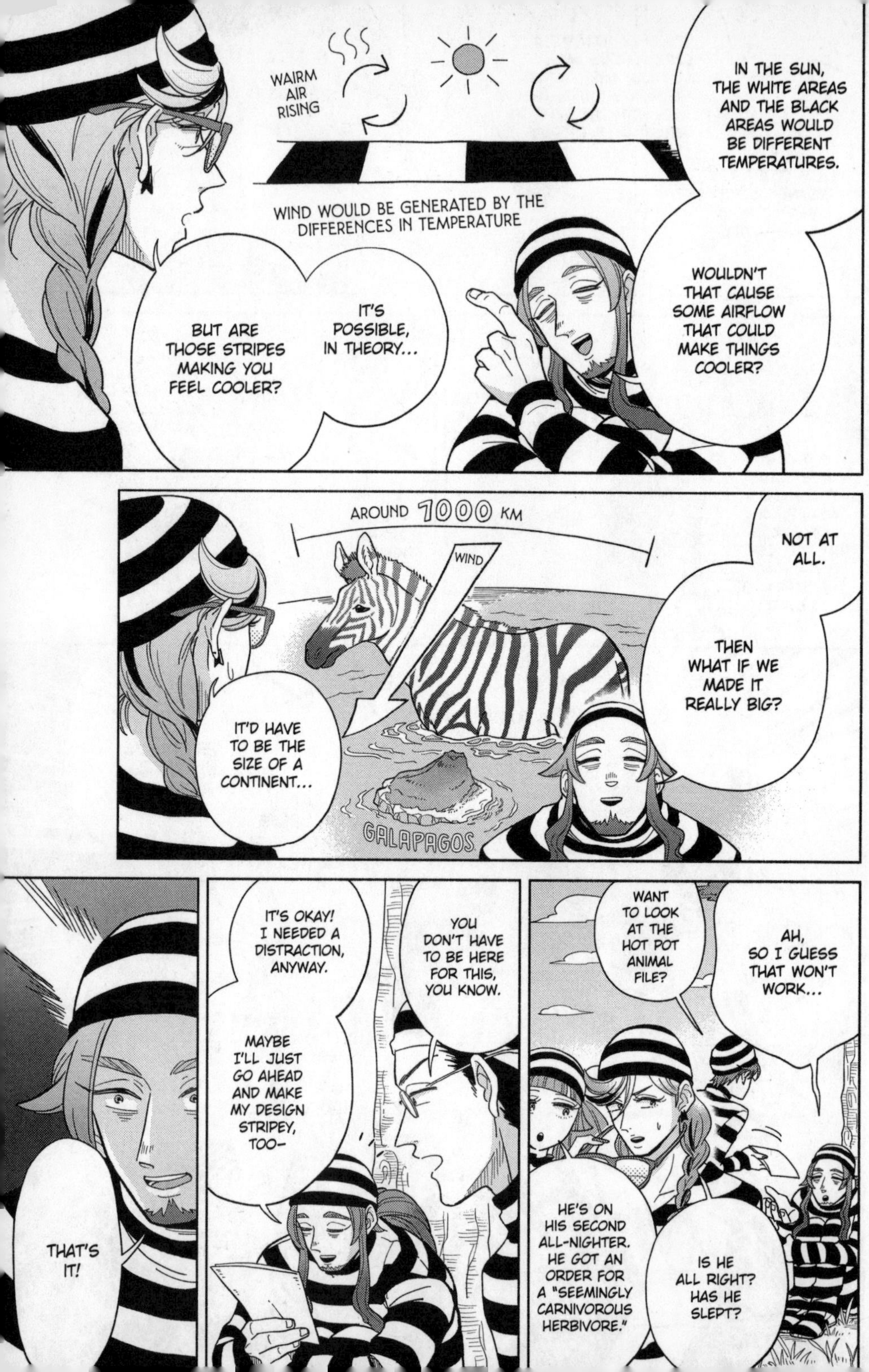
IN THE SUN, THE WHITE AREAS AND THE BLACK AREAS WOULD BE DIFFERENT TEMPERATURES.
WAIRM AIR RISING
WIND WOULD BE GENERATED BY THE DIFFERENCES IN TEMPERATURE
WOULDN'T THAT CAUSE SOME AIRFLOW THAT COULD MAKE THINGS COOLER?
IT'S POSSIBLE, IN THEORY...
BUT ARE THOSE STRIPES MAKING YOU FEEL COOLER?
AROUND 1000 KM
WIND
NOT AT ALL.
THEN WHAT IF WE MADE IT REALLY BIG?
IT'D HAVE TO BE THE SIZE OF A CONTINENT...
GALAPAGOS
AH, SO I GUESS THAT WON'T WORK...
WANT TO LOOK AT THE HOT POT ANIMAL FILE?
IS HE ALL RIGHT? HAS HE SLEPT?
HE'S ON HIS SECOND ALL-NIGHTER. HE GOT AN ORDER FOR A "SEEMINGLY CARNIVOROUS HERBIVORE."
YOU DON'T HAVE TO BE HERE FOR THIS, YOU KNOW.
IT'S OKAY! I NEEDED A DISTRACTION, ANYWAY.
MAYBE I'LL JUST GO AHEAD AND MAKE MY DESIGN STRIPEY, TOO-
THAT'S IT!

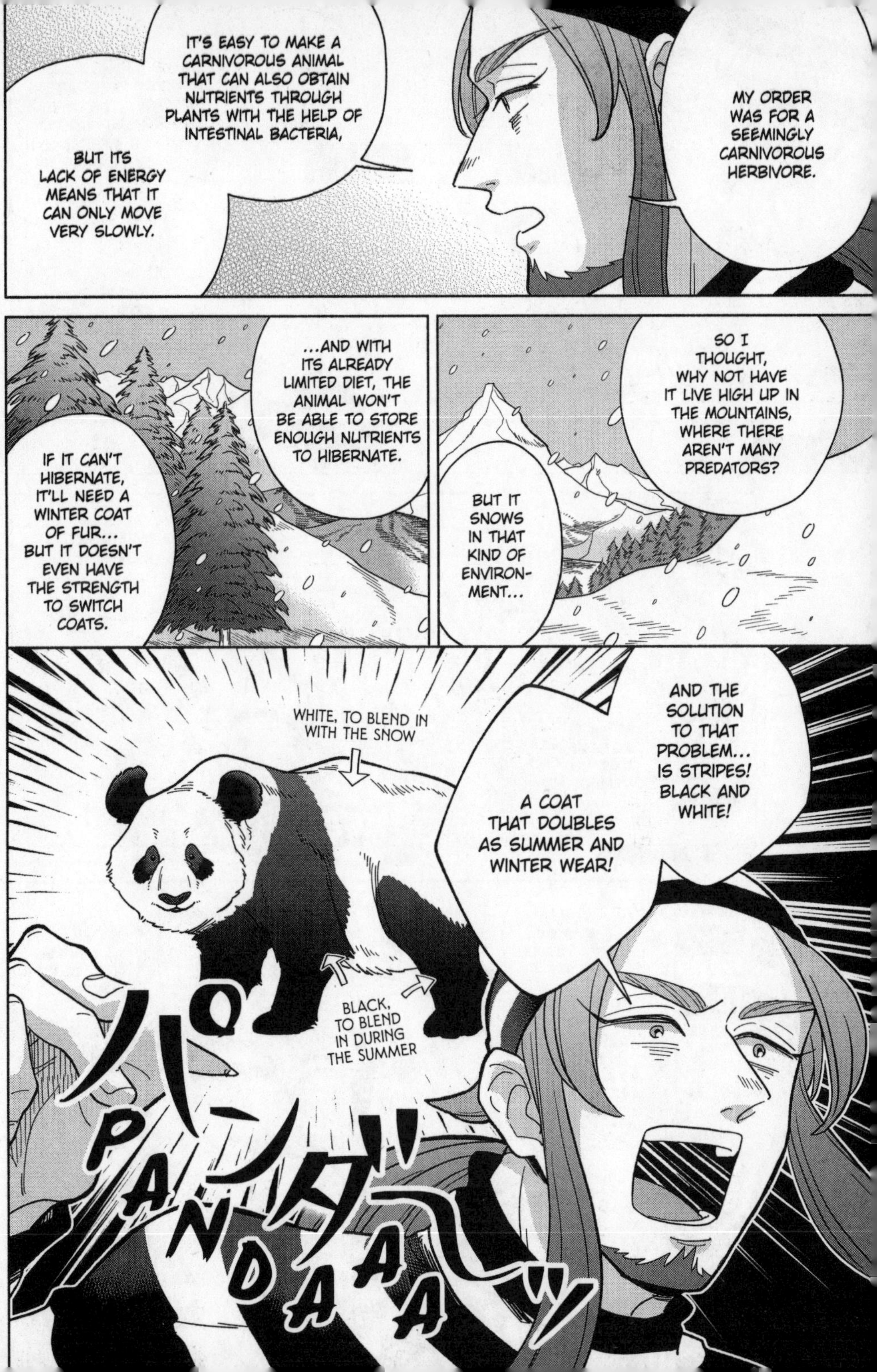
MY ORDER WAS FOR A SEEMINGLY CARNIVOROUS HERBIVORE.
IT'S EASY TO MAKE A CARNIVOROUS ANIMAL THAT CAN ALSO OBTAIN NUTRIENTS THROUGH PLANTS WITH THE HELP OF INTESTINAL BACTERIA,
BUT ITS LACK OF ENERGY MEANS THAT IT CAN ONLY MOVE VERY SLOWLY.
SO I THOUGHT, WHY NOT HAVE IT LIVE HIGH UP IN THE MOUNTAINS, WHERE THERE AREN'T MANY PREDATORS?
BUT IT SNOWS IN THAT KIND OF ENVIRON-MENT...
...AND WITH ITS ALREADY LIMITED DIET, THE ANIMAL WON'T BE ABLE TO STORE ENOUGH NUTRIENTS TO HIBERNATE.
IF IT CAN'T HIBERNATE, IT'LL NEED A WINTER COAT OF FUR... BUT IT DOESN'T EVEN HAVE THE STRENGTH TO SWITCH COATS.
AND THE SOLUTION TO THAT PROBLEM... IS STRIPES! BLACK AND WHITE!
A COAT THAT DOUBLES AS SUMMER AND WINTER WEAR!
WHITE, TO BLEND IN WITH THE SNOW
BLACK, TO BLEND IN DURING THE SUMMER
PANDAAA

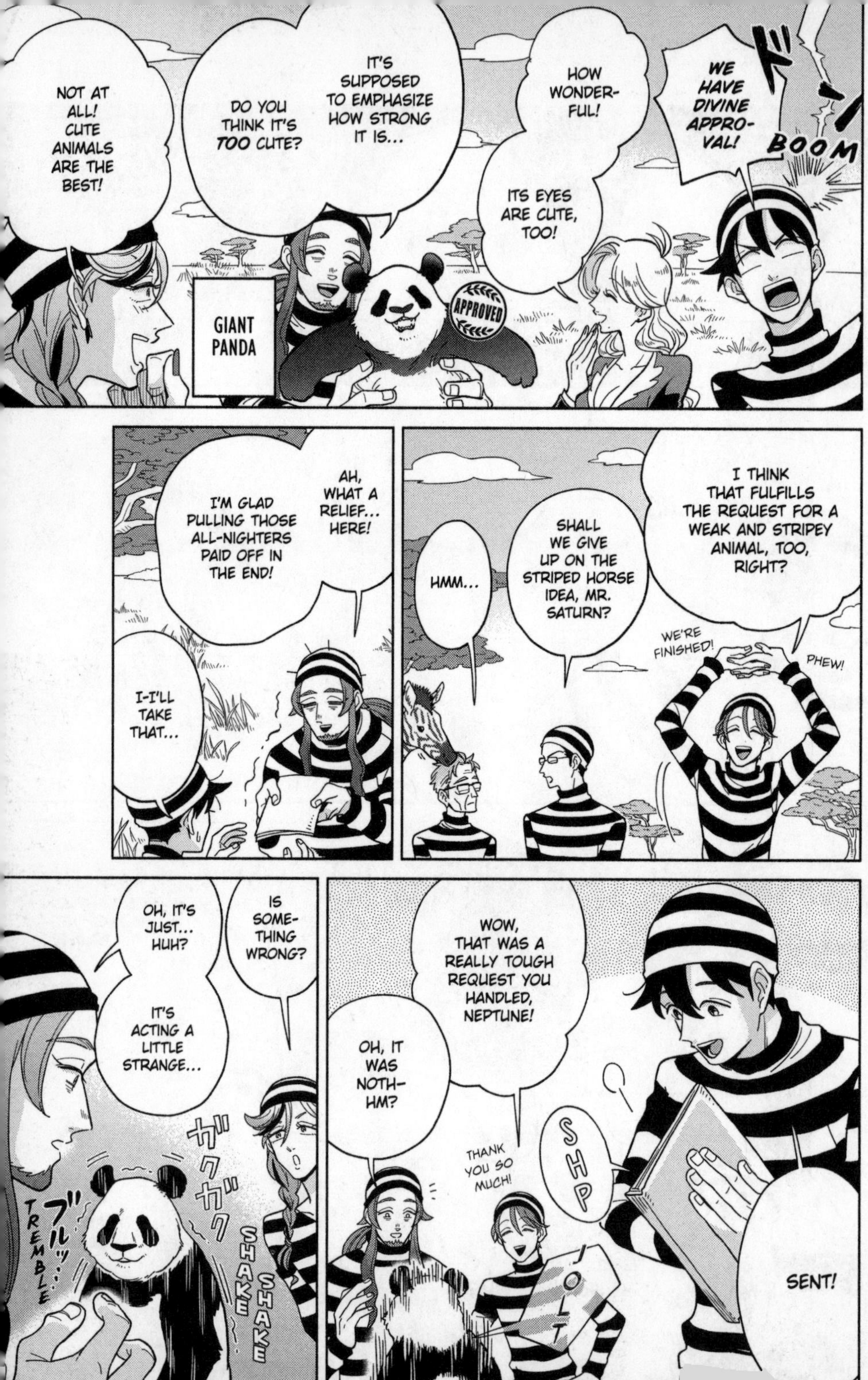
WE HAVE DIVINE APPRO-VAL!
BOOM
HOW WONDER-FUL!
ITS EYES ARE CUTE, TOO!
IT'S SUPPOSED TO EMPHASIZE HOW STRONG IT IS...
DO YOU THINK IT'S *TOO* CUTE?
NOT AT ALL! CUTE ANIMALS ARE THE BEST!
APPROVED
GIANT PANDA
I THINK THAT FULFILLS THE REQUEST FOR A WEAK AND STRIPEY ANIMAL, TOO, RIGHT?
PHEW!
WE'RE FINISHED!
SHALL WE GIVE UP ON THE STRIPED HORSE IDEA, MR. SATURN?
HMM...
AH, WHAT A RELIEF... HERE!
I'M GLAD PULLING THOSE ALL-NIGHTERS PAID OFF IN THE END!
I-I'LL TAKE THAT...
WOW, THAT WAS A REALLY TOUGH REQUEST YOU HANDLED, NEPTUNE!
SENT!
SHP
THANK YOU SO MUCH!
OH, IT WAS NOTH-HM?
IS SOME-THING WRONG?
OH, IT'S JUST... HUH?
IT'S ACTING A LITTLE STRANGE...
ガクガク
SHAKE SHAKE
ブルッ
TREMBLE

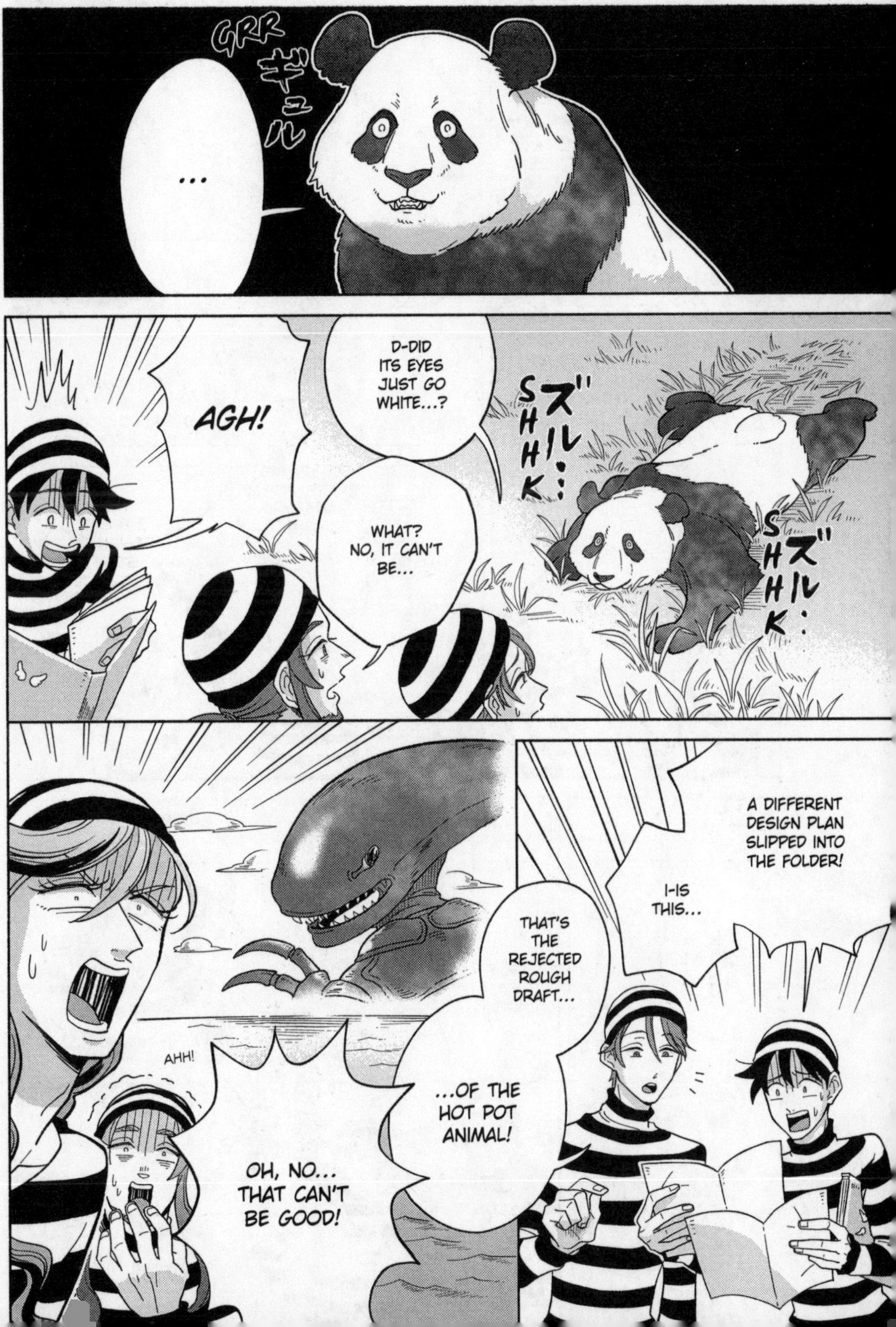
GRR
ギュル
...
ズル：
SHHK
ズル…
SHHK
D-DID ITS EYES JUST GO WHITE...?
WHAT? NO, IT CAN'T BE...
AGH!
A DIFFERENT DESIGN PLAN SLIPPED INTO THE FOLDER!
I-IS THIS...
THAT'S THE REJECTED ROUGH DRAFT...
...OF THE HOT POT ANIMAL!
AHH!
OH, NO... THAT CAN'T BE GOOD!

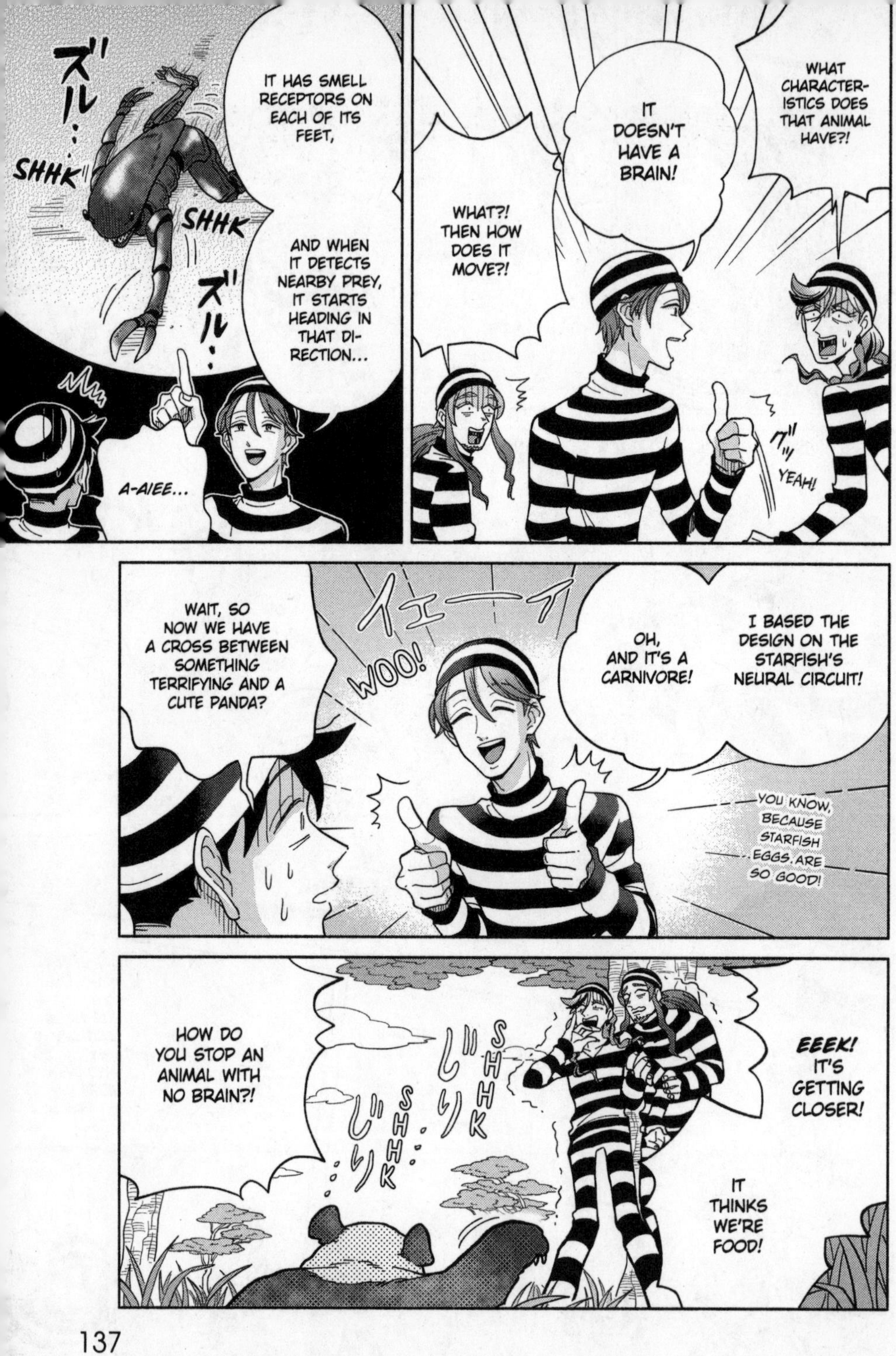
WHAT CHARACTER-ISTICS DOES THAT ANIMAL HAVE?!
IT DOESN'T HAVE A BRAIN!
WHAT?! THEN HOW DOES IT MOVE?!
グッ
YEAH!
IT HAS SMELL RECEPTORS ON EACH OF ITS FEET,
ズル…
SHHK
SHHK
ズル…
AND WHEN IT DETECTS NEARBY PREY, IT STARTS HEADING IN THAT DI-RECTION…
A-AIEE…
I BASED THE DESIGN ON THE STARFISH'S NEURAL CIRCUIT!
OH, AND IT'S A CARNIVORE!
YOU KNOW, BECAUSE STARFISH EGGS ARE SO GOOD!
イエーイ
WOO!
WAIT, SO NOW WE HAVE A CROSS BETWEEN SOMETHING TERRIFYING AND A CUTE PANDA?
EEEK! IT'S GETTING CLOSER!
IT THINKS WE'RE FOOD!
じり
SHHK
じり
SHHK
HOW DO YOU STOP AN ANIMAL WITH NO BRAIN?!

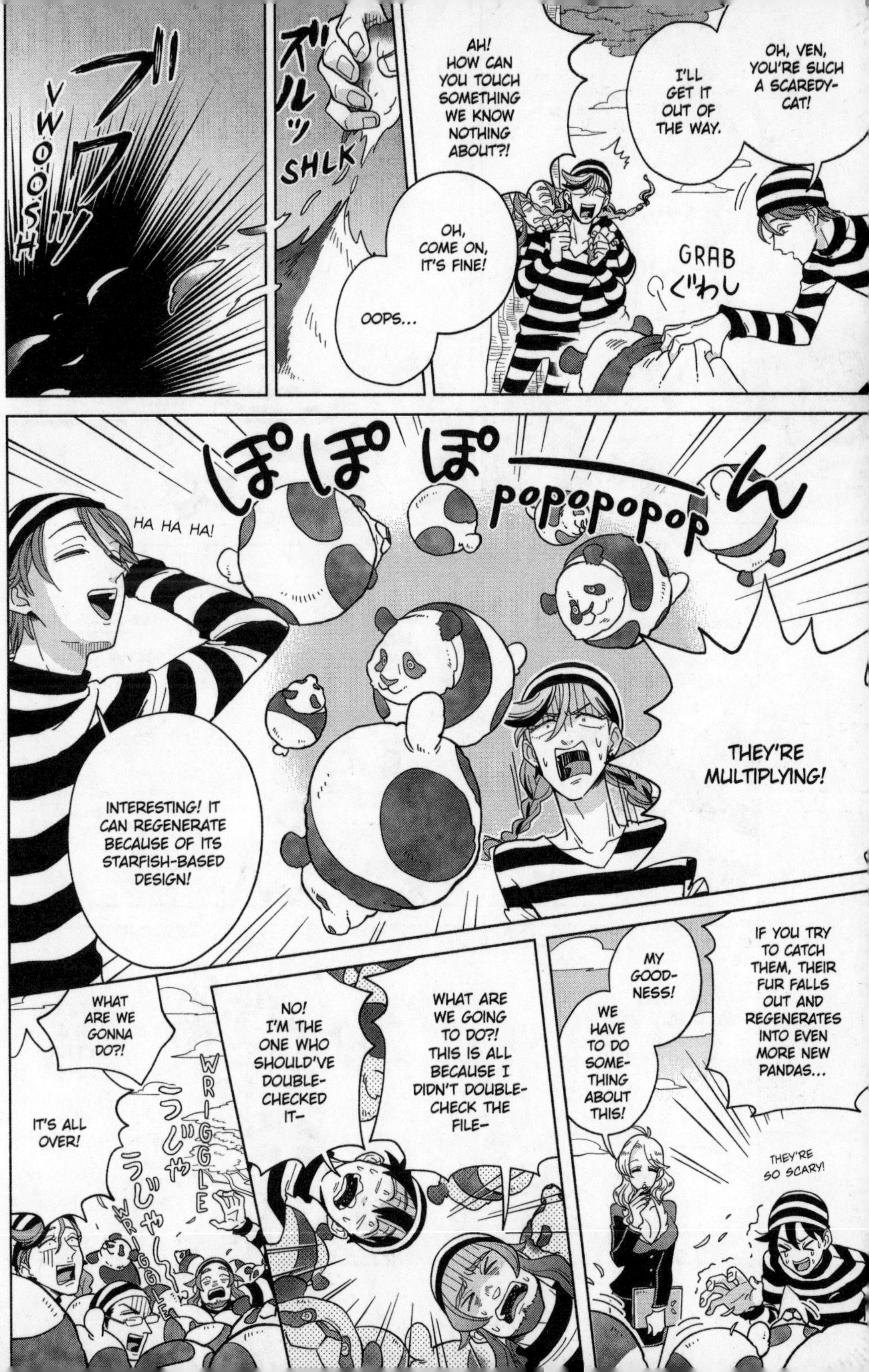
OH, VEN, YOU'RE SUCH A SCAREDY-CAT!
I'LL GET IT OUT OF THE WAY.
AH! HOW CAN YOU TOUCH SOMETHING WE KNOW NOTHING ABOUT?!
GRAB ぐわし
OH, COME ON, IT'S FINE!
OOPS...
ズルッ SHLK
ブワ VWOOSH
ぽぽぽーん popopopop
THEY'RE MULTIPLYING!
HA HA HA!
INTERESTING! IT CAN REGENERATE BECAUSE OF ITS STARFISH-BASED DESIGN!
IF YOU TRY TO CATCH THEM, THEIR FUR FALLS OUT AND REGENERATES INTO EVEN MORE NEW PANDAS...
MY GOODNESS!
WE HAVE TO DO SOMETHING ABOUT THIS!
THEY'RE SO SCARY!
WHAT ARE WE GOING TO DO?! THIS IS ALL BECAUSE I DIDN'T DOUBLE-CHECK THE FILE-
NO! I'M THE ONE WHO SHOULD'VE DOUBLE-CHECKED IT-
WHAT ARE WE GONNA DO?!
うじゃうじゃ WRIGGLE WRIGGLE
IT'S ALL OVER!

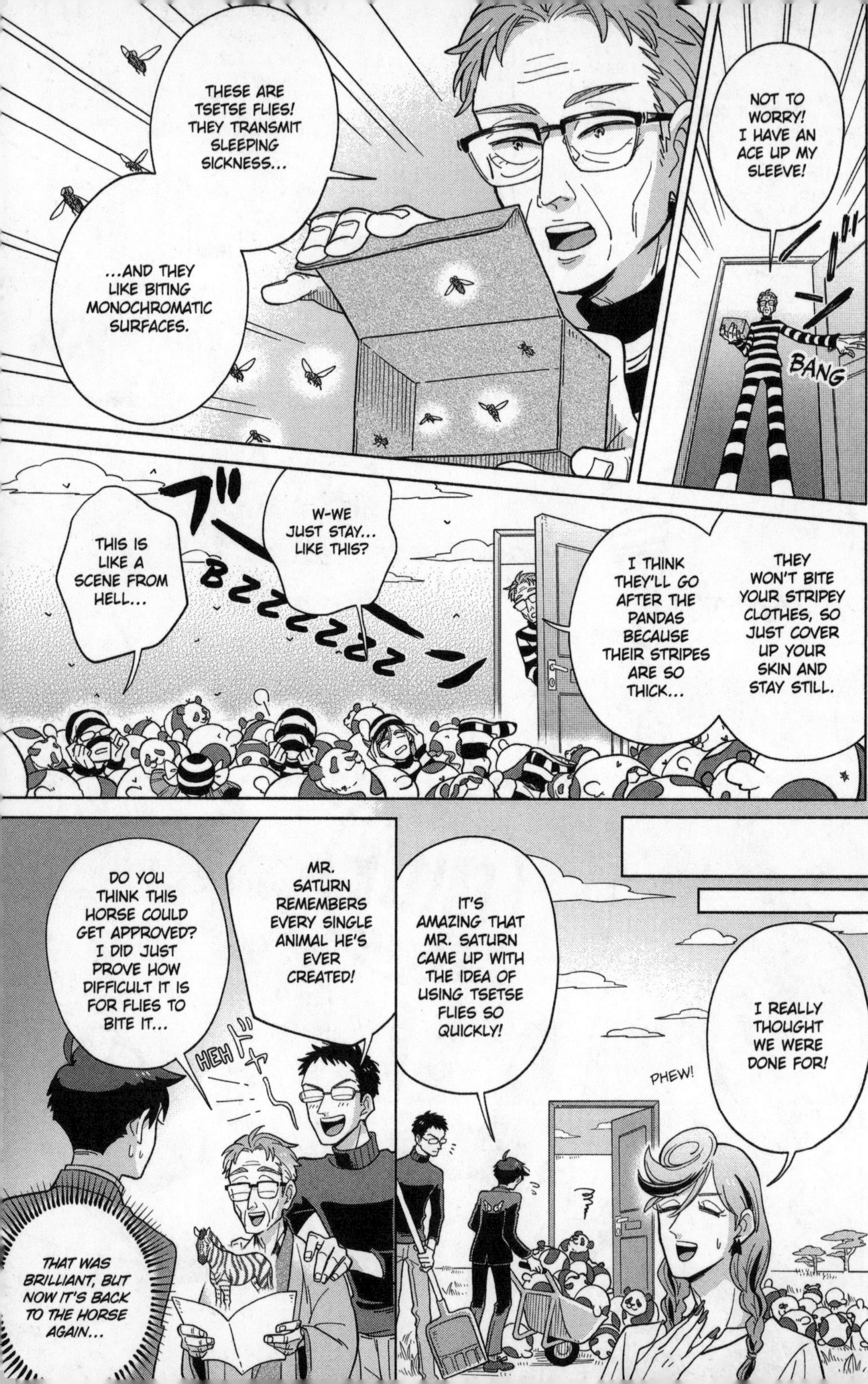
NOT TO WORRY! I HAVE AN ACE UP MY SLEEVE!
BANG
THESE ARE TSETSE FLIES! THEY TRANSMIT SLEEPING SICKNESS...
...AND THEY LIKE BITING MONOCHROMATIC SURFACES.
THEY WON'T BITE YOUR STRIPEY CLOTHES, SO JUST COVER UP YOUR SKIN AND STAY STILL.
I THINK THEY'LL GO AFTER THE PANDAS BECAUSE THEIR STRIPES ARE SO THICK...
W-WE JUST STAY... LIKE THIS?
BZZZZZZZZZ
THIS IS LIKE A SCENE FROM HELL...
I REALLY THOUGHT WE WERE DONE FOR!
PHEW!
IT'S AMAZING THAT MR. SATURN CAME UP WITH THE IDEA OF USING TSETSE FLIES SO QUICKLY!
MR. SATURN REMEMBERS EVERY SINGLE ANIMAL HE'S EVER CREATED!
HEH
DO YOU THINK THIS HORSE COULD GET APPROVED? I DID JUST PROVE HOW DIFFICULT IT IS FOR FLIES TO BITE IT...
THAT WAS BRILLIANT, BUT NOW IT'S BACK TO THE HORSE AGAIN...

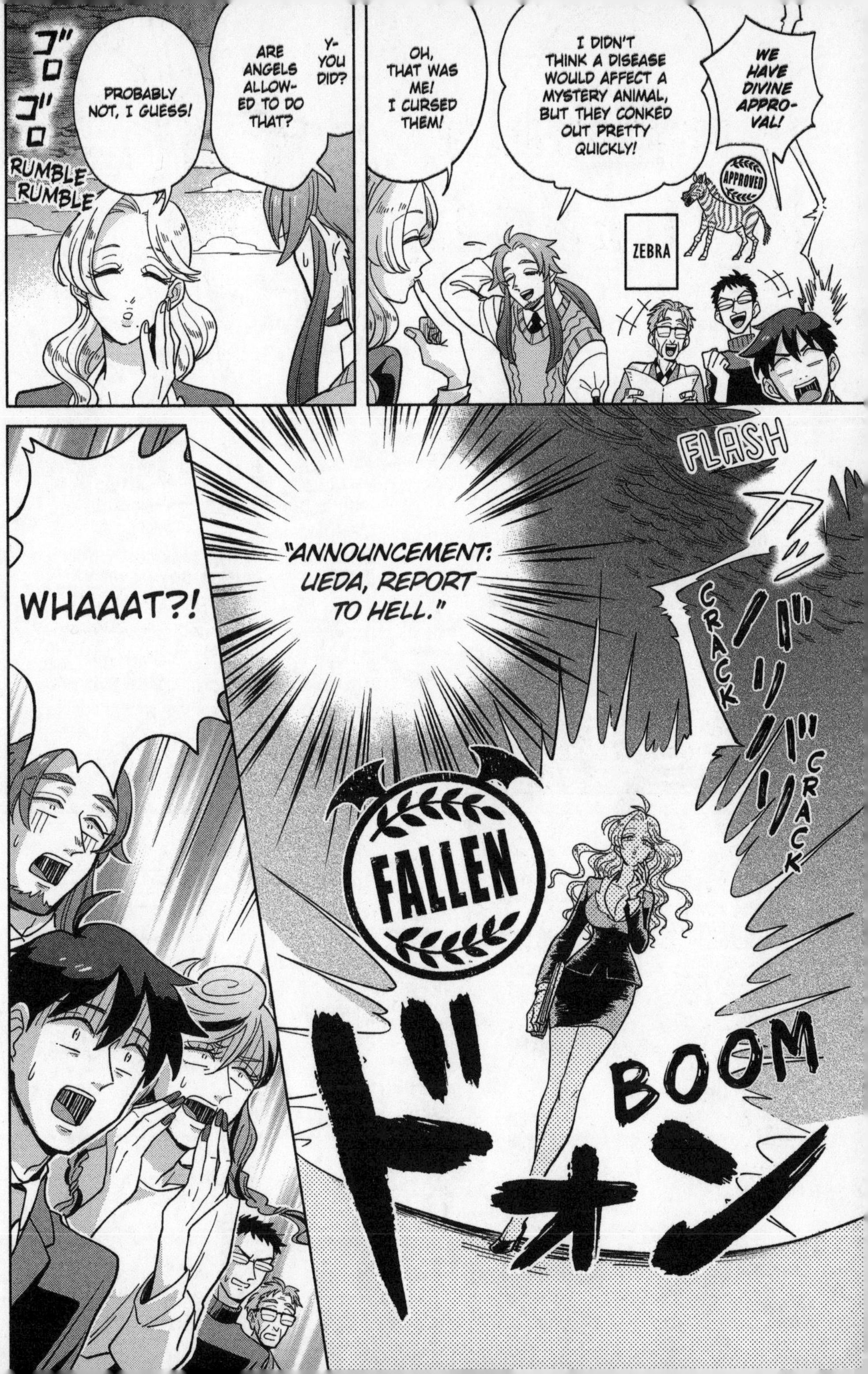
WE HAVE DIVINE APPROVAL!
I DIDN'T THINK A DISEASE WOULD AFFECT A MYSTERY ANIMAL, BUT THEY CONKED OUT PRETTY QUICKLY!
OH, THAT WAS ME! I CURSED THEM!
APPROVED
ZEBRA
Y-YOU DID?
ARE ANGELS ALLOWED TO DO THAT?
PROBABLY NOT, I GUESS!
ゴロゴロ
RUMBLE RUMBLE
FLASH
CRACK
バリバリ
CRACK
"ANNOUNCEMENT: UEDA, REPORT TO HELL."
FALLEN
BOOM
ドオン
WHAAAT?!

# THE ENCYCLOPEDIA OF
# REAL ANIMALS 14

| ANIMAL 39 | ZEBRA |
|---|---|

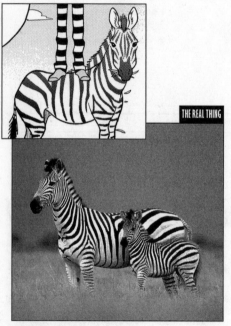

THE REAL THING

A zebra family in Botswana.
Photo: Minden Pictures/Aflo

Researchers are still speculating as to why zebras have stripes. Hypotheses such as, "in order to be less visible to predators," and "to make their bodies cooler," do not have much support these days, so the designers also questioned such theories in this chapter. The most plausible explanation is that the stripes keep disease-carrying tsetse flies from landing on the zebras' skin. Tsetse flies transmit single-celled trypanosomes which cause sleeping sickness (a disease that leads to coma and death) in humans. Recent research has found that tsetse flies can detect the polarization of light, and that while they can see big areas of homogeneous color, areas with vertical stripes may blend into the background and be difficult for them to differentiate. This means that to a tsetse fly, zebras are almost invisible.

| | |
|---|---|
| **[Name]** | Zebra |
| **[Classification]** | Class: Mammalia |
| | Order: Perissodactyla |
| | Family: Equidae |
| | Genus: *Equus* |
| **[Habitat]** | Eastern and Southern Africa |
| **[Length]** | Approximately 2.1-3 m (6.9-10 ft) |

## ANIMAL 40 | ZEBRA MORAY

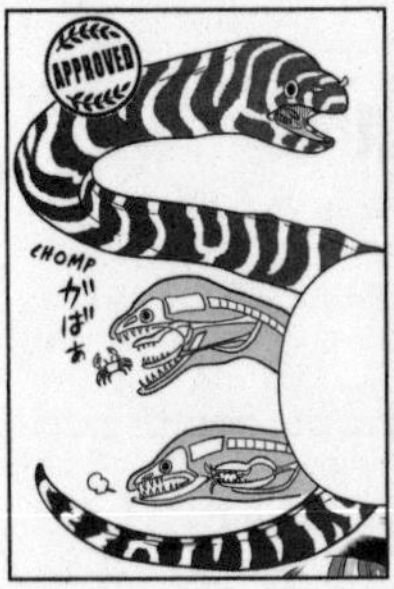
APPROVED
CHOMP
がばぁ

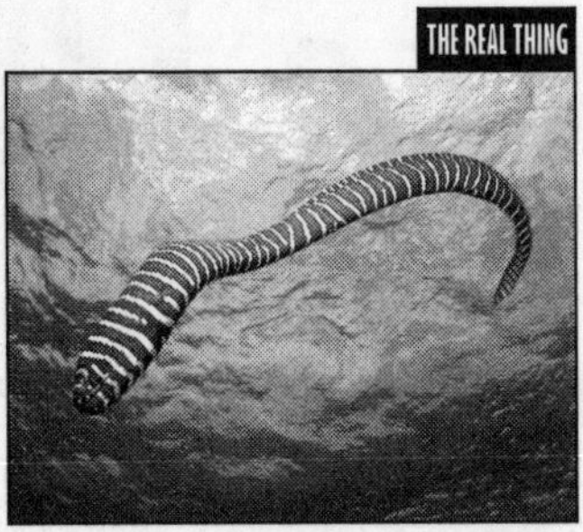
THE REAL THING

A zebra moray swimming in the oceans of Hawaii. They can also be found in some parts of Japan, including Yakushima Island.

Photo: Pacific Stock/Aflo

Like their namesake, zebra morays have beautiful stripes and are often kept in aquariums. They have a second set of jaws in their throats called pharyngeal jaws, which they use to drag their prey down their esophaguses. Though having a second mouth emerge from the throat of the first is quite alien-like, it's a feature necessary for bringing food deep into the morays' long bodies. To enjoy zebra morays at home, we recommend frying or braising the meat.

**[Name]** *Gymnomuraena zebra*
**[Classification]** Class: Actinopterygii
Order: Anguilliformes
Family: Muraenidae
Genus: *Gymnomuraena*
**[Habitat]** Pacific Ocean, Indian Ocean
**[Length]** 50-100 cm (1.6-3.3 ft)

## ANIMAL 41 | GIANT PANDA

The reasoning behind the giant panda's coloration has also long been a mystery, but recent hypotheses state that its coat doubles as both summer and winter wear. During the winter, the white areas help pandas blend into the winter landscape, while in summer, the dark areas help them blend into the shadows. Because they have the digestive organs of carnivores, they have difficulty processing bamboo efficiently. They also sometimes prey on animals such as mice.

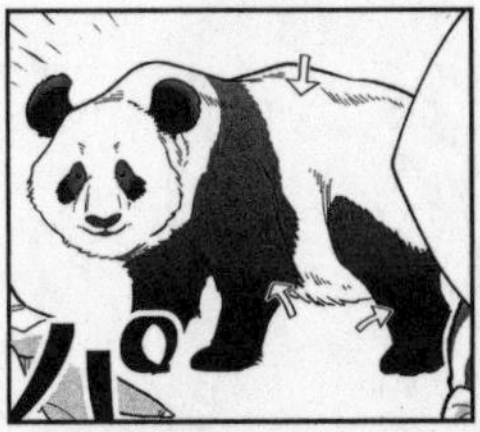

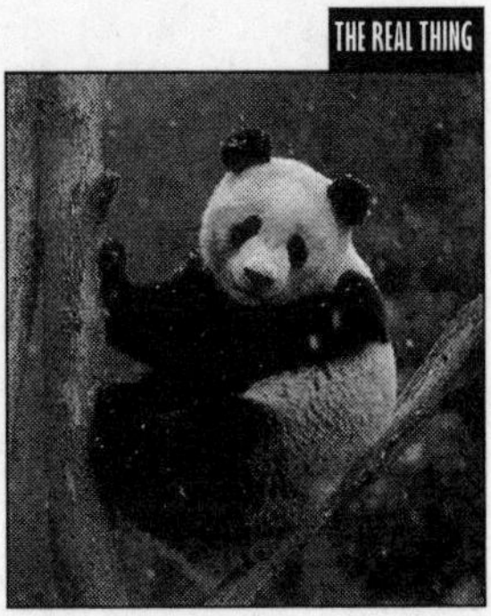
THE REAL THING

A giant panda in the snow at Wolong National Nature Reserve in China.

Photo: AGE FOTOSTOCK/Aflo

**[Name]** *Ailuropoda melanoleuca*
**[Classification]** Class: Mammalia
Order: Carnivora
Family: Ursidae
Genus: *Ailuropoda*
**[Habitat]** China
**[Height]** Approximately 1.5-1.8 m (5-6 ft)

# References

Kita, Masaki, Toshiyasu Inuzuka, Yasuo Nakamura, Hiroshi Kido, Michiyasu Yoshikuni, Satoshi D. Ohdachi, Yuichi Oba, and Daisuke Uemura. "Anesthetic substances from shrews." *Symposium on the Chemistry of Natural Products, symposium paper 45*, Session ID 31 (2003): 181-186.

Yamagiwa, Juichi. *Kodansha no Ugoku Zukan MOVE Doubutsu Shinteiban*. Japan: Kodansha, 2015.

Lavers, Chris. *Why Elephants Have Big Ears: Nature's Engines and the Orders of life*. Translated by Takao Saito. Japan: Hayakawa Publishing, 2002.

Smith, Martin R. and Jean-Bernard Caron. "Hallucigenia's head and the pharyngeal armature of early Ecdysozoans." *Nature* 523 (2015): 75-78.

Motokawa, Tatsuo. *Uni wa Sugoi Batta mo Sugoi: Design no Seibutsugaku (Chuukoushinsho 2419)*. Japan: Chukoron-Shinsha Inc., 2017.

Holden, D., John J. Socha, Nicholas D. Cardwell, and Pavlos P. Vlachos. "Aerodynamics of the flying snake *Chrysopelea paradisi*: how a bluff body cross-sectional shape contributes to gliding performance." *Journal of Experimental Biology* 217 (2014): 382-394.

*The New Encyclopedia of Aquatic Life Vol. 5: Aquatic Invertebrates II*. Edited by Andrew Campbell and John Dawes. Translated by Minoru Imajima, Toshihiko Fujita, Hiroshi Saito, Teruaki Nishikawa, Toshiaki Kuramochi, and Shunsuke Mawatari. Japan: Asakura Publishing Co., Ltd., 2007.

Barnes, R.S.K., P.J.W. Olive, D.W. Goldings, J.I. Spicer, and P. Calow. *The Invertebrates: A Synthesis*. Translated by Tatsuo Motokawa. Japan: Asakura Publishing Co., Ltd., 2009.

Funakoshi, Kimitake, University of Fukui, Kuniko Kawai, and Mizuko Yoshiyuki. *Koumori no Fushigi Sakasama Nano ni mo Wake ga Aru*. Japan: Gijutsu-Hyohron Co., Ltd., 2007.

Shiraishi, Taku. *Tondemonai Ikimonotachi: Nankyoku no Sakana wa Naze Kooranai no ka?!* Japan: Takarajimasha, Inc., 2006.

Adams, Rick A. "Ontogeny, Functional Ecology, and Evolution of Bats." Edited by Scott C. Pedersen. *Cambridge University Press*, 2000.

Gavelis, Gregory S., Shiho Hayakawa, Richard A. White III, Takashi Gojobori, Curtis A. Suttle, Patrick J. Keeling, and Brian S. Leander. "Eye-like ocelloids are built from different endosymbiotically acquired components." *Nature* 523 (2015): 204-207.

Teyssier, Jérémie, Suzanne V. Saenko, Dirk van der Marel, and Michel C. Milinkovitch. "Photonic crystals cause active colour change in chameleons." *Nature Communications* 6, 6368 (2015).

Yabe, Takashi, Supervised by Hideaki Kato. *Kodansha no Ugoku Zukan MOVE Hachuurui, Ryouseirui Kenrouban*. Japan: Kodansha, 2017.

Masuda, Modoki. *Sekai no Chameleon*. Japan: Bun-Ichi Co., Ltd., 2011.

Iwami, Tetsuo. *Nankyoku no Sakana no Seikatsu: Shuukan Asahi Hyakka Doubutsutachi no Chikyuu 94 Gyorui 10 Kasago, Karei, Fugu, Hoka*. Japan: Asahi Shimbun, 1993.

Team, Ben. *Panther Chameleon. Panther Chameleon Owners Guide*. IMB Publishing, 2016.

Holeton, George F. "Oxygen uptake and circulation by a hemoglobinless antarctic fish (*Chaenocephalus aceratus* Lonnberg) compared with three red-blooded antarctic fish." *Comparative Biochemistry and Physiology* 34, 2 (1970): 457-471.

Nakano, Hideki. *Umi no Gang. Same no Shinjitsu wo Ou. Verseau Books 028*. Japan: Seizando-Shoten Publishing Co., Ltd., 2007.

Nakaya, Kazuhiro. *Same no Ochinchin wa Futatsu. Fushigi na Same no Sekai*. Japan: Tsukiji Shokan Publishing Co., Ltd., 2003.

*Tori (I) – Dachou, Pengin, Washi, Kamo, Chidori nado*. (from The Picture Encyclopedia of Animals: *Sekai no Doubutsu*, vol. 5) Supervised by Tadashi Yoshii. Japan: Kodansha, 1982.

Ramsay, Jason B., Cheryl D. Wilga, Leif Tapanila, Jesse Pruitt, Alan Pradel, Robert Schlader, and Dominique A. Didier. "Eating with a saw for a jaw: Functional morphology of the jaws and tooth-whorl in *Helicoprion davisii*." *Journal of Morphology* 276 (2015): 47-64.

Tsuchiya, Ken. *Sekitanki: Perumki no Seibutsu*. Supervised by the Gunma Museum of Natural History. Japan: Gijutsu-Hyohron Co., Ltd., 2014.

Motokawa, Tatsuo. *Sekai Heiwa wa Namako to Tomo ni*. Japan: CCC Media House Co., Ltd., 2009.

Schilthuizen, Menno. *Nature's Nether Regions: What the Sex Lives of Bugs, Birds and Beasts Tells Us About Evolution, Biodiversity, and Ourselves*. Translated by Kyoko Tazawa. Japan: Hayakawa Publishing, 2016.

"Squirrels use old snake skins to mask their scent from predators." *ScienceDaily*, 25 December 2007. <https://www.sciencedaily.com/releases/2007/12/071219130305.htm>. Accessed 27 May 2018.

Melin, Amanda D., Donald W. Kline, Chihiro Hiramatsu, and Tim Caro. "Zebra stripes through the eyes of their predators, zebras, and humans." *PLOS ONE* 11, no. 3 (2016).

Caro, Tim, Amanda Izzo, Robert C. Reiner Jr, Hannah Walker, and Theodore Stankowich. "The function of zebra stripes." *Nature Communications* 5, 3535 (2014).

Caro, Tim, Hannah Walker, Zoe Rossman, Megan Hendrix, and Theodore Stankowich. "Why is the giant panda black and white?" *Behavioral Ecology* 28 (2017): 657-667.

Egri, Ádám, Miklós Blahó, György Kriska, Róbert Farkas, Mónika Gyurkovszky, Susanne Akesson, and Gábor Horváth. "Polarotactic tabanids find striped patterns with brightness and/or polarization modulation least attractive; an advantage of zebra stripes." *Journal of Experimental Biology* 215 (2012): 736-745.

*Kodansha no Ugoku Zukan MOVE Sakana Kenrouban*. Supervised by Tadashi Yoshii. Japan: Kodansha, 2017.

## Special thanks:

Editor / Yoshimi Takuwa-san (Institute for Liberal Arts, Tokyo Institute of Technology)
Kamome Shirahama-san
Saba-san
Ame Toba-san
Tomato-san

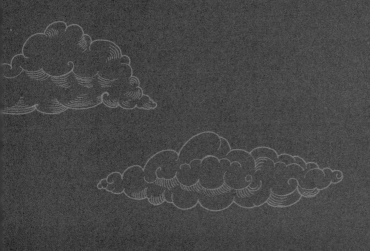

# HEAVEN'S DESIGN TEAM

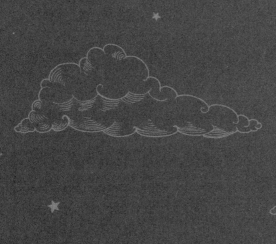

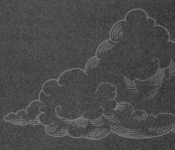

# Translation Notes

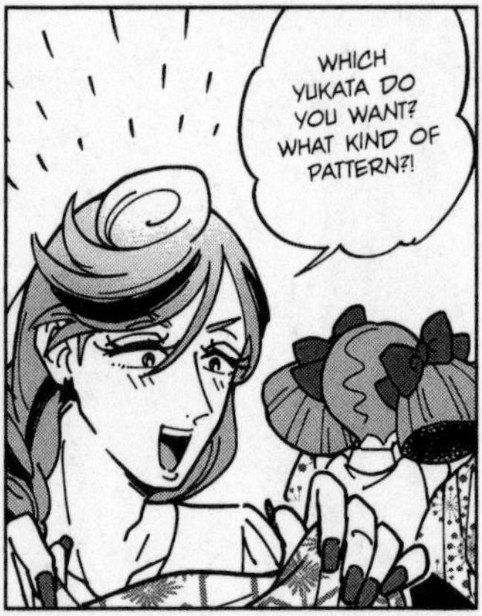
WHICH YUKATA DO YOU WANT? WHAT KIND OF PATTERN?!

## Yukata, page 103

A kimono-like garment worn primarily in the summer, where its light and airy design offers a solution for beating the heat. It is also common to wear yukata after bathing in a hot spring or bathhouse in order to cool down, and some establishments do include a simple yukata rental as part of their services.

## The culprit is among us, page 106

Jupiter is borrowing a catchphrase from Hajime Kindaichi, the titular crime-solving high school detective in the mystery manga *The Kindaichi Case Files*. The composition of this page, with all the "suspects" shown beneath the detective, is also reminiscent of the classic series.

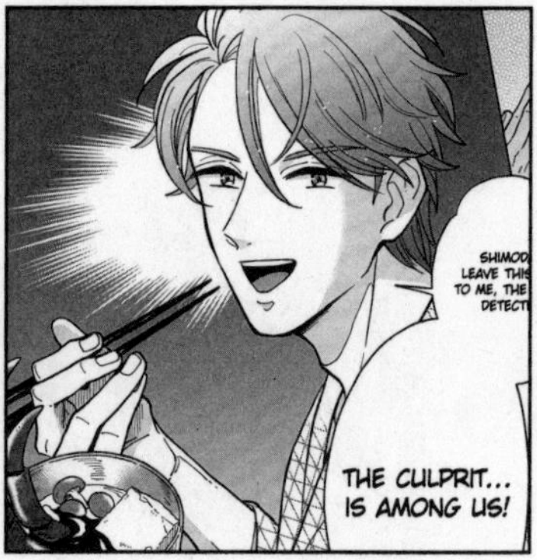
SHIMOD LEAVE THIS TO ME, THE DETECT
THE CULPRIT... IS AMONG US!

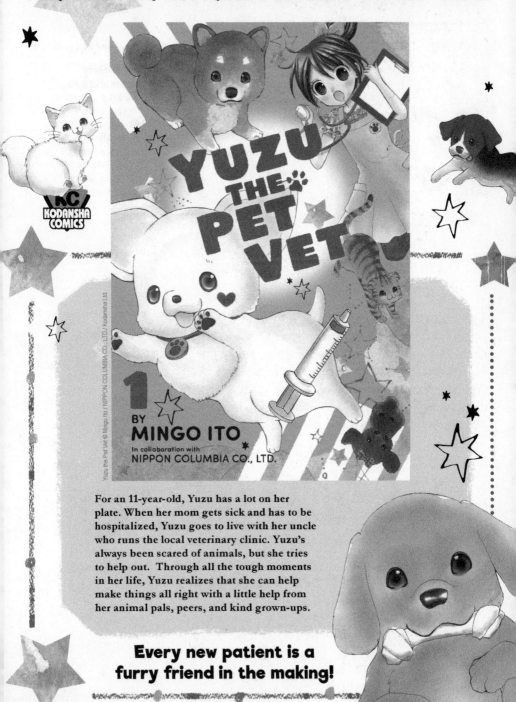

**The adorable new odd-couple cat comedy manga from the creator of the beloved *Chi's Sweet Home*, in full color!**

Praise for *Chi's Sweet Home*

"Nearly impossible to turn away... a true all-ages title that anyone, young or old, cat lover or not, will enjoy. The stories will bring a smile to your face and warm your heart."

—School Library Journal

# Sue & Tai-chan

### Konami Kanata

Sue is an aging housecat who's looking forward to living out her life in peace... but her plans change when the mischievous black tomcat Tai-chan enters the picture! Hey! Sue never signed up to be a catsitter! *Sue & Tai-chan* is the latest from the reigning meow-narch of cute kitty comics, Konami Kanata.

KC KODANSHA COMICS

A Kodansha Comics Trade Paperback Original
*Heaven's Design Team* 2 copyright © 2018 Hebi-zou&Tsuta Suzuki/Tarako
English translation copyright © 2020 Hebi-zou&Tsuta Suzuki/Tarako
All rights reserved.

Published in the United States by Kodansha Comics, an imprint of
Kodansha USA Publishing, LLC, New York.

Publication rights for this English edition arranged through
Kodansha Ltd., Tokyo.

First published in Japan in 2018 by Kodansha Ltd., Tokyo
as *Tenchi sozo dezainbu*, volume 2.

ISBN 978-1-64651-129-7

Original cover design by SAVA DESIGN

Printed in the United States of America.

www.kodanshacomics.com

9 8 7 6 5 4 3 2 1
Translation and lettering: JM Iitomi Crandall
Additional lettering and layout: Belynda Ungurath
Editing: Z.K. Woodbridge, Vanessa Tenazas
YKS Services LLC/SKY Japan, INC
Kodansha Comics edition cover design by My Truong

Publisher: Kiichiro Sugawara

Director of publishing services: Ben Applegate
Associate director of operations: Stephen Pakula
Publishing services managing editor: Noelle Webster
Assistant production manager: Emi Lotto, Angela Zurlo
Logo and character art ©Kodansha USA Publishing, LLC